Duke Paoa Kahanamoku c. 1918
Photo courtesy of Tommy Holmes

DUKE

The Life Story of Hawai'i's
DUKE KAHANAMOKU

JOSEPH L. BRENNAN

KU PA'A PUBLISHING INCORPORATED
Honolulu, Hawaii
1994

DUKE KAHANAMOKU
The Life Story of Hawai'i's Duke Kahanamoku
Joseph L. Brennan

KU PA'A PUBLISHING, INCORPORATED
(formerly Topgallant Publishing Co., Ltd.)
3180 Pacific Heights Road
Honolulu, Hawaii 96813
(808) 531-7985

ISBN 0-914916-96-3 HARDCOVER
ISBN 0-914916-97-1 SOFTCOVERS
PRINTED AND BOUND IN HONGKONG

OUTRIGGER DUKE KAHANAMOKU FOUNDATION

The Outrigger Duke Kahanamoku Foundation is a public institution created to
encourage athletes and scholars from Hawaii whose endeavors will contribute to the
growth and development of sports in Hawaii; to support athletic events and
participation by teams and individuals in state, national and international
competition; to support individuals in furthering their education; and to assist in
preserving, perpetuating and developing sports which have a special cultural or
historical significance to Hawaii.

The author and publisher appreciate the cooperation of the Outrigger Duke
Kahanamoku Foundation in granting the use of the Duke Kahanamoku image
through out this book.

*Special thanks to the Bishop Museum, Mr. Cedric Felix, the Hawaii State Archives, Mr. Bob Krauss,
Honolulu Advertiser columnist, the Honolulu Advertiser and my special and dear friend Tommy Holmes for
their kind use of their photographs. The photos with credit lines of Joseph Brennan photos are photos in the
collection of Joseph Brennan.*

To my dear and longtime friend Tommy Holmes

Postcard of Duke Kahanamoku in a diving stance   *Bishop Museum Photo*

Duke Kahanamoku in Swan Dive Formation, 1913   *A.R. Gurrey, Bishop Museum Photo*

CONTENTS

Duke's Waikiki   *Bishop Museum Photo*

Ala Moana near Kalia Road, Waikīkī 1900-1920   *Bishop Museum Photo*

FOREWORD

Kahanamoku—Kālia Road

IN THE AREA TOWNSIDE OF WAIKIKI, KĀLIA ROAD JOINS JOHN ENA ROAD. WITHIN THE AREA CREATED BY THIS MEETING OF ROADWAYS, ONE FINDS NOW THE HUGE MASS OF THE HILTON HAWAIIAN VILLAGE AND, SOMEWHAT FURTHER, THE BEACH FRONTING FORT DERUSSEY. A bus highway, once part of Kālia Road, now marks the old Kālia Beach settlement of home and canoe sheds (hālau or pāwaʻa) belonging to Hawaiian families: the Kahanamoku-Paoa clan, the Coit Hobrons, the Alapais, the Moehonuas and others.

In my youth (the 1930s) Kālia Road was still a quiet place, although traffic increased each decade. In time this created freeway conditions at a monstrously busy corner where Kālia Road joined Ala Moana Boulevard and John Ena Road. Gone forever are the days when Duke Kahanamoku and his family lived there.

At the corner of Kālia and John Ena Roads, at the Waikīkī side of today's Wailana Apartments, two large, green-stained, Hawaiian-style cottages sat side by side. Trimmed in white, making them resemble houses at Waimea, these homes sat on a large grassy lot perhaps nearly an acre in size. From them came and went the large families of the Kahanamokus and Paoas. Everyone in town knew these two homes. Side by side, they represented the best of 'ohana living in those times. Henry Paoa and Duke Kahanamoku were the family patriarchs. Mrs. Kahanamoku, Julia Paakania Paoa, was a sister of Henry Paoa. The Kālia land had been awarded to the Paoa clan in 1877 in a "Palapala Sila Nui" (numbered 1775) signed by King Kalākaua. The earliest claim by Paoa was made in 1847, then under terms of the "Great Mahele," certain lands were awarded to those native Hawaiians who could show good reason for such claims. The Paoa who claimed the 3.29 acre parcel in Kālia stated that his family had been given the area by Queen Kaʻahumanu, probably in the 1820s, when she was Kuhina Nui. The claim was verified by a chief known as Alapai, who himself claimed a nearby parcel. Alapai and his family had known the Paoa family a long time. This original Paoa claim later led to a Land Court Award (number 1775).

The Paoa-Kahanamoku house lot claim can be traced in the records as far back as 1847. Naming Queen Kaʻahumanu as the aliʻi who placed the Paoa family on their house lot leaves little doubt that a connection existed between the "Dowager

Queen" Ka'ahumanu and earlier members of the Paoa-Kahanamoku families. Alapai's supporting testimony regarding the Paoa application leaves no doubt that this claim was well founded.

Young Duke Paoa Kahanamoku, who was to grow up to be the world's greatest swimmer, spent his teenage years in a house near his neighboring Paoa cousins. It was a lively, pleasant, comfortable family neighborhood where everyone knew each other. For the most part there was peace and prosperity and, if they had lived there for any length of time, people certainly understood the importance of place.

At the beach end of Kālia Road the Ala Moana shallows provided fish and all kinds of crabs, wana, and limu to the dwellers of Kālia. It was a good life for all: happy, gentle, and free. Neighbors attended school together, they shared food and certainly enjoyed one another's parties, and frequently married one another. An atmosphere of human warmth pervaded the old Kālia Beach settlement, one of the last strongholds of Hawaiian life before the relentless spread of Waikīkī, emptied ponds and streams, opened paved roads, and drove Hawaiians from their patrimonial lands.

Duke Kahanamoku grew up in this neighborhood. He lived close to the ocean, close to the heart of Waikīkī, and close to the soil—the *'āina* where his mother's family had lived for generations. He was a true *keiki hānau o ka 'āina* of Waikīkī. Born and bred to it, as a world-class swimmer it became his destiny to bring world-wide attention to Hawai'i.

Duke Kahanamoku and his Paoa cousins are inextricably linked to Kālia and to Waikīkī. They go deep into the sands of this famous playground, with its "Pink Palace," its Natatorium, and its Waikīkī Shopping Center filled with chic and famous Parisian shops. Duke Paoa Kahanamoku rises above the waters of Waikīkī as a beloved presence. He was a great chief of our time, indisputably the *alii nui* of Waikīkī.

Early 1900's *Courtesy of Cedric Felix*

ACKNOWLEDGMENTS

THE AUTHOR IS DEEPLY INDEBTED TO MANY PEOPLE AND ORGANIZATIONS FOR MATERIALS GENEROUSLY SUPPLIED FOR THE WRITING OF THIS PROFILE OF DUKE KAHANAMOKU:

First would be my long-time friend, the late Duke Paoa Kahanamoku himself, with whom I fished, swam, sailed, and dined over many years. He attended my professional fights on the Mainland during my boxing years—and visited by dressing room to offer congratulations or, uh, succor...

My thanks certainly go to Duke's widow, Nadine Kahanamoku; to the State Division of Archives; the State Library of Hawaii; Janet Bell, formerly of the University of Hawaii Library; Mary H. Hendricks, Librarian for the *Honolulu Advertiser* and the *Honolulu Star-Bulletin* (now retired); Dee Prather, formerly with the Hawaii Visitors Bureau; Reverend Dr. Abraham K. Akaka, ex-Pastor of Kawaiahao Church; and author-teacher-historians, A. Grove Day and Ralph S. Kuykendall.

Also my gratitude and thanks must go to many deceased friends; such as

A busy Waikiki in the early 1900's   *Courtesy of Cedric Felix*

Duke's sister, Bernice; his brother, David; "Auntie" Marie Piikoi; Mrs. Bernyece Harvey of Guadalajara, Jal., Mexico; writer-historians Emma Lyons Doyle, Kathleen D. Mellen, and Gwenfread Allen; and Admiral Norris W. Potter. Among those I'm happy to say are still living would be Kimo Wilder McVay and Mrs. W. E. Huntsberry, plus all those wonderful "aunties" and "calabash cousins" of Duke's who were so helpful and kind with their answers to my endless questioning.

It stands to reason that the author was not present to hear some of the dialogue or to witness many of the incidents herein cited. So, depending upon Duke's almost infallible memory, the data has been extrapolated into a first-cousin of truth. Duke was privy to everything written here and gave it his unqualified approval. Also, when the story occasionally waxes omniscient and it has been essential to go into Duke's mind, the resultant lines stem from what Duke told his biographer in person. Duke's forty-four years of friendship with the author built a mutual trust and we hope the truth shines through the text.

PREFACE

To those who knew of Duke Kahanamoku's fantastic athletic accomplishments, his charm, and his integrity, this pure Hawaiian symbolized all that is best in Hawai'i. To his friends he was a warm, simple man of great dignity and courage. He had a massive gentleness that comes only from an inner sureness of strength. The two-time Olympic swimming winner lived a life of excitement, tension, mind-boggling successes—and heartbreak. He knew the disciplines and demands of being a competitive athlete and demonstrated the great heart it takes to be a world champion.

At Duke's funeral, Hawai'i's revered and respected Reverend Abraham Akaka spoke with tear-filled eyes and a face twisted in sorrow:

"Duke Kahanamoku represented the *alii* nobility in the highest and truest sense—

Duke Kahanamoku with Dad Center   *Courtesy of Cedric Felix*

concern for others, humility in victory, courage in adversity, good sportsmanship in defeat. He had a quality of life we are all challenged and inspired to emulate."

Today, years after Duke's 1968 death, he remains the patron saint to surfers and swimmers throughout the world. His stature and fame have grown in quantum jumps since he was first crowned world's aquatic winner in the 1912 Olympiad by the King of Sweden and again, in the 1920 Olympic Games, by the King of Belgium.

His magical feats filled the minds of cheering fans. Kahanamoku was wined, dined, and feted by royalty, celebrities, and sports aficionados wherever he went. Not until he lost to Johnny Weissmuller in the 1924 Paris Olympics was he uncrowned. He was then thirty-four and Weissmuller was twenty.

In the ensuing years he toured much of the world as ambassador-at-large for all of Hawai'i, demonstrating his swimming and surfing prowess. He served as Sheriff of Honolulu for twenty-six years and for decades officiated at major national and international surfing contests. Duke made some thirty movies opposite stars such as John Wayne, Ronald Coleman, Anita Stewart, Wallace Beery, George Brancoft, and others—mute testimony to the world's desire to see him in the water, on the water, and out of the water.

Today, when TV and movies make surfing regular international fare, Duke's name is still known to spectators and participants thronging the beaches of California, Hawai'i, Australia, and elsewhere. If anything, Duke's fame has increased. He is in the Swimming Halls of Fame at both Honolulu and Fort Lauderdale. In 1984 Duke was inducted into the U. S. Olympic Hall of Fame with a lavish ceremony in Los Angeles. Along with his athletic accomplishments, it was Duke's character and personality that truly generated his golden image.

To know Duke was a privilege.

Bishop Museum Photo

DUKE

Duke Kahanamoku surfing at Waikīkī with Diamond Head in the background. c.1919
Gurrey, Bishop Museum Photo

Alakea Slip   *Courtesy of Cedric Felix*

1

Explosion at Alakea Slip

EXCITEMENT RAN RAMPANT ALONG HONOLULU'S WHARVES, FOCUSSING ON ALAKEA SLIP THIS AUGUST DAY OF 1911. Hawai'i's swimmers were meeting contestants from many far shores—to say nothing of vying against each other—for recognition from the American Amateur Union. Every watching fan hoped that this day's contests would produce at least one qualified entry for the Olympics already less than one year away. Here was an island of gifted natural watermen, and many were sad that the world had not given them the respect they were long due. Particularly the fans' hearts were with young Duke Kahanamoku, their coppery Honolulu-born Polynesian swimmer determined to prove his worth as an Olympic contender. Something was stirring, and deep pride was in it.

No Hawaiian had yet been hailed by the world as a top swimming performer. These islanders knew that their home-grown Duke had already clocked sprint events with times that hovered close to official world records. Word of his feats had not yet been accepted by the mainland powers-that-be. Maybe today the officials would see for themselves. Tension was high, even the majestic green Ko'olau Range to windward seemed leaning forward to see the swimmers.

Those who knew Duke best knew that the tall, lithe twenty-year-old swam basically for the sheer love of swimming. To win was secondary. He swam for fun, for health, for joy. Ocean swimming was his shrine. Since this pure-blooded Hawaiian with the generous mouth and even teeth found it painful to embarrass an opponent, his coaches and fans had to coax him to go out and win. Duke raced only fast enough to beat the man who would come in second. A dream swimmer, yet one who, because of his unwillingness to humiliate his opposition, worried the life out of his coaches.

It was hoped that this day would be different for Duke; different, too, for the eager mob lining the wharves. AAU authorities would record the clockings, and the times would be sent to the U. S. mainland for the attention of a waiting, sports-conscious world. Rich in ocean history, Hawaiians well knew the water prowess of their bygone heroes. It seemed wrong that distant lands had claimed the aquatic spotlight for so long. The crowd felt that today could be the day when Hawaiian swimmers would get the recognition they justly deserved. Young

Kahanamoku had won the 220-yard race earlier in the afternoon with an astonishing two minutes forty-two and two-fifths seconds—a full fifty seconds under the world record. Next was the big one, the 100-yard sprint—the one Duke was primed for. The swimmers crouched for the takeoff, quality speedsters, each and everyone. Big of foot and hand, wiry and lean as a panther, Duke tensed for the dive. At the bang of the pistol, each contestant hit the water with a splat. This race meant so much, and the cry of the crowd was a begging, demanding thing. Swimmers dug in and churned water as if chased by sharks. Hysteria was in the air.

The first few yards saw speed merchant George Cunha sticking shoulder to shoulder with Kahanamoku, and the two of them pulling out in front of the pack. The duo beat the water to a froth, side by side, with no appreciable show of difference in their pace. But as they chewed up the route, Duke threw his piston-like arms and legs into another gear—a higher, faster gear—and his body forged ahead while the crowd roared. Porpoise-swift, the swimmers swept on.

No one before had seen this unbelievable burst of swimming speed. Water mounded up a glassy hill in front of Duke's chest. He clawed forward with a momentum that told of something new in the aquatic world. Spectators felt it, sensed it, saw it, and knew they would always remember it. When Duke shot to the finish line a full thirty feet ahead of Cunha, clapping hands drummed and voices shrieked a wild aloha!

Consternation gripped the AAU timers at the finish line. The clockers were standing stiff and tight, their eyes fixed on the stopwatches. Shaking in puzzlement, their attention swung to each other. Had they all caught this unknown Hawaiian in the same mind-boggling fifty-five and two-fifths seconds? Why, it was four and three-fifths seconds faster than the official American record!

The crowd was quick to see the perplexed expressions of the officials, and excitement began to spread like wild fire. When the judge took each timer's report and announced the startling figures pandemonium reigned. Cheering rose into the air and rocketed against the jagged cauliflowered clouds above. Duke Kahanamoku had bested the world's best.

Duke himself was thinking back on the pre-race words of his mentor, George "Dad" Center, "You can do anything you want, Duke, be anything you want; just listen to the music inside yourself and it will come out." In his own heart Duke had believed all along that there was that touch of champion in his Polynesian heritage—an island race that used water as naturally as others used air. Maybe today was proof positive...

He got back up onto the wharf in a dazed, heady condition. People were reaching for his hand, slapping him on the back and shoulders. Their words were a din of compliments and appreciation. Best of all was Dad Center himself, whose words put the seal of truth upon what all the others had been yelling.

After the initial furore, Duke made his way to a protected side of the wharf. He lay down for a short respite before the start of the 50-yard sprint, in which he was also entered. Duke later related that he knew that all islanders were counting on him to bring Hawaii its deserved recognition for swimming. They would not interfere with his few minutes of rest.

The rest was short, the call for readiness for the 50-yarder came quickly. With spine still tingling, he took his place on the jump-off platform. He could feel the crowd's faith, and it made the winning of this second event a very doable thing.

Curling his toes over the platform ledge for a solid purchase, Duke was a coiled steel spring. He needed only the bark of the starter's gun to slingshot himself out into space. To his left and right were other swimmers supercharged with desire—but they did not have the support of an entire race. Today Duke could be Hawai'i incarnate! The thought was a little frightening.

As in a dream, Duke heard the starter's shout, "On your marks," and then "get set!" The contestants hunched even farther. The pistol crack followed, launching swimmers into the air with elasticity known only to top swimmers. The splat of their bodies told of the force—and every swimmer churned and lashed to gobble up the yards.

Duke quickly took a slight lead, but he knew that he raced against swimmers from the mainland, faster than the local competition he had trained with. This challenge from strangers welled large within him, and he knew that it would take an all-out effort. There would be no quick, early lead and then a shift to automatic.

This race was the character builder coaches spoke of. Screams from the crowd told him this was so. Swimmers boiled to his right and left. They ate up the yardage, all of them bunched. There was a long interval of dig and dig, tough seconds with seemingly no ending. "Close!" flashed into Duke's mind, "Too close!" With the finish line just a few strokes away, he called upon his last shred of energy and drove to slap the wall with his open hand.

Sucking air and hanging for a dizzy moment, Duke allowed himself the luxury of feeling that he had won. Listening to the throaty roar of the fans, he had to believe that he was truly the winner. But, perhaps the applause was for someone else... Possibly another had slapped the wall a blink ahead... Yet here were congratulatory hands reaching from the platform. Even his competitors were grabbing at him. Duke looked to the officials and wondered what the clocks showed. Again AAU timers were transfixed by their stopwatches. Their hesitancy made a frightening vacuum for Duke, like the silence after a howl. Timers were looking at each other, shaking their heads and searching for confirmation. Duke gulped his panic.

Finally through the megaphone came: "Kahanamoku—first place! Time, twenty-four and one-fifth seconds—a new American amateur swimming record!" The place exploded. Duke's mind registered "tilt!"

Duke let the excitement run through him and thought of the debt he owed his coach, Bill Rawlins. His memory whirled back to the endless days Bill had worked with him on the ocean course at the foot of Diamond Head; the careful clockings, the studied instruction, and all the suggested changes in stroke, leg-drive, and breathing.

Now, here was Rawlins himself banging Duke on the back and congratulating him. "See?" Rawlins was saying gleefully, "You never knew I clocked you under Charles Daniels' world record on some of your trial runs!"

A little out of his head, Duke found himself in the grasp of close friend Vincent "Zen" Genoves, a class-A middle-distance swimmer. Genoves, too, was enroute to bigger things in the swim world, and his congratulations were like mana from heaven. "Great going," Zen was saying, "You're a champ!"

"I—I was lucky," Duke managed to stammer. He was still trying to comprehend what he had done.

Rawlins broke in with, "I knew you had it, kid!" Duke nodded and grinned his thanks, then added, "Congrats to you, too, Zen. You won the long-distance stuff." Zen Genoves had won the long-distance events of the mile, half-mile, and quarter-mile. His fluid over-arm stroke and rapid leg-drive had propelled him as though steam-driven. He and Duke viewed each other with well deserved and mutual admiration. Two finely-tuned young men full of the same heady wine of victory, their thoughts turning emotional cartwheels.

Best of all, Duke had shattered two long-standing swimming records! The realization was overwhelming. Would they believe the facts on the mainland when the race results were cabled in? No matter, Hawaiians went rabid with excitement over what their favorite swimmer had accomplished. He was their guy! The headline of the *Sunday Advertiser* shouted:

DUKE KAHANAMOKU BROKE TWO SWIMMING RECORDS!
Hawaiian Youth Astounds People by the Way He Tore Through Water
Vincent Genoves Proves to be Fine Distance Man.

A heavily-boxed paragraph gave these details:

Two American Amateur swimming records were broken yesterday by Duke Kahanamoku, the expert natatorial member of the Hui Nalu Club. The fifty and one hundred yards records went by the board, and the new figures established by Kahanamoku are, respectively 24 1/5 seconds and 55 2/5 seconds. The old record for fifty yards was beaten by 1 3/5 seconds, while the blue ribbon distance figures were reduced by no less than 4 3/5 seconds. The course was carefully measured three times in all, and tomorrow morning it will be measured again by a surveyor. Kahanamoku is a wonder, and he would astonish the Mainland aquatic sports if he made a trip to the Coast.

Then a more detailed account followed:

There were some great doings at the Alakea slip yesterday, when the first aquatic meet ever brought off under the auspices of the Amateur Union was staged. The affair was an unqualified success, and the fact was made plain that Hawaii has good and better, for that matter, swimmers than any other country. When a lad can get out and, in a hundred yards dash, beat the American Amateur record by four and three-fifths seconds, there is something doing for sure.

Duke Kahanamoku was known to be a fast sprinter, but not many people thought that the youth was a world beater. Cunha, who swam in the event, was at least thirty feet behind the winner, and as Cunha in practice has always just about touched 61 to 63 seconds, Duke 's figures must be right.

No less than five watches caught Kahanamoku's time as fifty-five and two-fifths seconds for the hundred, and there is no doubt that the record is correct. The only thing that might add a fifth or

Alakea Slip, Honolulu, Hawaii. AAU swim meet. August 11, 1911 is the day Duke Kahanamoku set the world swimming record for 100 yards. He did it in 55 2/5 seconds — 4 3/5 faster than the American record.

Joseph Brennan Photo

so to the figures is the fact that the finish was over an imaginary line which was directly under a thin rope that was fastened across the dock. Still, as all the men with watches caught the time the same, that should be all right.

The course was measured before the race, and at least three times was the distance checked. A surveyor will again measure the straightaway tomorrow morning, and then there can be no doubt about the records.

The fifty yards race was also an eye-opener, and the way Duke got through the water was wonderful. He was pressed for the first part of the race by Cunha, but when within twenty yards of the finish, the Waikīkī boy shot out and won easily enough in the amateur world record time of twenty-four and one-fifth seconds. Kahanamoku was cheered when he climbed out of the water, and well he deserved the ovation.

In the hundred yards sprint Kahanamoku set the pace from the report of the gun. He simply tore through the water and before half the distance was covered it was seen by those holding the watches that very fast time was being done. At fifty yards Duke showed clear of the rest of the bunch, and he had a lead of ten feet over Cunha. At seventy-five yards Duke was at his top, and he was drawing away rapidly from Cunha. When within ten yards of the finish, Kahanamoku sprinted at a wonderful rate, and shot under the rope in a record time. Cunha swam gamely and he can rest happy in the fact that he made just about his best time over the distance and lost to a coming world beater.

Another great swimmer who did fine work over the longer courses was Vincent Genoves. He is a powerful swimmer and he captured three events—800 yards, one mile, and 440 yards races— in the best style...

The column continued, giving additional details about other swimmers in other events. However, its impact lay in the news that Duke Kahanamoku's sun had risen. Suddenly he was involved with swimming experts and officials all over the world. He'd be a very watchable young man from here on in...

*The MID-PACIFIC MAGAZINE published a surfing article in its January 1911
issue written by Duke Paoa (Kahanamoku).   Courtesy of Tommy Holmes*

The AAU meet at Honolulu Harbor, Alakea Slip.   Courtesy of Cedric Felix

Duke Paoa Kahanamoku   *Joseph Brennan photo*

2

Who Are You?

WORD CAME BACK TO THE ISLANDS THAT DUKE'S FANTASTIC RECORD-SMASHING AT HONOLULU HARBOR WOULD BE ACCEPTED. The news was knee-buckling to Duke. Abruptly, his private life came to a close as he catapulted into the public domain, where he would stay until and beyond his death. The news media embraced him in a heavy hug and wanted to know about his background. Duke's first records predated radio and TV, but the print media of newspapers and magazines were powerful forces and wanted to know everything. The world hungered for stories with a championship shine, so the search began.

Previously Duke had only been recognized locally as a beachboy with an extraordinary flair for surfing and swimming. Now he had instantly gained world-class aquatic stature. Reporters began delving into his past. What sort of person was he? Who were his people? What was his ancestry? Where had he been all this time?

Many questioned his being addressed as "Duke." Before few had ever asked about the name, colorful nicknames being common among the beachboys. There was "Panama" Dave Baptiste, Sam "Colgate" Kaluhiolani, John "Boss" Makua, Alfred "Molokai" Horner, William "Chick" Daniels, Dick "Brains" Janda, Frank "Indian" Telles, Harry "Curly" Cornwall, Louis "Sally" Hale, Sam "Steamboat" Mokuahi, "Turkey" Love, and Kepoikai "Splash" Lyons; colorful, exciting men, all. Newsmen dug back into Duke's beginning. They talked to him, his brothers, and his sisters; they talked to every relative and friend they could corner.

This is what they found: On August 24, 1890, a strong golden-hued infant was born to Duke Halapu Kahanamoku and his wife, the former Julia Paakonia Lonokahikini. The birth was at Haleakalā (the home of Princess Bernice Pauahi Pākī Bishop) at King and Bishop Streets in Honolulu (where today the Bank of Honolulu is located), the same home where Duke senior had been born in 1869.

The name "Duke" implied no actual royalty, rather it commemorated an event involving royalty. Hawaiians often remembered important events by naming babies after the participants. The name was given originally to Duke's father, Duke Halapu Kahanamoku, at the suggestion of Princess Bernice. The big event in 1869 was the visit to Hawaii of Alfred Ernest Albert, Duke of Edinburgh, second son of Queen Victoria of England. Duke Alfred had sailed in one of her majesty's ships to Honolulu that year, and the baby Kahanamoku was named "Duke" to commemorate the event.

Duke junior's birth in 1890 was a time of great unrest in Hawai'i. King David Kalākaua was in disfavor with many of his people. Certain segments of the populace—the sugar interests, for example—sought drastic changes. Island politics were in a state of flux. The King's sudden death in January of 1891 during his San Francisco visit proved to be the catalyst. Lili'uokalani, his sister, fell heir to rulership of Hawai'i. Her reign lasted but briefly; her abdication was immediately sought by dissenters. By 1893 she no longer ruled. It had been a short, stormy office for her. The last Hawaiian monarch, Lili'uokalani lost her throne to powerful commercial factions supported by the U. S. Navy. Sanford Ballard Dole became president of the islands' Provisional Government. Little Duke was not quite four years old at the time, too young to know that history was being made and foreign nationals were taking over the stewardship of his homeland.

Hawai'i became a Republic on July 4, 1894, presided over by President Dole as Chief Executive. By July 7, 1898, when Duke was eight years old, the American flag flew over the Hawaiian islands. Two years later, on April 30, 1900, the Organic Act made young Duke an American citizen.

He was receiving his education at the old Waikīkī Grammar School on Waikīkī Street (renamed Kalākaua Avenue) across from where the Moana Hotel stands today. His education progressed later to the Kaahumanu School on Beretania Street. In 1904 at age fourteen, he went to Kamehameha School and studied blacksmithing and the machinist's trade. Ultimately he entered McKinley High School and signed up for commercial studies.

In true Hawaiian tradition the Kahanamoku family expanded. After Duke, the first born, came brothers and sisters: David, Bernice, Bill, Sam, Kapiolani, Maria (who died early), Louis, and the last baby, Sargent. "Sargent," the sixth son, was named to commemorate the fact that Duke's father had just been promoted to sergeant of police.

Nine children brought the Kahanamoku home alive in the old Kālia district of Waikīkī. The Hilton Hawaiian Village hotel currently occupies the site where the old homestead formerly stood. Father Kahanamoku's limited salary often made for tight going, but the home blossomed with a camaraderie and love. The Kahanamoku family had very little that money could buy and everything worthwhile that it could not. The Kahanamokus were quality human beings.

Duke's years of growing up were, for the most part, as easy as swinging in a hammock. There was school, planning, dreaming and playing. Young Duke however, found his greatest excitement in swimming. With the ocean practically the backyard, he and his five brothers made the most of Māmala Bay's blue, clean waters.

Duke had a certain charisma right from babyhood, loved by his family at Haleakalā, and by those in his grandparents home at Kālia in Waikīkī. He was fawned upon by his Uncle David Piikoi and his first cousin, Maria Kanehaikana Piikoi, both descendants of Hawaiian *alii* (royalty). The Kahanamoku family preserved the Piikoi name by giving it as a middle name to Duke's brother, David. David always seemed to feel the name gave him a master's degree in dignity. Duke felt likewise about his own middle name, Paoa, which also had illustrious connotations. Histories of old Polynesia were rife with *alii* named Paoa. To Duke it was reminiscent of "chieftains" and "kings"— and always a source of pride. Still, his brothers used to kid him with the literal Hawaiian interpretations of the name: "Strong odor, whether pleasant or unpleasant; fragrant bones." They made much of it in their rollicking way. "No wonder you get the stink-eye from us!" they'd laugh. Despite their jesting, Duke the oldest of the six, knew they loved him.

Aquatics of all kinds were young Duke's passion; swimming, body surfing, surfboarding, and canoeing. He swam with a natural instinct. The Polynesian blood of his forefathers bubbled in his veins and fostered a rare talent. As he grew in stature, Duke turned to bigger boards for bigger waves and longer, wilder rides. As his brothers and friends, too, grew and excelled, the joyful competition pushed each to new heights. In time, clubs were formed, and they joined in organized competitive swimming, sailing, outrigger canoeing, and surfing programs. Away from the water Duke was something of a lost soul.

Waikīkī of yesteryear had not yet been touched by today's tourism and commercialism, so the oldtime values still held. Pure Hawaiians like the Kahanamoku's lived as though tomorrow held no threat and life was lived and enjoyed on a day-by-day basis. Meeting on the beach near the old Moana pier at Waikīkī Beach was a daily routine for Duke, his brothers and their friends. When they were not in or on the water, there was always the strumming of 'ukulele or guitars. Hours of "talk-story" and laughter embellished their time away from school. At the harbor they dove for coins tossed by passengers on visiting

Duke Kahanamoku carries a young boy on his shoulders while surfing in front of the Outrigger Canoe Club in 1910.
                                             A.R. Gurrey, Jr. Bishop Museum

steamers. Utopia and cash were theirs for the taking, and they revelled in it.

Even the horse trams furnished ease and fun for these carefree boys who knew laughter as few do today. Young Duke captured the fancy of the tram driver and arranged for free transportation for his younger brothers. Smiling, in later years he explained: "We used to ride to the end of the line at Kapi'olani Park, unhitch the horses for the driver, then bring them around the tram and hitch them to the other end for the return trip to town. He got to knowing us pretty well and was always glad for our help. Of course, we knew that the hour-and-a-half drive from town had him fed up with the horses. Free fare was important to us those days, for my dad's salary as a cop was pretty skinny for a family of our size."

The Kahanamoku family was a tightly-knit group of loving people. Day and night, happiness was the currency for all. Year in and year out, their warm regard for each other remained unchanged. (Friends, relatives, neighbors, a very integrated and strongly knit community.)

Laughter leavened the hours; one story tells how the boys would leave the house wearing their shoes of stiff, squeaky leather—only to yank them off and hide them in sand or bushes immediately on leaving sight of Mama. Mama felt that unshod feet did not become sons of an officer of the law. Out of sight, the boys reveled in their barefooted freedom, but on returning home, they always retrieved and donned shoes before entering the house. Duke grinned when telling how their father always knew of their trick, but simply acted ignorant as they came squeak-squeaking across the floors. Father, too, had once been a boy who loved the old barefoot Hawaiian ways.

From infancy the Kahanamoku brothers were exposed to swimming, surfing, and canoeing. Along with other beachboys, they used to meet under an old hau tree on the shore where the plush Royal Hawaiian Hotel stands today. Youthful and exuberant, they wore life like a loose garment and referred to their spreading hau tree as "the poor man's clubhouse."

Although the boys wouldn't have known, it's recorded that surfing had been a prominent pastime at Waikīkī up to the end of the eighteenth century. After King Kamehameha I consolidated Hawai'i into a single kingdom, surfing mostly became a sport of royalty. During Duke's youth, shortly after 1900, the sport again flamed into popularity. This was at least partly due to Duke's flamboyant shows at Waikīkī. His spectacular rides kept the tourists talking. Other surfers vyed for the same attention, though few could match his skills.

As Duke grew into strong, young manhood, he rode the waves the way he'd heard the *alii* warriors had ridden them—proudly and handsomely. He began making the biggest boards to ride the tallest waves. Peers who shared the surfing with him strove to copy his finesse, but Duke's gracefulness was that of a bird in flight.

Camaraderie among the surfers was such that Duke dreamed of forming a club. In time he did organize one—a moneyless one and with only the spreading hau tree on the beach for headquarters. They did the best they could with what little they had. This small club was the forerunner of many others that later produced exciting competition.

From ancient days Hawaiians had prized their surfboards. They were works of art, hand-smoothed and designed with meticulous care. Lacking a skeg (rudder), they were heavy, often exceeded ten feet in length, and made of the finest island woods available. Thinner ones were called *alaia;* thicker ones were known as *olo.* Stories say the *alaia* was developed to supplant body surfing and was usually made of *koa*, the sickle-leaved Hawaiian acacia, or wood from the breadfruit tree. However, some chiefs made surfboards from a strong, lightweight, balsa-type wood called *wili-wili*, a tree related to the symbolic tree of India—the Tiger's Claw. *Olo* were made of a light-weight wood and generally used by surfers of smaller stature and lesser talent.

A third type of board was used by more experienced surfers. Called a *kīko'o*, it was designed for surfs that broke bigger and farther out. Duke and his friends favored longer and more streamlined surfboards. They experimented with hollowed-out boards to attain more buoyancy, maneuverability, and speed. Competition spawned inventiveness and originality.

Outside of Duke and several others, few had the raw strength or nerve to ride the type of boards used by the ancient *ali'i*. The massive old boards displayed at Bishop Museum in Honolulu are a distant shout from those used in modern surfing. Bishop Museum's collection includes two boards weighing respectively 148 and 160 pounds. Reportedly, they were used at Waikīkī around 1830 by Abner Pākī, a high chief and father of Bernice Pauahi Bishop. Pākī supposedly towered six feet four inches in height and weighed over 300 pounds. Stories say this giant of a man found it no great strain to handle the 160-pounder with its 16-foot length. After studying the board to estimate its age, museum archaeologists concluded it had been used by *alii* many years before Abner Pākī 's birth in 1808.

Formation of the Outrigger Canoe Club in May 1908 also contributed to the renaissance of surfing. Alexander Hume Ford and others organized the club and charitably invited some of the hau-tree beachboys to come in as members. The new club was a quantum leap in comfort and style for the beachboys. Here was a large grass-covered house on the beach with ample room for storing surfboards and canoes. It had a touch of class, and most of the boys went over to the "fancy" new club. Some, however, did not. Among the holdouts was Duke; his loyalty to the more pedestrian club was rock-ribbed. Not until nine years later did he forsake the club he had helped to organize. "Prestige" could wait.

Throughout his youth, Duke strove to perfect his body and his skills as a waterman. Swimming, surfing, and canoeing were his passion. Dreaming of someday becoming an aquatic champion, he practically lived in the water.

Swimming, surfing, sailing, and canoeing challenges developed between the beach clubs. Once the Healanis, an up-and-coming club, asked Duke to paddle for them in one of the bigger and more important contests. He competed as an unattached member and performed impressively. But later, when he applied for membership, he was rejected by the board. Hypersensitive Duke was greatly embarrassed.

Daunted he was not. He redoubled his efforts and became an even better athlete. He used to say that God had given him a gift and a whip. "The whip," he added with a grin, "is to flog myself into getting the most out of the gift."

When top Australian swimmers visited the islands in 1910, Duke inspected their performance almost microscopically. Day after day he and Frank Kalani, his close friend, studied their special crawl stroke. To master the unfamiliar Aussie kick the two spent hours hanging onto short boards and kicking. Deciding that the stiff-leg kick in the Aussie style used more energy then necessary, Duke went with his natural instincts. He came up with a slightly bent-leg kick and improved his speed with less effort. Religiously he practiced and perfected his innovation. In 1911 Duke was still pushing himself to improve. One summer's day he was practicing off Sans Souci, near Waikīkī, with the Hustace brothers, Harold and Curtis. They were moving pretty well; the brothers, too, were top-quality sprinters. William T. "Bill" Rawlins, an island attorney from Yale University and veteran swimming buff, watched with stopwatch in hand. He got them to swim the measured 100-yard course and clocked them. He was astonished at the way Duke slashed through the course.

Agog at what his stopwatch showed, Rawlins told Duke, "I'd like to manage you!"

"It's a deal if you think I've got it," Duke responded. "I'd like to go to the top of the world... "

They closed the compact with no more than a handclasp and a smile.

For several months Rawlins worked with all three of the young swimmers. The team soon expanded with the addition of Lew Henderson, a Pearl Harbor architect, and Dude Miller, a beachboy.

To obtain official recognition for any records, swimmers had to belong to a recognized club. Accordingly, they organized their own club in 1911 and named it Hui Nalu.

Duke had concocted the name when all were in a dilemma over finding one that would challenge the already-organized Healanis and Myrtles. Sitting on their boards off Waikīkī one afternoon waiting for a rideable swell, Duke pointed seaward and said "The name of our club is out there." He explained, "The swells coming in spill into a hui (a gathering). And nalu (surf) is what we ride. See? Add them up and you get hui nalu—the surf club!"

By unanimous consent, the club was born and christened.

The newly-formed club had scant funds, so a clubhouse was a figment of the members imagination. Material assets were their surfboards and swim suits. They had something else, though, a great spirit of camaraderie, a mission. In their zeal they constructed bigger boards with sleeker lines and better balance, all in the interest of gaining more speed and maneuverability. Two top surfers, Zen Genoves and Ken Atkinson, developed the first ten-foot competition boards. The innovations, called "gudgeons," were three inches thick and made of northern-California redwood.

Not to be outdone, Duke developed a 114-pound board. With his rare expertise and outstanding strength, Duke handled it well in booming surfs. He used to defend his giant board and kid fellow surfers with, "Don't sweat the small stuff. Reason? Because it's small stuff." Gentle laughter took the bite out of his good-natured gibe. Hui Nalu grew. It included such capable watermen as George and Lawrence Cunha, Sam King, Henry Steiner, Dad and Mike Center, Bill Roth, Norman Ross, Ted Cooper, Kenny Atkinson, Atherton Gilman, Lane Webster, Dude Miller, David Larsen, Knute Cottrell, Zen Genovese, Steamboat Bill, Tough Bill, and the Hustace brothers, Harold, Henry, Tom, and Curtis.

The fledgling hau-tree club of swimmers, surfers, and canoers had started as an all-male group. But when they moved up to a name like Hui Nalu, they also added a couple of women. Two excellent female surfers were invited to join. Mildred Turner was one, a petite young woman known as "Ladybird." The other was Josephine Pratt, another expert surfer, usually called "Jo." Both gave an extra dimension to the club. It made for a close-knit, even happier organization.

These are the stories eager news reporters dug up about the young swimming sensation. They learned little from him personally, for modesty and humility made him somewhat of a reporter's nightmare. When pressed he used to say, "I guess I'm the scarcest talker I ever met." His habit of living inside himself gradually gained a public understanding that he was a very private person; pleasant, but private. However, his record-breaking efforts at Alakea slip put his swimming ability out in the open for the world to see.

Obviously born with a body and health fine-tuned to athletic success, Duke took full advantage of his gifts. However, he realized that others were comparably gifted, so the difference would have to come from dedication, faith, and luck. With evangelical conviction, he worked at improving his leg-drive, arm-stroke, and general physical condition. His will—yes, his immense will—was tied to every facet of the program. Unceasingly, almost religiously, he pushed himself.

Time alone would tell...

Standing left, Duke Kahanamoku and other Waikīkī watermen near the Seaside Hotel, 1914.
Ray Jerome Baker, from the Baker-Van Dyke Collection, Bishop Museum Photo.

Duke head-standing in the surf at the foot of Diamond Head, Waikīkī Beach in the 1920's.
Joseph L. Brennan Photo Collection

Duke with surfboard   *Bishop Museum photo*

3

The Essence of Modesty

HABITUALLY QUIET AND SELF-EFFACING, THE BEACHBOY KNOWN AS DUKE GREETED INTERVIEWS WITH LITTLE ENTHUSIASM. Despite this, newsmen came with incessant questions. Trying to maintain a low profile wasn't easy. Newsmen questioned him particularly about a rumor that he was a direct descent of King Kamehameha the Great.

Softly, Duke disclaimed all relationship. In all humility, he said that he had no claims to belonging to any of the old *ali'i* families. His contentment lay in being accepted as a good Hawaiian. That sufficed for him. Questions on Duke's genealogy were smothered early, and further questioning turned to what might come of this promising young talent.

Almost a week after the Honolulu swimming event, a reporter from the *Sunday Advertiser* made it a point to find out Duke's personal reaction to the events. The reporter was a little astonished that nowhere had there been any mention of what Duke himself thought about his spectacular wins. To correct this omission, the reporter made an appointment with Duke for an interview on Waikīkī Beach. An appropriate spot, that was where Duke managed to earn a few dollars during the week as a beachboy. He was at home there .

Duke and his brother David once described the meeting. At 2:30, the appointed hour, a fat reporter showed up on the beach with his staff photographer. There was no evidence of Duke. The newsmen scanned the shore with its many bathers and loungers. "This will be like trying to find a needle in a haystack," the reporter complained. He and the photographer asked the other beachboys, but no one admitted having seen Duke.

One of the beachboys shrugged his shoulders and said, "Duke's a shy guy y'know, an' keeps himself pretty scarce most of the time." Another said, "He's like clockwork with his swims; hits the water every day at two-thirty." Their eyes raked the tumbling surf; no sign of Duke.

After some diligent searching, they found Duke asleep under one of the coconut trees fringing the sloping sands. He had his swim suit on and his big surfboard lay at his side. One of the beachboys woke Duke, who looked up, blinked his eyes, and smiled. "I was having a good dream," he said apologetically.

A little abrasively, the reporter came back, "I thought you had run out on our appointment."

The powerful Hawaiian shook his head "No," and got up. "Sorry," he said almost wistfully. He stared with interest at the photographer's paraphernalia. "Where should we shoot the pictures?"

"You pick the spot," the reporter suggested.

Duke's still-blinking eyes danced around the several people standing by. "What's wrong with in here?" he ventured, pointing at the courtyard of a small beach cottage.

At a nod of approval from the portly newsman, Duke lifted the mammoth surfboard under his arm and headed for the courtyard and its privacy. The newsmen followed. "They tell me, Duke," said the reporter, "that you're such a private gent that you don't even talk to yourself." Those within earshot grinned and laughed sparingly at the jibe.

Duke just nodded and went along with the ribbing, finally saying, "Guess, at that, I'm no chatterbox."

Inside the courtyard Duke was the essence of co-operation, following the photographer's suggestions. "Suppose we take a shot of you with your board up on end?" the cameraman asked.

"Right," Duke agreed. He turned to fighting the out-sized surfboard upright. The effort brought his back, biceps, and forearms alive like vibrant bars of steel.

The photographer studied Duke's muscular development and said admiringly, "This is a cinch, like going hunting in a zoo."

They got that shot and others from different angles. The reporter explained, "I'm doing a special article for the *Honolulu Advertiser's* Sunday issue."

"I'm complimented," Duke said quietly, and resumed posing with the board as the cameraman requested.

The reporter continued, "Duke, you guard your privacy like a Doberman. But how does it really feel to swim faster than any other man on earth? Makes you sort of a superman." Obviously trying to restrain the awe in his voice, it still came through.

Maneuvering his surfboard to still another position, Duke analyzed the question. Quietly, he said, "It—it's bound to make a guy a little prideful." A touch of self-consciousness intruded, "Outside that, things are the same."

Surprised, the newsman went on, "Hey, you're a phenomenon. Everybody in the islands has lost their minds over you."

"Ah," Duke defended, "they think I'm great if I just blow up a balloon."

"Just the same, kid, you showed us front-burner stuff at Pier 3. Those two records you busted have stood since 1907!"

Modesty showed in Duke's face. He was surprised at a newsman having a long-ago record so readily at hand. "I didn't know," he said meekly.

Eager to prove his knowledge of swimming, the reporter added, "C. M. Daniels set the 50-yard record in twenty-five and four-tenths seconds. Also that year he swam the 100-yard sprint in a new time of sixty seconds. It took you to break both of them." He faltered for an instant to suck in more air. "That's two world records—unbeaten for four years—you've dumped in the ash can!"

Duke's face took on a smile as he began to better assess his Pier 3 achievement. "It was really that important?" he ventured quietly .

"Right. You made aquatic history!"

This kind of talk was music to Duke's ears. He wanted to know more about the great swimmers of the past. It was his passion. He coaxed with, "You know swimming history?"

"Lots! Been following and reporting it for years. Take your style—it's much like the original trudgen, at least as far as your arm stroke goes. In 1873 it was introduced in Europe by J. Trudgen. He picked it up in South America and did so well with it that everybody and his uncle latched onto it."

"You were a swimmer, too?" Duke asked.

"Yup, before I took on all this lard." He slapped heartily at his protruding stomach. "Now I just report it." Having found an avid listener, the newsman went on, "A top trudgener holds his head high out of the water, the way you do, and keeps his arms working in a circle, out wide on the recovery and pulling them alternately under the body to gain forward thrust. It's a sort of double over arm motion with a scissors kick. You follow me?"

Nodding, Duke said, "Sure, I know that stroke and I've done something about it. I've even improved on it, speeded it up."

The reporter elaborated, "It was revolutionary. In 1877, an amateur using it made the mile in twenty-nine minutes twenty-five and one-half seconds. That record was busted in 1892 and again in 1909. T. S. Battesby made it in twenty-four minutes one and one-half seconds." He looked up searchingly. "Wonder where those old-time champs have gone..."

More people were coming into the courtyard, most eyeing the big, loose-jointed boy being photographed and interviewed. Some of the older beachboys who were not too overawed at finding one of their number now a subject for the press started their usual ribbing. They laughed and kidded when Duke took additional positions suggested by the cameraman. Despite the hazing, it was clear they all loved Duke.

Duke was toiling at trying to please the newsmen. Looking to get clear of the hazing, Duke said to the newsmen, "Maybe you'd like pictures of me in the surf riding a wave."

Eagerly, the reporter assented.

"Yeah, sure," agreed the photographer.

Relieved at the chance to escape, Duke lifted his board and headed for the ocean. They made their way across the Waikīkī side to the concrete breakwater between the Outrigger Canoe Club and the Moana Hotel. Bystanders followed along. Watching Duke on the move was a visual treat. His hard, coppery, symmetrical body wasn't fire-engine-big, but the raw power showed. The word went out that Duke was on the beach and another couple of newsmen joined them.

As they walked, the reporter unloaded more swimming history. "Swimming got a shot in the arm when the crawl stroke was introduced. Alex Wickham adopted it from Solomon Islands natives. But the combined flutter kick and double overhand stroke—the freestyle—was introduced to Australia by Frederick Cavill. Frederick had taken his family through the South Seas in the early nineteen hundreds and saw islanders in Samoa swimming and generating terrific speed without the use of their legs. Being swim champions of Australia at the time, the Cavills closely studied the natives and, from that, developed the Australian crawl. They really had something!"

"Those Cavills must've been something!" Duke broke in.

"Exactly, Duke. Between himself and his six sons, they introduced the crawl to Australia and began just smashing long-standing records. In the beginning swim experts predicted the new stroke would cut seconds off the sprint races, but would prove too exhausting for middle- and long-distance stuff. But when Daniels, using the new crawl, smashed every American record from the 50-yard dash to the mile, the crawl was in like a porch climber."

Duke interrupted quietly, "I've always used the flutter and crawl. I think Hawaiians have always used it—with slight changes." He smiled, "I call it the 'Hawaiian crawl.'"

Duke dropped his board on the sand and waded into the small surf.

Meanwhile, the two newsmen mounted the walkway atop the pier. They strode toward the seaward end, watching the young Hawaiian swimming parallel.

Duke was a captive fish released to the freedom of the sea. No longer was he the shy young man taking awkward poses to please a photographer. Now he was in his natural element, doing what he knew best, sliding and speeding through the water. With his fabulous crawl stoke, he swept close to the pier so that the cameraman might get an action shot.

"Why so full throttle?" the cameraman shouted as he bent to his equipment, trying to get the swimmer in focus. "Circle and come at us again!"

"Slower!" called the reporter.

Duke rolled lazily, went into a powerful backstroke, and grinned. He made a run seaward to return for another close-up. He swung back, a little slower this time, putting great armfuls of seawater behind him and driving those powerhouse legs with a rhythm beautiful to behold.

Frowning into his finder, the cameraman called again, "Too much speed!" His camera had clicked, but he had missed keeping the swimmer in the image.

Once more rolling on his back, Duke glanced up. "Maybe I should dog-paddle!" he kidded.

"Nope," cried the reporter. "Give us the crawl that broke the world's record, but slower!"

"Right," agreed the cameraman. "Show us low gear."

Duke circled out and called back, "I'll put it in real low gear!" He straightened and came head-on. His technique was sheer elegance; effortless, rhythmic, and laden with power. He cut the pace to avoid defeating the slow-speed shutter of the camera.

Another click of the camera mechanism, and both newsmen called, "Again!"

Duke swam as the camera clicked and clicked. He looked wild and free out there.

The reporter yelled through cupped hands, "There's safety in numbers, if you don't mind!" It wasn't hard to convince Duke to swim a while longer.

With picture-taking finished, Duke barreled to shore and got to his feet. As he strode the sloping beach sand he glistened like a Greek god. Newsmen joined and there was more aquatic talk. They got to the subject of the beach clubs and Duke waxed a bit more articulate. Hui Nalu, his own club, was one of his great loves. His wide, sable eyes sparkled as he spoke. "You see," he explained, "I'm lucky to be a member. There were only three of us at first. Kenneth Winter was number one. He's gone to Chicago. I was number two. William Cottrell was number three. Now there are twenty-seven of us." He told of the wonderful assortment of top watermen who were club members. In a low voice he named other members. It was plain that he felt privileged to belong. It was a long talk for Duke. A statement of this length amounted to a major speech. Suddenly self-conscious, Duke blinked and went quiet. He hoped he hadn't sounded too silly.

As the interview closed, the newsmen thanked Duke for his time. The swimmer said, "My pleasure," stepped into the surf, and swam like a mahimahi (dolphin fish) escaping free from a hook.

Newsmen watched the fluid grace of his stroke, as different from the norm as night from day. Their assessments of his personality had sharp differences. Some felt he was a card-carrying loner; others thought he was just an inarticulate twenty-year-old Polynesian with a language handicap. All agreed he possessed a great swimming gift. They kicked their thoughts around and tried to reach a reasonable consensus. One response was featured in the *Honolulu Advertiser's* Sunday issue of August 20, 1911:

> Let our psychological analysis start right here. Duke Kahanamoku was neither disinterested, interested, bored, pleased or indifferent about being interviewed. If you can analyze that state of mind, you are welcome to the result.
>
> You cannot tell by his smile if he would like to throw you overboard for taking his time or hand a lei around your neck for taking his picture. On the whole, there can be little doubt that he was pleased. Perhaps that is a conclusion made in self-defense, but at any rate the day after, he asked how the pictures came out, and from that you can draw your own conclusions. His attitude while being interviewed was nothing more than pleasant courtesy.

It's possible the reporter's uncertainty stemmed from not recognizing Duke's extreme shyness. Once when chided about his scanty wordage, Duke apologized, "I never overegg an omelet." Modesty was in him like a heartbeat and when questioned about his tendency toward self-effacement, he replied, "I try not to bother people." A psychologist might attribute such responses to a lack of self-esteem, but they were more a measure of Duke's inherent humility.

4

A Touch of Discrimination

DUKE'S SENSATIONAL CLOCKINGS WERE SENT TO THE MAINLAND AND, TO THE CONSTERNATION OF HAWAIIAN OFFICIALS AND LOCAL SWIMMING DEVOTEES, THE TIMES WERE NOT ACCEPTED. The numbers were so startling that mainland officials refused to believe them. Duke was crushed, thinking that August day in Honolulu harbor would not be recognized.

One sarcastic reply came from the mainland with the remark: "What are you using for stopwatches over there—alarm clocks?"

It hurt Duke to the bone. "If I could just get the chance to do it over there in the States," Duke said. "I'd show them." With that thought, his hopes began stirring again; a little.

Later stories carried the inference that the AAU would take the island reports under advisement; authorities would investigate, check with other officials, and, in general, give the reports additional study. A decision could be long in coming.

Honolulu papers rose up in arms over the doubt displayed by mainland authorities. Angry headlines punched back at mainland dailies. The insult was especially painful because Hawaii had long been striving to be recognized for her great aquatic stars. Despite the AAU's failure to accept the records, word of Duke's times in the 50-, 100-, and 220-yard freestyle events swept the athletic world.

Incensed at the non-acceptance of the records on August 20, 1911 one local paper blasted:

> As a matter of fact his [Kahanamoku's] record has not yet been approved by the Athletic Olympia which decides such things. It matters not, even discounting that inch and a sixth shortage in the course, that Kahanamoku actually swam faster than is recorded of any man is beyond reasonable dispute. If our Olympia decides otherwise his efforts count for nothing. There is bound to be a protest in that sun-afflicted region called "the East" about his record.
>
> We are some sporting nation, but it must be admitted that that part of "we" which hangs around the corners of Tecumseh, Maine, and Forty-fifth

Duke   *Courtesy of Cedric Felix*

Street, New York are sometimes inclined to turn a collection of supercilious noses skywards over an American or world's amateur record of any sort being held by a "South Sea Islander" whom they might actually think of at this moment is blowing the ashes under a pot destined for the par-boiling of a missionary.

Even if they admitted that the record was broken they might even refuse to admit the existence of such a place as the Hawaiian Islands, if such drastic action was necessary to continue "we" on the high plane of athletics where we have proudly set ourselves. They have been known to do such things.

Happily, there are hardly such characters on the amateur committee.

Perhaps, on the other hand, our "sports" will cheer for Duke and recognize his prowess instead, in which case we will humbly retract and eat our sacrilegious words.

Much bitterness was displayed in the local press. Other Territorial writers hit back from other angles, equally as acidly. News scribes pointed to Hawai'i's history as a home of great swimmers, starting with the Polynesians who first settled the islands. They stressed past kings and chiefs and told of magnificent swims of years gone by.

One paper cited the authenticated instance of seventy-seven-year-old Captain Sam Manu who swam fifteen hours after his boat was rammed and sunk in Hawaiian waters. They documented the 1909 instance where fifty-two Hawaiian children survived the sinking of a vessel off the Moloka'i reef. When the boat sank the youngsters, averaging ten years of age, swam two miles through writhing seas and made it safely to shore.

John Turnbull's book *Voyage Around the World (1800-1804)*, was quoted to show that Turnbull had witnessed Hawaiians diving to incredible depths and remaining under water for unbelievable lengths of time. Turnbull's documentary told of natives hired to dive beneath large vessels to nail copper sheeting to the ships' bottoms. It was common for them to remain below from three to four minutes at a time. Occasionally they surfaced with swollen faces, red-raw eyes, and blood issuing from nostrils. To Turnbull's recorded amazement, the sturdy Hawaiian watermen promptly recovered and went back to complete the job.

Another historical swimming record dealt with the sinking of the vessel *Keola*. The boat, despite its known leaky condition, lifted anchor at Lahaina, Maui, and sailed for Kawaihae, Hawai'i, on a Saturday, May 8, 1840. She had some thirty-odd people aboard and moved heavily through choppy water. After dinner on Sunday they were in sight of Kaho'olawe Island when a battering gale hit the craft. Poorly secured barrels of molasses and casks of water shifted and rolled around crazily on the main deck.

The crew fought frantically to halt the runaway cargo to stem the rush and crush of fat wooden missiles. Crewmen and passengers alike jumped and ran to keep from having their legs smashed and broken. Iron-hooped containers rolled heavily with every plunge of the ship.

Suddenly a following sea lifted the vessel's stern and propelled all the barrels forward. Screams and shouts pierced the air. The loose cargo smashed into the bow and the load was too much. Stone ballast in the ship's hold shifted forward, wrenching timbers. The vessel's bow dove into a swell and never came up. Those above deck grabbed anything that could possibly keep them afloat. Cries from those trapped below ended as the vessel submerged. With the wind beating the water to a froth, everyone was on their own.

Kaluawahinenui, a Hawaiian woman, found herself clinging to a wooden bucket for support in the wild sea. Seeing her crippled husband, Mauae, struggling to remain afloat she pushed the bucket toward him and told him to hang on. He did but they found the bucket wouldn't support their combined weight. Kaluawahinenui swam to another bucket, and reaching it, she made her way back to her husband to help him. The wind was relentless, the sea savage.

They clung to their buckets through the night, hoping that their strength would hold—and that sharks would not attack. One by one, others near them disappeared beneath the surface. It was a night of horror, waiting for daylight and the possibility of rescue. In the first rays of Monday's dawn, Kaluawahinenui's bucket came apart. She dared not take hold of her husband's meager float, so she treaded water and stayed close. They tried to work their way toward distant Kaho'olawe. Death was in the wind.

Mauae's strength ebbed and his wife pleaded with him to hang on. Morning passed, as did noon. By early afternoon Mauae had become too feeble to make any progress. Kaluawahinenui took the bucket, and had her husband grasp her hair while she kicked. She towed him for hours toward the far shoreline. Finally the second bucket disintegrated. Mauae's strength gave out and he could no longer grip his wife's hair. She pleaded with him to pray and just keep his head up. She hung onto him and heard him mutter words of prayer. The wind and chill were relentless, Kaluawahinenui pulled Mauae's arms around her neck, held them with one hand, and desperately struck out in a slow, agonizing swim for the island. Between swimming and towing, they had been in the water about thirty hours when she realized he was dead. Numb with grief and exhausted, Kaluawahinenui released the corpse and weakly swam on alone.

She swam all the rest of that day. Long after dark she managed to gain the shoal water of Kaho'olawe. She crawled through the shallows and to the sandy shore. She lay limp and beaten for a long while. As strength gradually sifted back, childhood memories told her she had landed on an uninhabited shore of the island. Trance-like, she got up and staggered inland in search of fresh water. Despite the rains, pools were difficult to find. Finally locating a lava pocket of rain, Kaluawahinenui dropped to her knees and slaked her terrible thirst. In almost total collapse, she wandered across the island in hope of finding someone, anyone. Prayers were answered when a fisherman came to her aid. The story of Kaluawahinenui's survival in time became legendary.

Hawaiians were rightfully proud of such aquatic marvels. Given their history, islanders were especially provoked over AAU's refusal to accept Duke's feat as an official record. Didn't those officials realize that Hawaiians were capable of such swimming excellence? Mainland officials believed that no man could swim as fast as the unknown Hawaiian had been clocked.

To get Duke to the mainland to prove his swimming prowess was the first priority. Apparently curiosity and a sense of challenge prompted the AAU to invite Duke to swim at a mainland meet scheduled for the near future. Duke's heart raced at the prospect. The absence of any funding with the invitation looked to be an insurmountable problem for the Kahanamoku household—money was painfully scanty in that little home.

Fortunately, in Honolulu there were proud and imaginative men, like Bill Rawlins (later a federal judge), who arranged various benefits to raise money to send Duke—and Genoves, the middle-distance swimmer, as well—to the meet. Rawlins and other instigators contributed heavily themselves. Friends even put on a play, *"Pinafore,"* on the deck of an abandoned ship in the harbor. Money was tight in 1912 and the show didn't draw well. Just the same, all the box office receipts were turned over to the fund. Three men, Duke, Lew Henderson, and E.K. "Dude" Miller, sailed for the West Coast aboard the *Honolulan.* Henderson went as manager and Miller as trainer. Rawlins had originally planned to manage the team but had been compelled to let Henderson go in his place, due to

Duke aboard ship   *Courtesy of Cedric Felix*

business. The others left with high hopes and little money.

On the mainland, Duke eagerly drank in the excitement of strange places, new people, and new experiences. He had thought of his friends Dude and Zen Genoves as globe trotters, for they had traveled to Seattle in 1909 to be part of the big fair. Along with Bill Morgan and Guy Rothwell, they had gone aboard the transport *Dix*. Dude and Zen gave canoe exhibitions on Lake Washington and Lake Union and helped show off a Hawaiian exhibit. Worldly men, those!

Duke was so unaware of what he'd find on the mainland that he had totally neglected proper clothing. The thin-blooded islander soon found mainland air biting right through his cheap Honolulu-bought suit. Years of living in a semi-tropical climate had not prepared him for even California's winter weather. He resorted to fending off the cold by stuffing cardboard inside his coat and keeping it tightly buttoned.

Duke's cardboard shield was secret until the day he started to undress in the Chicago Athletic Club's locker room. With friends standing around, he unthinkingly pulled off his coat and allowed the cardboard to spill to the floor. Good-natured laughs rang through the room.

Embarrassment covered Duke. "You know what?" he said, looking in mock shame at the scattered cardboards, "That's what causes half the misery in the world. Caring—wanting—and not getting." It was no Freudian slip.

Duke's humiliation actually worked to his advantage. Windy City clubmen soon had Duke down at Marshall Fields where they had him fitted out with clothes fit to withstand the Great Lakes' wintry blasts. Zen accompanied Duke on that safari through the store. With the mahogany hue of their skin, they were mistaken for Indians. Unpardonable questions, normal for that era, were asked. Duke was quick to add to their confusion. He and Zen even helped the misconceptions by feigning no knowledge of English.

Speaking to the salesmen and salesgirls in Hawaiian, they soon had the haole (white people) totally confused. Bargaining went on, with the "language barrier" causing customers and clerks to stand by eavesdropping. Strange colored men, indeed! When the islanders had milked the situation for all it was worth, they broke into clear English and enjoyed the last laugh.The crowd found it hilarious.

Finally walking out, Duke looked down at his new raiment and blinked. He felt like a fox in the chicken house. The grin wouldn't leave his face.

Duke was to have such experiences again and again. Wherever he went he was taken for either an Indian or a Negro. On buses and street cars, among crowds on the avenues, in restaurants and shops, he found people gaping insolently at him. Friendliness was scarce.

"Look—an Indian without feathers!" he heard a girl remark as he came out of his hotel. In Pittsburgh, he was refused service at a restaurant. Humiliated, he rose from the table and made his way toward the exit. Another diner, sitting with a smartly attired group, spotted him and called, "Hello, Duke! How about joining us?"

Duke smiled his recognition of an old friend who had visited the Islands for years on end. Still embarrassed, Duke just wanted to leave. He quickened his step, but his friend had risen and hurried after him with outstretched hands. He embraced Duke like a long lost brother. They were the center of attention. The head waiter, now wholly aghast, stood to one side.

With obvious pride, Duke's friend introduced the islander to the other diners with handshakes all around. Duke felt so welcome that he had to fight back tears. His friend joked, "Bet your problem is that there's no poi on the menu!"

Duke said quietly, "No, it's just that they made it clear that I'm not wanted in here..."

"You mean they refused you service? Impossible!"

Duke looked down at the carpeting and, rather than make an issue of it, answered, "No, I really did come in just for poi—and they don't have it." It was a lame joke, he realized, but anything was better than hurting someone's feelings. He thought of the hospitality—the aloha—which his own people lavished on visitors from the continental United States and tried not to be bitter.

The man didn't accept Duke's joke for an answer. "You haven't eaten!" he said; it was a statement, not a question. Then he insisted that Duke join his party and dine with them. While Duke was making an effort to politely dissent, the man signalled for the maitre d'hotel. "Tony, please!" he called.

That individual hurried to the table as though escaping from a firing squad. "Yes, Mister Melton?"

"Please have another place set at my table here," Melton ordered. "And, by the way, Tony, meet the sensational Hawaiian swimmer, Duke Kahanamoku—my good long-time friend." Then turning back to his invited guest, he said, "Duke, this is Mr. Anthony Scalise, boss man here for many years..."

A chair was brought and a place arranged for Duke. He sat down, his embarrassment still strong. The experience had been as brutal as a street accident. He noted the maitre d'hotel whispering an apology to his host, who dismissed it with a nod.

Such blatant racial prejudices were repeatedly slapped in Duke's face during his mainland travels. Only his strong focus on the competition and distant Olympic dreams would take some of the sting out of the insults.

Duke Paoa Kahanamoku as a young man.   *L.E. Edgeworth Collection - Bishop Museum photo*

5

Deep Skepticism

THE HAWAIIAN GROUP WAS MET WITH CYNICAL SKEPTICISM WHEREVER THEY TRAVELLED. Swimming enthusiasts and most "experts" simply would not believe that this swimmer from a far away Pacific island had the water speed claimed. Still, or perhaps especially because of the controversy, he was always terrific copy for the media. Photographers shot hundreds of pictures, and writers described him as a mysterious, strange-looking dark native from distant coconut islands.

The hype continued. Despite doubts of his being a record-fracturing swimmer, he was constantly photographed. Duke found himself being posed in a ridiculous grass skirt, strumming an 'ukulele, and various absurd settings to please newsmen. It was all set up by mainlanders and left Duke feeling pretty silly. Henderson, Miller, and Genoves went along with the gags, hoping their pal would not weary of the nonsense and decide to return home.

But the silliness bothered Duke far less than the too frequent doors closed to him for racial reasons. He continued to eat alone to avoid Henderson and Miller being embarrassed because of his presence. Sometimes waiters or waitresses left him to sit, unattended and ignored. This deliberate neglect was as subtle as a punch—only it hurt far more. Those times the blues knocked hardest at his heart, and he would sit cursing the neglect and avoidance. He saw people grinning like sharks, or, worse, staring with contempt. Times he wished he was a one-man fighting brigade—to rise up, turn tables with a crash, and stomp out.

Not until the group reached Chicago did Duke get a chance to swim. On March 14th he entered a 100-yard exhibition meet. Duke was confident before the start of the race. Cameras and spectators alike focussed on his massive, coppery frame. With competitors lined up on the pool's edge, all eyes were on the island man.

At the gun's crack swimmers made long, flat dives and came up churning. Duke knew he was on trial with those haole watchers and swam as never before. His style startled the mainlanders, who had never seen a man swim with his head lifted high and with arms curving into the water like motor-driven blades. Duke took the lead, stayed in front, and finished in fifty-seven seconds flat. Fans went into a frenzy, not only over his remarkable time, but also over the spectacular new form he demonstrated.

Duke had his next chance in Pittsburgh, Pennsylvania. After the newspaper coverage on his performance in Chicago, Pittsburghers were fighting to see him. Doubts about his clockings still survived, but swimming devotees wanted to see for themselves.

In Pittsburgh Duke was again the center of attraction. Lined up with his competitors, he knew he was going to have to prove himself in every race he swam. Tonight would be just one more in a long series of tests.

The gun fired, and Duke leaped with the rest. He landed fine, but found the water biting cold. He dug in hard and felt the water churn, He led the pack to the last twenty-five feet. Then, with the crowd yelling hysterically, his legs locked with cramps. He came to a crippled, dazed halt. The others plowed past, and the feelings inside him were worse than the pain of his calves.

Like a broken-winged bird, he slowly made his way to the pool's side where they helped him out of the water. Anguished, he heard boos from the audience and listened to the unintelligible murmur from all sides. Most of all, he felt the numbed disappointment of the crowd.

Manager Henderson was quick to explain to the officials. "Maybe the chill of the water had something to do with it," he pointed out . "Too, my boy entered this event without practice since leaving Honolulu. Don't forget, he's had this long, tedious train ride across your continent..."

He was repaid with lifted eyebrows and cold stares.

Duke was questioned personally about his collapse. "I guess," he answered, "I tried too hard, too fast." He wanted to hide, to get away. He knew this would not have happened swimming in the warm waters of home.

Ensuing hours were a nightmare at the hotel that evening. His shame grew beyond understanding, for he had always thought of himself as almost unbeatable. The following morning he loosened up in the same pool and gradually worked the lameness out of his legs. He worked more that afternoon and evening, the same the following day. He took pride in his body and he was a work horse for effort. The kinks gradually left his legs, the wonderful feeling of indestructibility returned, and he knew his speed was still there.

He knew it the following night when he had a second chance in the Pittsburgh Athletic Club pool. These fast watermen each wanted their place on the forthcoming Olympic team, and they too were dedicated swimmers. This time

Duke was in better shape, but he still worried about the chill of the water.

While others were getting organized preparatory to the start, he asked the official if he could test the water temperature. With the official's approval, Duke jumped in and paddled a few yards to adjust to the chill. Hoots rang out from the audience. "Grandstander!" came a shout. "Show-off!" yelled others. Obviously others had some inkling of the islander's problem and held their tongues. Duke swept back to the tank's rim, lifted himself in one rhythmic motion, and stood there, tall, wide and metallic in the lights. The water made his rope-like muscles glisten, and he was something to see. On the inside it was something else, he knew he was a stranger in a strange land among strange people—who doubted him. Duke hit the water this time and demonstrated a speed no local had ever before seen. It was a 100-yard test and Duke wasn't used to turns, but his speed on the straightaways overcame his one weakness.

He won with seconds to spare. Fans applauded and Duke grinned, drunk with the joy of self-vindication. He won again in the 50-yard swim, and again beat the existing world's-record time. The crowd was in an uproar; with Pittsburgh swim fans acknowledging the newcomer as the king of sprint swimmers.

Newspapers, too, went berserk. Next morning they featured the young Hawaiian in picture and prose. They tried hard to identify his new crawl stroke. The trudgeon was still used by most top swimmers, but Duke's form of freestyle caught their imagination. Where did it come from? Who was the originator? Speculation ran in sports pages throughout the nation.

Duke's powerful flutter kick came in for lengthy discussion and analysis. "Where did he get it?" was the big question. Modestly, Duke disclaimed any credit for having invented it.

One paper pointed out that Charles Dana, adventurer and writer, once watched a Hawaiian messenger swim from his ship to shore. Dana had seen a distinct wake of foam made by the churning flutter kick. He insisted that no wake such as that could be left by the usual scissors or frog kick employed by American and European swimmers. The writer contended that the ancient Hawaiians used the flutter kick and had probably developed it body surfing. There a swimmer has to be moving extremely fast to catch a breaking wave and ride its forward momentum.

It was also mentioned that possibly the Hawaiian habit of surfing with small boards led to their using a flutter kick. The fast up-and-down thrust of the flutter assisted in catching a breaking wave. With the flutter kick furnishing the speed and buoyancy used for surfing, Hawaiians supposedly combined that with an overhand swimming stroke to give them their crawl.

One fact tended to dispute all this so-called evidence. History books indicated no tradition of competitive speed swimming among the ancient Hawaiians. It appeared they swam only for distance and endurance. Their swimming was portrayed as a leisurely type of cruising, with heads out of the water and arms moving in something resembling a combined breast stroke and dog paddle. Swimming was a form of bathing or for fun—certainly not a competitive contest. Hawaiian's only competitive water sport was surfing. One top swimming coach went on record saying, "There are three styles of the crawl stroke—The Australian, the American, and the Hawaiian. Each of these divisions is a distinctive style embodying the main characteristics of the stroke, that is, the double overarm stroke and the dragging leg kick. Yet each is a different stroke and each has its representative champions and proponents."

Arguments went, pro and con, none really proving much of anything. However, Duke himself had become controversial. He brought swimming to the notice of those who had never bothered to read about swimming, let alone attend a meet. Duke had that special quality which made people want to see him perform.

With Duke's performance in Pittsburgh, he was given his chance to vie in New York City for a berth on the American Olympic team. The four—Miller, Genoves, Henderson, and Duke—entrained for the big city, which Duke had thought of as a "never-never land" too far away to ever visit.

In New York he duplicated his feats of Pittsburgh and was officially picked to go to Philadelphia for the finals. Duke was jubilant. Henderson kept talking Olympics to him; Olympics, Olympics, Olympics! Duke tried to talk Olympics back, but his talk was akin to nervous drumming on the table. Anything could still happen—he remembered the disappointment following his unrecognized win at Alakea slip and his first race in Pittsburgh.

Public interest in the islander was intense when the group got to Philadelphia. The young man of few words still had difficulty with the never-ceasing questioning from curious crowds and eager reporters. By nature he was as effusive as a wooden cigar-store indian. Trying to explain his emotions was always a problem. With a friend, Duke would just thump his chest and say "Things inside are hard to get at."

Talkative or not, Duke had become an exciting symbol. He and Henderson strove to give the public what it wanted—color and uniqueness. At the

Left to right: Genoves, Dude, Duke and Ned Steel   *Courtesy of Cedric Felix*

Philadelphia meet they got caught up in the frenzy. Duke came to the pool clad in a Nile-green swim suit, over which had been wrapped an American flag. When he took off his robe and exposed the colorful regalia a roar went up from the crowd. The Territorial swimmer from faraway was suddenly their boy.

Again Duke demonstrated that his Hawaiian crawl was superior, and went on to set more records. He still lost fractions of seconds on the turns, but his speed on the straights kept him in front at the finish. He was now one notch closer to the games in Sweden.

Duke's chances improved when Coach Chilton helped him with his turns. Duke's previous swimming had been in open water off O'ahu, and he'd never had to contend with cement walls and reversing his course. Spectators in droves watched Duke practice under Chilton's tutelage. Standing on the pool's rim, Duke's six-foot two-inches and 188 pounds was an impressive sight. With the rich features of a Polynesian chief, he presented a handsome specimen of Hawaiian manhood.

It was said that Duke's pigeon-toed kick left a wake at one end of the tank while he was actually hitting the opposite end. His shoulders rose up from the water unlike those of other swimmers. Having body-surfed and paddled surfboards all his years, his chest and arms were like those of a weight lifter.

When he turned on full power in his stroke and kick, his body lifted up and forward, leaving half his back exposed under the pull of his burly arms.

Duke's life was fine, except for one thing. Zen Genoves had not shared equal success. Genoves had failed to qualify for the United States Olympics team. Zen, Dude Miller, and Lew Henderson returned to Hawaii. Although Duke was staying with Lew's parents in Germantown, Pennsylvania, the departure of his manager, trainer, and teammates left him painfully lonely.

Luckily for Duke, he now had the good fortune of being able to train under George Kistler, famed University of Pennsylvania swimming coach. Kistler spent endless hours working with the island prodigy. He particularly stressed helping Duke with his turns. It took time to develop the best technique, but Duke was a perfectionist and happily slaved at Kistler's instructions.

Fans continued attending Duke's practice sessions. His new style excited everyone. Even his name was something to reckon with. People found that the syllables "Ka-ha-na-mo-ku" had a delightful roll as they came off the tongue. The name was freighted with the romance of distant places. One lady newspaper reporter wrote that the name summoned up visions of waving coconut palms, blue lagoons, and soft, sunny skies with white thunderheads high-piled on the horizon.

In many answers to the natural question, it was repeatedly made clear that "Duke" was a given name, and not a title. Many refused to believe it, for Duke's tall, dignified appearance, straight carriage, and gracious manner all smacked of royalty. His personal charm made him a hero of the crowds, and it was hard to resist investing him with royalty.

With his reputation building, Duke found that pressures, too, were growing. More was now expected of him. He always wanted to please. In silent moments at night, he whispered to himself: "If I don't measure up, my life will be in the sewer."

All the straining of his daily swimming finally paid off. Duke was selected to represent the United States in the sprints at the Olympics in Stockholm, Sweden. Swim buffs, sports reporters, and officials who had formerly sold Duke short now extolled him as the best of swimmers. His homeland—tiny islands in the Pacific—now received greater attention. What sort of people lived in that distant archipelago? Whenever Duke was questioned about home, he was both modest and proud in his answers. It was as though he had been delegated ambassador-at-large for "paradise." He did love talking about "Hawai'i."

6

The Stockholm Games

Duke was getting ready to board the Red Star liner *Finland*—the Olympic ship—and sail for Europe. A fever of excitement climbed upon him.

"I can't even eat!" he said to other members of the team. His zeal was still a hard, gem-like flame, but so much had happened so fast that his appetite was, he said, "Sort of *kapakahi* (lopsided)."

Before going to the dock that morning, he first telegraphed a public message to Hawai'i. He expressed his "sincere and grateful thanks to everybody for the financial assistance and encouragement by which I am enabled to take part in the great Olympic Games." He pledged "to put forth my best efforts to win and to add to the glory of the United States and Hawaii."

Duke, still a small island boy at heart, boarded the ship with his body finely honed, but wondered if he still carried all of his heart. Much of it seemed to have been left back in his island home. To ease the loneliness, during the voyage he wrote many letters and cards to those he loved, particularly his mother, father, brothers, and sisters.

The *Pacific Commercial Advertiser* of Honolulu noted:

> Duke is very regular in his correspondence, and there is not a
> mail comes in from the Coast, but brings letters and postals to
> his loved ones here. He always concludes with "Aloha to all
> and regards to the boys."

One card to his father on June 24th points up how he tried to keep his spirits up as the vessel tirelessly put miles between him and home: "Here at sea. Having a good time, and all well aboard. Rained this morning quite a lot, but it's over now. Have been swimming in a little tank (aboard). Some traveling, Daddy! Bought a little camera in New York. Hope results will be good throughout. Fine bunch of athletes. Sang *Aloha Oi* for Colonel Thompson (a millionaire) last night on board. He appreciated it very much and shook hands with us. The boys also appreciated my singing. Aloha nui and regards to the boys. Duke."

On the reverse side were signatures of "the boys," "Duke Paoa Kahanamoku,

Practice tank aboard ship.   *Courtesy of Cedric Felix*

Duke Kahanamoku in practice tank aboard ship.   *Courtesy of Cedric Felix*

Otto Wahle, James H. Reilly, T. Nerich, M. McDermott, Ken Huszgah, Harry Hebner, Perry McGillivray, Arthur McAleeman, Jr. and C. W. Gaidzik." Other items, such as this from another card, further revealed his hunger for the sight of familiar faces: "Met George MacFarlane in New York and he was glad to see me. So was I to see him, you bet!" As the days continued to pass, Duke gradually adjusted and got caught up in the excitement of travel. It shows in later mailings. One dated June 26th, to his father read: "Arrived at Antwerp at 10 a.m. Went all round the city. Had a swim in a tank—swam 100 meters in 60 4-5. Will sail for Stockholm on Wednesday. All well, Best regards to all. Aloha nui. Duke."

Arrival at Stockholm, Sweden, was an incredible thrill for Duke. He had been saying "Stockholm" with the same awe that others accorded to religious shrines. "I'd always wondered if I'd ever get to the West Coast," he said, "let alone to land in Europe." He could hardly believe it. Looking up at a sky of cold, aluminum-colored clouds Duke realized that he was far away from warm, sunny Hawai'i. The strangeness of new places shook away the last of his blues. There was something new at every turn; to see, hear, taste, and smell. He even began to enjoy people who stared at the first Hawaiian they had ever seen. The Swedish language was delightful to hear and he wrestled with their strangely-accented English questions as best he could. Frequently, though, he had to use an interpreter.

The days just before the swimming events were a mishmash of coming and goings. The U. S. team captain watched every American competitor to make sure each remained in top condition. Reporters hustled about, talking with the athletes, always seeking stories. Writers from publications covering the world sought interviews with the most colorful contestants. Duke was constantly in demand by the newsmen. Photographers were continually snapping pictures and commotion was the order of the day.

With the tension and excitement of the events before the races, Duke feared—as he worded it—"My clock might run down before I even get in there."

Duke had one tremendous advantage, he was blessed with a wonderful capacity for sleep. This very advantage almost doomed him the day of his big chance. Wanting to be strong for the coming race, Duke found a place to lie down and rest. Grateful that only a few remained aboard the Finland, he sauntered below deck and lay down on an unoccupied bunk.

He had only meant to relax for a few moments, but Duke slept like he swam—all-out. In no time he was out like a dead man.

An hour quickly slipped by and word was signalled in the stadium pool that the 100-meter race would begin shortly. Duke's coach and teammates began looking for him. They searched, but couldn't find him. The American team became frantic in its hunt. They announced Duke's name in the stadium.

"Kahanamoku wanted on the starting platform!"

Finally, Michael "Turk" McDermott, the U.S. backstroke champion and a good friend of Duke's, said, "Maybe the guy is still out on the boat, grabbing a snooze!"

With that he headed dockside fast. It was quite a run to where the *Finland* was moored. McDermott raced the gangplank and started combing staterooms. Sure enough, he heard Duke snoring in a far cubicle. Duke was notorious for his snoring; when he "sawed" he could cut—not a knot, but—a nail. McDermott lost no time in wakening him.

"You're wanted on the starting platform!" he yelled. "They're ready for your race!"

Blinking, Duke got up, shook his head, and joined McDermott in the run back. He almost died at the thought of having come this far and then sleeping through his big chance. Guilt sped his feet, and he quickly outdistanced McDermott.

Frantically, Duke ran, twisting through the crowds near the stadium. On a dead run he burst through the athletes' gate. People shouted, "There's the Hawaiian!"

He raced to the starter and panted, "Can you please wait 'til I get a swim suit? I—I'm sorry."

"Where've you been?" asked the official.

"I guess my dad fathered a fool. I've been sleeping."

While annoyed by the delay, the starter agreed. Duke plunged toward the lockers to get his suit.

McDermott, the breast stroker, was just arriving. "You won't have anything left for your race!" he gasped, "I sure don't."

Duke kept right on, pulling off his shirt and piling into his swimsuit, all the while thanking McDermott for finding and waking him. In a minute he was on his way. By this time the crowd knew the delay was due to Duke's absence. Mostly good-natured guying poured from the audience as he made his way back to the pool. Some was less than good natured, from those who had hoped the race would be swum without him.

Duke ran to the platform and panted his thanks to the officials for the additional time to get ready. There was scolding and angry words of censure from

King Gustaf of Sweden applauds after awarding Duke the gold medal for winning the 100-meter freestyle at the 1912 Olympic Games held in Stockholm. *Joseph Brennan photo*

Duke in his suit.

Courtesy of Tommy Holmes

several, but they allowed him to join the other competitors. No one had ever come closer to missing an Olympic event. The young Hawaiian gave silent thanks for reprieve. He sensed the vast crowd seemed to be with him.

On this July 6th, 1912, Duke had strangely enough become the sentimental favorite. His big test in the Stockholm pool had gripped the attention of the world. Duke faced a strong field. Any of the contestants might press him as he had never been pressed before. Great events bring great efforts—and great efforts sometimes bring startling results.

An audience exceeding ten thousand watched Duke line up with Bretting and Raume of Germany, Longworth of Australia, Huszgah of the United States, and Healy of Australia. The air was electric as the swimmers locked their toes on the jump-off for this 100-meter dash. Even Duke, always so confident, now felt the fever. Royalty lent a special flavor to the contest, with the audience including King Gustavus V, the Queen, the Crown Prince, and the Crown Princess. Diplomats, and VIPs, high-ranking military from many countries helped fill the royal box, making it a gala event.

The pistol crack sent six finely-trained athletes into the water in one lunging splash. Duke was up first and churning fast. With twenty-five meters covered, the Hawaiian turned and looked back to see his competitors. The nearest was a full ten feet behind. Seeing the comfortable lead, Duke actually lessened his effort and dropped into a lower gear.

Watching him ease off, the crowd gasped. Could he really be this good? The other swimmers were straining to the limit, shortening the distance to the islander. Duke seemed content to let them gain. When he hit the end he had only a six-foot lead on the Australian Healy, who placed second. The other American, Kenneth Huszgah of the Chicago Athletic Association, splashed in a close third.

The crowd roared until the time was announced. Electrically clocked at sixty-three and two-fifths seconds, it was only one second slower than the record established by Duke in prior heats. Pandemonium reigned, the Hawaiian swimmer became a hero. Most observers believed that if the others had swum faster, Duke could easily have increased his own speed and probably set a new record. To him, the win was enough. Duke had again proved himself, and proved it where it counted. Fans were especially excited by the way he had done it. Duke was unique.

Years later Michael "Turk" McDermott, the U.S. breast stroke champion from 1909 to 1918, said, "It wasn't that he [Duke] was unorthodox. His stroke was very symmetrical and easy. And he had plenty of rhythm. Besides, he was strong, had a good heart and had big feet. I think that's where they got the idea to manufacture those swim fins to make you go faster."

Duke, his coach, and the whole U.S. team were joyous. Duke had broken the record established in 1907 by the American C. M. Daniels. The locker room was wild as the Americans pounded each other's backs. Duke couldn't wait to get outside to send word of the victory home to his family and friends.

Four days later, July 10th, was a royal day for Duke. Contest medals were being awarded by the King. It was a brilliant scene with the huge crowd banked high above the royal box. Also there was the Queen and batteries of diplomats, courtiers, and army and naval attaches. Ceremonies had not been long under way when King Gustavus leaned forward and motioned to Duke, standing below with the swimmers. The crowd saw the gesture and came alive. It wasn't like the dignified old monarch to be so outgoing.

In disbelief, Duke saw the King beckoning him to the royal box. Duke hesitated while his fellow Americans urged him on.

"Go on Duke!" they urged. "You're wanted by the King!"

Zombie-like, Duke walked to the royal box. The tall, slim bearded King rose, leaned down, and clasped Duke's hand in a warm grasp. A smile swamped Duke's face as he wrestled with the King's Swedish accent. Much went over Duke's head like the summer thunder; perplexed, he tried to comprehend. He slowly understood that he was being presented to the Queen and the royal family. Duke found it mind-boggling, but happily nodded his gratitude.

More congratulations were offered by the King, and despite the language barrier, Duke knew the words were heartfelt. A quick second handshake and Duke nodded goodby to the royal family. He then turned and strode trancelike back to the other swimmers.

His coach reached out and squeezed Duke's bicep. "Now this crowd knows you're a quality guy!" The crowd's yells drowned out the rest of the man's words.

Tears came to Duke's eyes.

7

Olympiad Furore

C OMMUNICATION BEING WHAT IT WAS THEN; DISHEARTENING NEWS HAD COME TO
THE ISLANDS THAT ALL WAS NOT WELL WITH H AWAI'IS EFFORTS IN THE O LYMPIAD.
The *Advertiser* had headlined on Monday, July 8th:

DUKE MAY LOSE HIS RIGHT TO SWIM IN FINAL HEATS

The subhead said:

*Misunderstanding Regarding Semifinals May Cost Him Place—Hawaiian
Boy Creates Furor in Stockholm—People Wild Over His Masterly
Performance.*

The column had a Stockholm dateline of July 8th and explained:

Owing to a misunderstanding regarding the semifinals in the hundred-
meter swimming races, America may lose what she has already won
through the efforts of Duke Kahanamoku, the wonderful swimmer from
Honolulu. The misunderstanding appears to have arisen over the dates of
the semifinals. Efforts are being made to straighten matters out and it is
possible that they will be successful.

Duke himself has carried the city and its thousands of visitors by storm.
He is easily the most popular of the swarms of athletes here from all over
the world. His work in the water is appreciated here most thoroughly and
he is being asked out as if he were a social lion.

The president of the British Life Saving Society yesterday visited him
at his quarters on the *Finland,* and offered him an extremely handsome
gold cup if he succeeds in covering the one hundred meter swim in a
minute flat.

Kahanamoku may take up the offer later.

This led to much confusion in Duke's staunch supporters home in the islands.
They were totally unprepared for the electrifying news that their boy had been

declared the world's 100-meter champion. Not only had he beaten his rivals, but he had also established a new world's record. Negroes and Indians had also carried the American banners to victory. But Duke Kahanamoku, the Hawaiian, was the only non-white team member to win his event and also set a world's record. It was noted by the press that Duke had comported himself as a gentleman and had accomplished much in promoting international friendships.

Duke's victory brought an extra dividend. Hawaii—a small territory of the United States—had now been brought to the attention of the whole world.

Days passed before the misunderstanding of Duke's status was cleared up in Hawaii. Even with the report of his triumphs, a cloud seemed to pervade the picture.

The *Honolulu Star-Bulletin* made the first attempt at correction when it ran this box item:

DUKE KAHANAMOKU WORLD'S CHAMPION
San Francisco, July 16,1912.
Duke Kahanamoku won July 10. Time, 1 minute, 3 2-5 seconds.

This dispatch was received by the *Star-Bulletin* yesterday afternoon and cleared up the misunderstanding regarding the performance of the Hawaiian swimmer at Stockholm. In the cable received by the *Advertiser* the night of July 10 there was, as will be remembered, a description of the ovation given Kahanamoku, but not a word which indicated that the race he had won that day was the final in the 100-meter swim. Previously the Associated Press had announced that the first race would have to be "reswum." It was believed in this office that the race reported July 10 was that recontested event.

The Advertiser tried to further clear the air with this column:

MIX UP OVER DUKE'S SWIM
AT STOCKHOLM IS NOW EXPLAINED

That there was general mix up in the 100-meter swimming race at Stockholm, Honolulu was already aware of some days ago, and the Coast papers which arrived yesterday confirmed this feeling.

One San Francisco paper says:

The semifinals of the 100-meter swimming race was a fiasco, the Americans remaining aboard their ship in ignorance that the events were to be staged that day. The races however, were run without the attendance of the Americans, the first heat going to Healy of Australia in 1:05 3-5 and the second to Bretting of Germany in 1:04 3-5. Through this misunderstanding the Americans may lose the finals of this event.

The Hawaiian, Kahanamoku, is the talk of the town for the easy, nonchalant manner in which he performs, he taking his heat in the 100-meter swim in 1:02 2-5, a new world's record. The president of the British Lifesaving Society has offered the kanaka a beautiful trophy if he does the distance in a minute or better.

The Americans did not, however, lose the finals of the event, the Duke won easily, after the committee decided to allow the Americans a chance in the race.

There had been some criticism as to whether the Hawaiian should compete as an American, but it was pointed out that he is in the same position as the Indian, Ranji, who for years represented England in cricket.

There was a difference of a full second in the times reported in the dispatches and in the news columns. It mattered little, Hawai'i was simply jubilant over her son bringing home an Olympic championship. One second more or less—who cared?

After the first exciting headlines, later items continued to play up the event. On July 11th, the *Pacific Commercial Advertiser* ran :

SWEDISH ROYALTY CONGRATULATES DUKE
BEFORE CROWDS IN STADIUM

Under the capitalized heading with Stockholm dateline, was this:

Duke Kahanamoku is by all odds the most popular Olympian in Stockholm. For several days the people have gone wild over him and yesterday Royalty itself unbent to welcome the Hawaiian swimmer into the Royal box in the stadium while the vast throng of more than ten thousand people cheered and yelled and gave him an ovation that he will remember as long as he lives.

Duke was brought into the stadium to hear the announcement of the results of the swimming heats yesterday. There was the usual enormous crowd, lines upon lines of humanity apparently stretching away to the sky, and banked high above the Royal box, at one end of the huge oval. The King, Gustav V, the Queen and a throng of courtiers, diplomats, ambassadors and military and naval attaches, all in uniform, were in the box. The scene was a most brilliant one.

When the announcer made the official statement that Kahanamoku had won the heat in the time hitherto unequalled, of one minute, three and two-fifths seconds, faster than anyone had ever gone through the water before, there was a tremendous roar from the crowds, and it swelled and beat against the sides of the arena until it sounded like the rumble of thunder.

As it reached its height King Gustav, who has taken great interest in the games and particularly in the aquatic sports, leaned forward from his seat and beckoned to the Hawaiian lad, standing alone, slightly forward of the little clump of swimmers. Kahanamoku hesitated and then as others called him, mounted to the box.

King Gustav rose and clasped his hand, and congratulated him heartily, declaring it was a pleasure to meet the man who had lowered the pride of the world's best swimmers, with so little preliminary experience. He then introduced Kahanamoku to the Queen, who was sitting smiling at the big, dark-faced lad, who accepted the ovation given him modestly, and without apparent embarrassment.

Kahanamoku is only one of the Americans here who have been winning against odds, and outclassing all who have gone against them. The Americans have succeeded in placing thirteen contestants to England's six and Germany's six, in the six finals, the preliminaries for which have been played off to date. In all, America has won 72 points to Great Britain and her colonies' 65, and Sweden's 57.

Two days later, with the Olympiad still in progress, the same paper ran:

HAWAIIAN BOY ONCE MORE SHOWS WORLD'S SWIMMERS WHAT HE CAN DO. AMERICANS NOW FAR IN LEAD IN STOCKHOLM, WINNING OTHER RECORDS.

Dated July 13th from Stockholm, it read:

Duke Kahanamoku, the Hawaiian swimmer again proved his superiority yesterday when by his great speed he enabled the American 800 meter relay team, of which he, McGillivray and Hebner were members, to win first place in the big race.

The big Hawaiian boy was given another ovation by the enormous crowd when he left the water after making a great showing. His popularity is increasing rather than decreasing every day.

None of this was lost on Duke's family. The Kahanamokus adored him. On July 13th, one of Honolulu's largest papers went into great detail on Duke's father's reactions. Readers found it warming that the father of a now renowned athlete remained modest.

One reporter went to the Kahanamoku home on Kalia Road (where the Hilton dome currently stands) to interview the gray-headed police officer. It wasn't much of an interview, for the policeman was so humble he would hardly say anything about his now-famous son.

"Now that your boy is an Olympic champion," the reporter said, "the whole world wants to know about his family, his ancestry."

"He's the same *keiki kane* (boy) today that he was last week." smiled the elder Kahanamoku. "He's still our young Paoa."

The reported startled. "Paoa?" This was new. "That's his name?" he asked.

The father nodded. "His middle name. Those closest to him call him Paoa; he likes it."

Proud and loving Mrs. Kahanamoku, who spoke little English, stood by quietly and proudly, obviously delighted that her oldest son had so distinguished himself.

It was clear that both parents were reluctant to say much about their boy, so the reporter deftly switched to other topics. He found they were members of the Reorganized Church of Latter Day Saints, and that Duke was also. He learned that the tall, well-built father was formerly a receiving clerk at the police station, then sergeant, and now a captain. He recorded that the father and all the sons were good swimmers and top surfers, though it was Duke who had always excelled.

"Does the name Kahanamoku have any special significance?" the newsman asked.

"It signifies 'shipbuilder'," he was told.

Feeling frustrated in his first effort to get a satisfactory story on the family's reactions, the reporter finally put the question point blank "Just what do you really think of your son now, Captain?"

"He's a pretty good boy" was the answer.

Grinning at the understatement, the newsman pushed on with, "Surely, you read everything about him in the papers."

Captain Kahanamoku looked away. He was so proud of his oldest boy's successes that he could not bring himself to talk about it. The reporter made what few notes he could, then beat a retreat. He could now well understand where the young Duke had learned his humility—and this was a news item itself. The newsman hurried back to his paper.

Not only did Duke's Olympic feat continue to be featured in island papers, it engendered many other surprising activities. One was the commercial use of Duke's name. The following ad appeared in the *Advertiser* of July 15th, 1912.

While Duke was still in Europe a committee of Honolulu's most prominent citizens (including Prince Jonah Kuhio Kalaniana'ole, then delegate to Congress) started a campaign to collect funds for the returning hero. They wanted to present him with a tangible expression of Hawai'i's appreciation and esteem.

No one had ever brought as much world-wide attention to the islands as had this youth. He was the most famous Hawaiian alive. Hawai'i was already turning an eye to the tourist trade. Who could be a better advertisement? Publicity given Duke was publicity for this Pacific paradise. All the work of a visitor's bureau could not compare with Duke's power; he had focussed the world's eye on the islands as no one ever before. It wouldn't do to lose Duke Paoa Kahanamoku, so it was decided to give him a home to assure his remaining in Hawai'i. The Kalia district was selected and a respectable little house and lot was picked out. Adjacent to Waikīkī, the home shaped up as one that would please Duke no end.

It was felt that Duke's presence would attract tourists and encourage water sports of every kind. Sensing that questions about the so-called "ugly head of professionalism" might rise up, the powers-that-be worked out arrangements to avoid any problems. Duke's amateur status would be unblemished.

Plans were taken over by the *Star-Bulletin* and the *Advertiser,* and the papers cooperated in fund collections. However, progress was slower than had been anticipated. On July 14th, the *Advertiser* ran a column reading, in part:

KAHANAMOKU FUND IS GROWING FAST

The Duke Kahanamoku fund is growing fast, several donations having been secured in this office yesterday. Yesterday's amounts contributed through the *Advertiser* were:
James Austin Wilder $ 4.00 A.
A. Wilder 10.00
A. L. Castle 1.00
Woodrow Wilson enthusiasts
at the University Club 16.00
                    Total $31.00

Meanwhile there were other hurried suggestions as to what Hawai'i should do for the young man who had already done so much for the islands. On July 20th, the *Advertiser* ran a column reading:

GIVE DUKE EDUCATION IS LATEST SUGGESTION

Ideas as how to properly honor our world championship swimmer, Duke Paoa Kahanamoku, keep coming in steadily to the sporting editor of the *Advertiser*. The last one to find its way to the scribe's desk is not a bad one after all and deserves serious consideration.

"Just tell them for me," said a sport last night, "that it may be very well to give Duke a house and lot, but I doubt if that is the best way to honor and boost the boy.

"Now, my way of thinking is to send Duke back to the
Mainland for a real good education. Of course, let him come
back here for a spell, but an education that will fix him for
life is what he should have coming to him. It is true that he
cannot make Pennsylvania University now, until he prepares for
it, but it would be well to pay his way through some good
school near the Quaker seat of learning, and if necessary fit
him for the university later. There, he would be near George
Kistler, the great swimming instructor, who would have him in
hand and keep him in trim to defend his title four years hence.
    "Kistler has said that Duke is not near the height of his best
form and the way he turned in the finals at Stockholm to see
how his competitors were doing shows that he could have
made the distance in better time and probably beaten the
record he made in the trials."

Suggestions for rewarding the Duke were coming in from everywhere. In the
eyes of Hawai'i he was a king in his own right. People were wracking their brains
to come up with a suitable gift of appreciation.

Other means were developed to help swell the fund for Duke. One that went
well was first introduced through an *Advertiser* headline:

POSTCARD SALE WILL GO TO AID DUKE FUND

The article described how *malihini* (newcomers) and *kama'āinas* (long-time
residents) alike could contribute to the Duke Kahanamoku fund by purchasing
hand-painted postcards of the new world's-champion swimmer. The pictures had
been taken by J. J. Williams, the veteran photographer of the city and the cards
would be displayed in the window of the Honolulu Photo Supply Company.

The cards would sell for ten cents each and that all anyone needed was a
postage stamp and an address to have them sent to distant friends. It was also
explained that gross, not net, receipts would go to the fund. The cards sold well.
People bought them as souvenirs for themselves as well as for friends throughout
the world. Most bought them simply to contribute to a worthy cause.

The pictures had that certain intangible Duke Kahanamoku appeal. One showed him moving through the water with his famous "Kahanamoku stroke." A second had a humorous touch. It was captioned "Canoeboy of Waikīkī" and showed Duke atop an overturned bucket with his thumbs curled little-boy-like under the straps of his bathing suit. A third simply pictured him standing on the beach.

The papers played the fund like a brass band and the money rolled in. Mayor Fern handled one subscription list. Board of Health employees initiated another. Others came from Honolulu Iron Works people and one by the local brewery employees. One paper later mentioned that "The Police Department will also show its regard for the son of their captain of the third watch by contributing a neat fund."

Clubs, schools, and individuals pooled contributions for the Kahanamoku fund. A benefit baseball game was organized by the Athletic Park and Oahu League. It was a play-off of the Star-J.A.C. tie for the championship. More than one hatful of currency and coins swept into the swimmer's fund from the crowd.

It was only much later that Duke learned of the character and extent of these fund-raising efforts. He felt both complimented and embarrassed. On one hand he was touched with pride to realize that the people of Hawai'i had so much faith in him and wanted him to represent them. On the other hand, he was troubled by the flavor of huckstering; it smacked a little of begging. But Duke kept his own counsel and said nothing lest he appear unappreciative. He realized that these friends had made their efforts for a cause that matched his own.

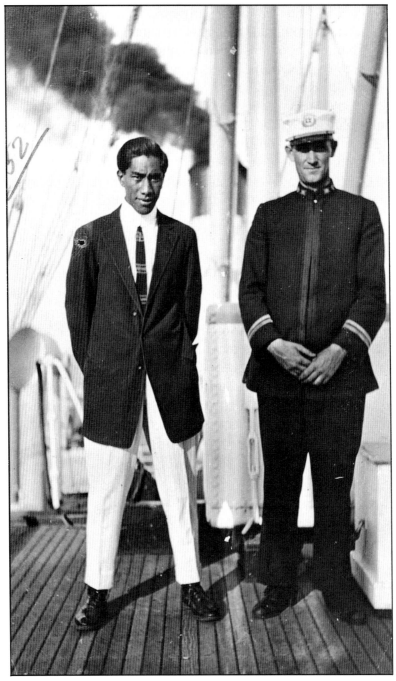

Duke with ship's officer aboard S.S. Wilhelmina c. 1912
Bishop Museum Photo

8

Junket—European Style

HAWAI'I CONTINUED TO REVEL IN DUKE'S SENSATIONAL WIN. On July 16th the *Pacific Commercial Advertiser* ran:

AMERICANS, WINNERS, TO SAIL FROM OLYMPIC GAMES TODAY

> *The Olympic Games for 1912 are over, leaving America with 128 points, Sweden with 104 points, Great Britain with sixty-six points and Germany with twenty-four points.*

Highlighted by the column was James Thorpe, the great all-around member of the American team, a Carlisle Indian athlete who had won the decathlon. It also noted that America took a second in the 800-meter four-man relay swim.

But nothing touched the Hawaiian islanders like the news that their Duke Kahanamoku had won his event. After that everything else was anticlimactic. Their boy had won and was expected to return home with the other winners. So there was some shock in the islands when it was learned that Duke was delaying his return for a performance tour before coming home. He was obviously enjoying life.

Duke had become more than just an Olympic champion. He had an extra dimension not found in all champions—style. His charm, background, personality and speed were all part of one big beautiful package. Wholly in sync.

Duke added showmanship to his swimming and he was in demand everywhere. Every city in Europe and America with a swimming pool wanted to see the big Hawaiian swimmer. Once they even abandoned the pool, when in Paris Duke swam in the Seine River. His was a class act.

For a while Duke and his beloved islands were in different worlds. Over the next nine months, Duke competed in races and exhibitions throughout Europe and the United States. Other prominent Olympic athletes also engaged in these barnstorming shows and records continued to fall. In Hamburg, Germany, on July 22nd, Duke again set a new record for the 100-meter freestyle. He clocked a time of one minute and one-fifth of a second, breaking his own earlier record of one minute two and two-fifth seconds set during a preliminary heat in Stockholm.

Public speculation immediately focused on Duke's one day soon swimming the 100-meter dash in a minute flat. What had formerly seemed incredible, now looked distinctly possible. Everybody wanted to be there when it happened. Crowds turned out in legions, each time eagerly expecting some spectacular new clocking.

Islanders were again agog when reading in their July 23rd *Pacific Commercial Advertiser:*

> Give our Duke another chance and he'll make the hundred meter water dash in a minute flat. The Hamburg sports pulled off a meet all their own in that free town yesterday and Duke surprised the good Hamburgers by making the hundred in just one-fifth of a second over the minute, which is a new record even for Duke, who made the distance in one of the Stockholm heats in sixty-two and two-fifths.

Duke's supporters rejoiced in his victories, but they were impatient for him to return home. They wanted to publicly honor him. With Duke's ever expanding international fame, nothing could halt the continued probing of his personal history. This wasn't easy, for Hawaiians were frequently uncommunicative about their family trees. When reporters confronted Duke with questions about his ancestry he modestly answered, "I'm just another beachboy from Waikīkī." As long as he continued to duck the question with his modesty and humility, the press had to investigate in the one place where the facts might be found—at home.

That wasn't easy. Hawaiians had no written language until the missionaries devised one in the 1800s. Throughout centuries they had successfully passed the history of their race by word of mouth. They used *mele* (chants) to record historic events and genealogies. With the repression of the Hawaiian traditions by the missionaries, much history was lost entirely, and much was distorted.

Newsmen ransacked all available sources of Kahanamoku history. They interviewed the former Lady-in-Waiting to Queen Lili'uokalani, who explained that grandmother Kahoeha and grandfather Kahanamoku of Duke Paoa Kahanamoku were *kahu* (retainers) of Bernice Pauahi Paki Bishop. She clarified the fact that to be a *kahu* of royalty was to be a close, intimate friend and almost invariably a blood-relative or *kahuali'i*. Mrs. Webb defined it further by saying,

"Queen Lili'uokalani had a habit of reminding people, 'When royalty is born, those who work for them, *kahu,* also are born.'"

Haole reporters had not known much Polynesian tradition. Mrs. Webb further explained that Hawaiian children were disciplined against exposing family relationships; neither would retainers or *kahu* speak of their relationships. In this, family histories were kept vague and sacrosanct.

Vague or not, newsmen sensed they were on the trail of an exotic genealogy for the athlete who carried and comported himself in such a royal manner. Perhaps because of his humility, this full-blooded Hawaiian had something kingly about him. He epitomized decency and dignity.

In an effort to substantiate what they had been told, reporters combed the records of the State Library, Punahou School Library, State Archives, and Bishop Museum. Much they unearthed seemed contradictory, and much of the rest ambiguous. They could only pick and choose the pieces they had unearthed to the limits of their abilities and honesty.

Another source of authentic information on Duke and his ancestry was his first cousin, Maria Kanehaikana Pi'ikoi. She was called "Auntie" Maria by those who knew and loved her. Generously, she filled in more of Duke's genealogy. Her family history paralleled that of another informant, the late Emma Ahuena Taylor. The latter explained that Duke's ancestors through his mother, Julia Paakonia Lono Kahikini, contributed to his *ali'i* ancestry. One of Duke's great-grandfathers (on the maternal side) was Paoa Hoolae of the Big Isle of Hawai'i. His wife was Hiikaalani. Their son Paoa—Duke's grandfather—assumed the family name of Paoa in lieu of Hoolae. Paoa's wife (Duke's grandmother) was Mele Uilama. This explained where Duke got his middle name. It also revealed how the name Paoa (not Hoolae) appears in the Great Mahele of 1848 for acreage in Kālia, Waikīkī, registered in that book of land grants. This is the area where the Kahanamoku and Paoa homes were later built.

Taylor traced the Paoa family tree and showed where Duke was a descendant of Kina'u (*kuhina nui* or premier) of the Kamehameha blood. She pointed out that Duke's mother, Kahoeha, was the granddaughter of Makue and Halapu (Duke's father's middle name), who were descended from the ancient Alapainui line. The "Alapai" family named survived as a middle name for Duke's brother Samuel. The Alapais became neighbors of the Kahanamoku-Paoa families. An Alapai gave testimony to the land court on behalf of the Paoa claim for the piece of land at Kālia Road. The land board commission accepted his statement without question.

Piece by piece, a mixed bag of these facts went into print.

Sports-minded people throughout the world were eager to learn more about Duke's ancestral background. In time it was reported that the swimming idol was full-blooded Polynesian with royal blood coursing through his veins. The public was even more enchanted. Here was a top athlete with kingly blood in his veins. He was a product of ancient men who, in the dim past, had sailed away from the southeast mainland of Asia, and, in their powerful sailing canoes, had become masters of the sea. They were watermen in every sense, sailing, paddling, surfing, diving, and swimming.

Duke became a symbol of all that was respected and loved in Hawai'i. He publicly represented its people and he secretly cherished this idea. This realization etched deep into his brain and he knew he'd have to work hard to live up to his image. It would not be easy for this fun-loving islander.

The challenge to maintain his image rode with him day and night. The thought was infectious; he hugged it to himself. There must be no juvenile acts, nothing in his behavior to show that the beachboy had not yet developed into a man. He intended to hold tight to this image, let it grow, and keep it shining. He felt he owed it to his family and to Hawai'i.

Yet, in a moment of simple love for swimming, he did something that almost wrecked the very image he wanted to preserve. After the close of his continental barnstorming, Duke was aboard the old slow-moving steamer *New York,* en route from Europe to America. In mid-Atlantic the big vessel developed engine trouble and was momentarily adrift in choppy seas. The ship had no swimming pool so Duke had not been able to swim for quite some time. So, with the steamer stalled for mechanical repairs, he donned his bathing suit and, to the astonishment of passengers and crew alike, dove over the side.

Not until Duke had swum well away from the ship did he have any idea of how fast it was drifting. In addition, it was only after he was actually in the water that he realized just how choppy the sea really was. It was a far cry from the flat water in which he was used to swimming.

Faint glimmers of worry began. He turned toward the ship and made no progress. Yells of delight from passengers lining the rails now turned into cries of alarm. Realizing too late how fast the *New York* was receding, Duke turned on all his swimming power and dug hard for it. It was a hopeless battle. Passengers, crewmen, and officers were mesmerized by the sight of his predicament.

"Man overboard!" rang the cry. Bells sounded. People rushed up from below. The ship's rail became even more jammed as Duke's head and shoulders grew smaller in the distance. Meanwhile the ship's engines were still dead and she had no power to move.

"Lower the lifeboard!" an angered captain finally called out.

Immediately a lifeboard was manned, and swung out from davits for its slow descent. By the time the sailors got to their oars and started rowing, Duke's head was only a pinpoint in the bouncing sea. It took heavy, fast sweeping of the oars to reach him. When they finally picked up Duke and returned him to the still drifting *New York,* the vessel's skipper was fit to be tied. Olympic hero or not, Duke was roundly chewed out by the captain. Nothing in the way of any apology the Islander could make would placate the officer.

During the next several days, Duke's almost disastrous swim gave rise to much shipboard talk about his still being only a kid at heart. This wasn't the image Duke wanted to present. He felt considerably less than the perfect image of the noble Polynesian which the press and the public had created for him.

Duke   *Courtesy of Cedric Felix*

9

Hawaii Could Ask No More

HISTORIANS TELL US THAT WHEN CAPTAIN COOK SAILED INTO HANA, MAUI IN 1778, THE HAWAIIANS GREETED HIM WITH CEREMONY AND GIFTS. They believed that the great Polynesian god Lono—long absent—had finally returned.

Runners brought word to King Kalani'opu'u that strange floating *heiau* (temples), with great wings, were in the bay.

The *Resolution* and *Discovery,* the British ships, appeared huge to the Hawaiians. Accompanied by a fleet of gift-laden canoes, Kalaniopu'u and many retainers met the strange floating "temples" and gave Cook and his crew a magnificent welcome.

That welcome was probably no more elaborate, sincere—or noisy—than that given Duke Paoa Kahanamoku when he returned to Honolulu on October 1st, 1912. He was aboard the Matson liner *Wilhelmina,* which was arrayed with the flags of many nations, honoring her famous passenger. Cannons on the forts boomed and boats on the waterfront gave forth with a bedlam of whistle blowing. Thousands of supporters clogged the wharves and hundreds more yelled and waved from nearby small craft as the big liner docked. Her own horn answered the pandemonium. This day was for a returning hero, away from home too long.

As the gangway was attached shouts rattled the sky. Duke Kahanamoku, with his best smile, strode down to meet the outstretched arms. Those closest saw no boastful returning hero. They saw a modest—even shy—boy who had won at what he liked best, thrilled to be home, but still embarrassed by the overwhelming show being lavished upon him.

Friends and relatives poured up the gangway to meet him, grabbing hands, arms, and piling lei around his neck. His suitcase was suddenly gone—David had it. His mama was there, hugging him and crying. Papa was shaking his hand and squeezing his arm. Duke was almost in shock, "Aloha nui!" was all he could say, "Aloha nui!"

Before Duke could hardly even greet his friends and loved ones, he had lei heaped so high he couldn't even see. He looked like a flower-bedecked Kentucky Derby winner.

Next, strong hands hoisted him to the shoulders of two stout supporters. There he rode like a chieftain, his smile a yard wide.

"I'd rather walk!" he protested, but his huge grin proved him a liar. They carried him, yelling until they were hoarse.

The rest of the day and night was a tangled skein. They threw a massive lūau (feast) for Duke at the home of Henry Paoa (his mother's brother) on Kālia Road. His parents, brothers and sisters, and all his other relatives and friends were on hand.

Duke had brought great honor to Hawai'i and popularized it to the world as no one else had ever done. News of the swimmer with the magic name always created news of his fabulous homeland. He had not only won a title, he had won the hearts of people throughout the world. Fourteen years earlier the world had thought of Hawai'i, if it had at all, as pinpoints of Pacific land annexed as a minor territory by the United States. Now the world saw Hawai'i as a living place, filled with people like Duke Kahanamoku.

Hawai'i could ask no more.

After all the parties ended, succeeding days began to present Duke with his life's great dilemma—making an income. With a limited education, he wasn't really trained for anything. Having gone no farther in school than six months at McKinley High, his "drop-out" status was now a problem.

Adulation Duke had, but he still needed to make a living. Being popular was one thing—but earning a dollar was quite another. In the past Duke had made a little money stevedoring on the Honolulu Harbor docks and had picked up some extra change beachboying at Waikīkī. Now, quite naturally, he wanted better. But, being unequipped in a business sense, Duke would have to take what he could get. Lucrative offers to turn professional with his swimming were brought to him, but he turned them down. "I owe it to my friends to stay amateur," he countered. "There will be more Olympics." Amateur he remained.

He could have stayed on the beach as a tourist attraction and accepted the largess of a doting public, but Duke elected to take a respectable job with the city. He wound up doing many things. He was a water inspector, reading meters, for the Public Works Department. He worked in the drafting department at 'Iolani Palace, copying and tracing lines until he ached for the sight and feel of the Waikīkī waters. For a while he was a chainman on surveying jobs, and at least that kept him outside. He was even approached to turn to professional boxing, but quickly decided that the fight game had more characters than character.

To help support his big family, Duke still spent much of his spare time as a

Duke returning from victorious swimming tour in Europe and U.S.A.
Arriving aboard S.S. Wilheminia at Honolulu on October 1st, 1912.
Joseph Brennan photo Collection

Duke's trophy collection as it appeared in August 1913.
L.E. Edgeworth Collection, Bishop Museum.

Duke at AAU swim meet, June 1913 (above and facing page)   *Courtesy of Cedric Felix*

Duke Kahanamoku image on a Mid-Pacific Carnival Poster.   *Bishop Museum*

A group of expert swimmers. The champion is in a bath-robe.   *Bishop Museum*

Duke Kahanamoku congratulates Bob Small as winner of the fifty yard dash (23-2/5 seconds), Febraury 21, 1914.   *Bishop Museum*

beachboy. He liked that it helped him stay in shape. Saturdays, Sundays, and holidays he helped with the outrigger canoes at the beach hotels. It didn't pay much, but every dollar was important. With his power and boat sense he was often the steersman. Oldtimers still talk of how, rather than use his paddle, Duke would steer and bring a canoe around with his immense feet. He picked up odd dollars here and there by teaching tourists to surf and swim. It was all income—as little as it was.

Duke found it rough, being a big star yet having such little income. He was a grown man, recently returned from being dined and wined like royalty. It was a bitter pill to settle for a meter reader's routine or an office boy's pay. Trying to adjust left him confused and bewildered. He continued to flounder, trying to scrounge out a living.

What made it even worse was that, with his fame and good looks he was an outstanding attraction to women on the beach. The paradox was that he could not afford to take out the very lovelies who made such a fuss over him. He was too proud to let them pay. There were moneyed female tourists, including visiting heiresses and well-to-do kama'āina women who sought his companionship. It humiliated him to realize just how insignificant his income was. He wondered how his swimming talent could possibly gain him entry into something profitable.

In his Hawaiian way, he reminded himself that there are two lives for each of us—an outer one of action and an inner one of the heart and mind. He recognized that one can always see a man's deeds and outward character, but not the inner self. There was always that secret part to everyone that had its own life, unpenetrated and unguessed by others. In that secret life Duke quietly rebelled at being a celebrity without funds. He was celebrated and honored, but without the ability to hold up his own end.

"People are always doing for me," he confided sadly to his family. "Dinners, gifts, trips, parties. I never had money to square accounts."

His father reminded him, "You could take the pro offers that keep coming in."

Mixed guilt and loyalty prompted Duke to say, "But after all the AAU has done for me, seems like I should stay amateur."

"They probably expect it," his father agreed.

Duke wrestled with the dilemma of living in Hawai'i on the kindness of islanders and tourists alike, or accepting one of the proffered commercial propositions. To escape into further amateur tours and exhibitions would be the easy way out. But that still left him with the shame of not being able to reciprocate for new generosities from those whom he was already under personal obligation. It rankled his sense of justice. Duke and his father discussed all aspects of the situation, but coming up with an answer was no simple thing. The dilemma continued.

Duke as a young man in his twenties.　　　　　　　　*Hawaii State Archives*

10

Runaway Boy

DUKE FOUGHT WITH AN INSIDIOUS FEELING THAT HE WAS STAGNATING IN THE ISLANDS. He wrestled with the desperate alternative of turning fugitive, and decided that he would grab every possible opportunity to go on tour. Weary of being a moneyless celebrity, in 1914 he took refuge in a trip to San Francisco. There he swam at a festival meet of local swimmers and Chicago competitors. He continued cracking records in the freestyle events, bettering his own times from Europe. He was a sure thing for the next Olympics.

Duke, George Cunha and manager Francis Evans sailed November 30th, 1914, on the *SS Ventura* for Australia. They arrived in Sydney on December 14th to an excited reception. The Aussies, very swim-minded, had read about the islander and were anxious to see him in action. As a guest, at the New South Wales championship meet, Duke was again a much-heralded athlete—and in no need of funds. Once more he was being graciously boarded and dined by others.

Duke confided to Evans, "I know I'm just running away from my problems, but ..." In his own heart he knew that all of the traveling wouldn't alter his difficulties back home in Hawai'i. Evans could only nod understandingly.

Sporting bright yellow bands on their hats—symbols of their club—the three island men sat in the Hotel Australia lobby being interviewed by William F. Corbett of the *Sydney Sun*. Most questions were directed at Duke, the star of this junket.

Duke was quick to ask, "When do we race?" To him nothing counted more than the next chance to compete.

"January the second," the newsman answered, impressed by the Hawaiian's eagerness. While the interview continued other reporters strode up and also made notes.

One, Cecil Healy, was a correspondent for *The Referee*. He had swum second to Duke two years earlier in the 100-meter swim at Stockholm. Healy stepped up and grabbed the visitor's hand, "Remember me?" he grinned.

Duke, great on names and faces, joked, "You're getting fat, Cece." To save the man any embarrassment, he added, "We're all getting fat." But it was a white lie, for the former competitor could easily see that Duke was still in top condition.

Another, William Longworth, who had swum against Duke at Stockholm also ambled up to say hello. Old friends and new barged in from every side. Duke was back in stride. The twenty-four year-old from Waikīkī beamed as he shook scores of hands. He was again somebody; somebody without financial worries.

Sydney newspapers described Duke as "an intelligent, bright fellow with an attractive personality and a modest reserve." His visit was important to the people of "Down Under." The country had been at war with Germany since the preceding summer, and people needed a lift. Duke proceeded to furnish it.

At the formal reception Duke was called upon to talk. Speeches were never his strong point, but he knew he had to say a few words. "I'm not as good a speaker," he said modestly, "as others here." His eyes dwelt on Cunha, Evans, and some of his competitors. "But, in the water, I'll do my best to please everybody."

Duke sat down to resounding applause. It had been a long speech for him, but the ring of sincerity and his obvious modesty had captivated his listeners. The Aussies loved him, even believing that he would beat their men in the upcoming meet.

Cunha and Evans rose and spoke their thanks for their heart warming reception. Others made speeches welcoming all who had come to Australia to compete. Most declined to try and pronounce "Kahanamoku," calling him simply "Duke."

The greetings and hospitality again had Duke feeling like a man of substance. Water-meter reading, stevedoring, beachboy work, and pencil pushing all vanished for the moment.

"I feel almost successful for a change," he confided to his manager. "I don't feel broke."

His anxiety to perform in the water grew. He knew he would feel even better as soon as he started racing. It had always been this way. Duke sometimes said, "Out of the water I'm nothing."

Duke was relieved when he, Cunha, and Evans were driven to the Domain Bath, a pool of exceptional beauty. Examining its size and decor, the Americans could not help expressing their admiration.

"A few days of loosening up," mused Duke, "and maybe we'll set some new records." He grinned and headed for the dressing rooms. Few steamers boasted swimming pools those days and it had been a long time since his last swim.

George and Duke were soon swimming, with a goodly crowd observing. Experts and reporters watched with interest, blinking at what they saw. Duke finished up several fast laps, came to a stop at the tank's rim, and did his own blinking at the excited observers. He turned to Cunha. "George," he said in a low voice, nodding at the jabbering spectators, "what's wrong? They sound like a treeful of wet mynah birds."

"They can't get over your style," Cunha replied.

Cunha was right. Next morning all the local sports pages carried descriptions of Duke's form. Some were written in praise, some in censure, but all admitted that the young Hawaiian must have something to have set all his records.

One reported, "The 'Kahanamoku Kick' is a method of propulsion different in some respects to the Australian Crawl-stroke leg-movement and different also to the alleged improvement that swimmers of the Middle-West and East of the United States claim they have discovered."

Another wrote, "The 'Hawaiian Kick' is much different from that of other swimmers. His is the movement of a crew-propelled boat. The legs are much more in service than the arms. Experts hold the opinion that his unusually large pedal extremities are an advantage to him."

Experts like William F. Crobett and Frank Beaurepaire discussed Duke's style. Corbett noted that "No one has used this kick and stroke to win like Duke has...The 'Kahanamoku Kick' is unique in that it takes advantage of kicking under water as well as on the surface."

Duke's first Australian demonstration had swimming enthusiasts astonished.

Two weeks passed while Duke practiced daily and acclimated to Australia's summer, preparing for the thirty-three-race tour. The first event was January 2nd, 1915, at the Domain Bath in Sydney.

Cecil Healy, the correspondent, described how the crowd waited for the islander with the hard-to-pronounce name. They shouted, "There he is!" when they spotted his smiling face in the row boat carrying Duke and Cunha from the far end of the Bath.

Healy wrote: "The Duke, with a beaming countenance was assisting to propel the craft and both he and Cunha waved their salutations to the crowd as they passed along."

Reaching the starting point, both swimmers stepped from the rowboat to the pool and nodded to the yelling fans.

Before the packed audience Duke took a preliminary dip to loosen up and adjust to the temperature. Australian fans hadn't seen this before, and a typical comment would have been: "My word, the lad will lose the ryce!"

Duke grinned self-consciously, took his few strokes down and back, and climbed out. His muscle-strapped body shone like a lacquered statue.

Cunha and Duke lined up with the best sprint swimmers in Australia: Page, Stedman, Longworth, and Barry. After being introduced, they toed the pool's rim and waited for the starter. They all got a good start, six bodies hitting the water simultaneously. Machine-like, they moved in an almost unbroken line, shoulder to shoulder.

Murmurs broke from the crowd. Fans had anticipated Duke breaking into an early lead. They immediately questioned whether Duke had lost his touted speed. "Had he ever been as good as the reports?"

At the halfway there was still no appreciable difference. Spectators bubbled with surprise. Were their own boys swimming faster than they ever had, outdoing themselves?

The noise grew until, at about three-quarters of the distance, Duke's head, chest, and shoulders rose from the water as his arms and legs began digging. He seemed to be climbing right out of the water under the mighty pull of his arms and the thrust of his legs and feet. He hit the finish in high gear and looked as though he'd go through the wall.

Duke's strong finish swung the applause from the local swimmers to Duke. The Aussies recognized a champion. The second- and third- placed men, Cunha and Barry respectively, swept up to the end and congratulated Duke. It hadn't really been a race once Duke fully opened up.

Always good sportsmen, the Australians became staunch admirers of the colorful Hawaiian. They next wanted to see Duke race against their middle-distance swimmers. The sprints were conceded, how about the 440-yard swim? Australia had some good men for that distance.

Happy to accommodate, Duke agreed to enter any event. The next meet was set for the 6th of January at the same pool, the 440-yard championship of New South Wales. Because of illness the powerful Bill Longworth was out, but four other top men would face Duke; Adrian, Page, Thomas, and Fitts.

Again excitement gripped the Aussies; they felt they had middle-distance men who could take the Hawaiian. Some believed that Duke's wide-margin win only four days earlier might lure him into a false sense of security. Maybe he would fatally underestimate his opponents.

The lineup brought the usual momentary hush to the crowd at the Domain Bath. Starter Fred Williams' hand rose, there was the gun's dry bark, and the quintet hit the water as one unit. They stayed that way for the first lap, arm to arm, head to head. There was one Aussie who would not be denied that day, Adrian. At the very last Adrian swept ahead in a driving finish, capturing first.

The applause was deafening. Duke was first to reach for Adrian's hand, "My congratulations!" he panted.

Town and Country Journal reported next morning:

> There never was so much excitement crammed into a short space of time as during the seconds it took the swimmers to cover that last lap. The Bronzed Islander put forth his supreme effort, but was beaten by a touch by Adrian.

It was good therapy for Duke to be beaten for a change. The 440 was not his distance—he knew it. But he had tried. He took the defeat well, knowing he had stepped into an event for which he was not properly trained. He wrote in detail to his father, ending: "Papa, Adrian won the race by six inches. I should have won. Really, I didn't try hard enough."

It was his first defeat in a long time, and only drove him to training harder and concentrating even more. He reviewed what George Kistler had taught him and all the tips he had gotten from other coaches and performers.

On January 9th, again at Sydney's Domain Bath, he won the 100-yard freestyle in the New South Wales Amateur Swimming Championship. He beat his fellow teammate, the dangerous Billy Longworth, and the record holder A. W. Barry. It was a big win.

The *Sydney Referee* reported:

> Duke took the plunge in the style popular with Americans, that is to say, they "flop" on their chests. At sixty yards, the Duke had but a lead of only a head over Billy Longworth, and A. W. Barry, the record holder. With the spectators figuring that the Duke was on the verge of defeat, he suddenly flashed ahead, leaving the others behind, as if they were stationary objects. George Cunha, the young "White Native of Honolulu" took second place from Barry and Longworth, who finished in that order.

It was a double victory for Duke, for he also won the 220-yard freestyle. Page was second, Cunha third, Thomas fourth, and Boardman fifth.

By this time, Duke's unique style had thoroughly captivated the Aussies. Experts debated it, pro and con. Some writers could see great things coming from the new style. Corbett of the *Sydney Sun* insisted that, despite Duke's world's record, the swimmer's condition suggested that he could do even better. Corbett added, "Duke has mastered the art of securing maximum of speed with minimum apparent effort."

The *New York Times* correspondent in Sydney went even farther:

> It is predicted by sporting authorities that the Australian "crawl" will have to give way to the "Kahanamoku Kick." The Duke's kick serves all the purposes of the "crawl" and it is much faster and needs less exertion than the Australians' method of locomotion in the water.

The same correspondent pointed out that Duke did not "bury" his head in the water, thereby lessening both drag and displacement.

When word of Duke's victory reached Honolulu, the *Advertiser* headlined on March 3rd:

DUKE KAHANAMOKU KICKS THE CRAWL OUT OF THE AUSTRALIANS!

The story pointed out that this particular newspaper had predicted that the "Kahanamoku Kick" would supersede the "Australian Crawl."

The *New York Times* correspondent wrote that before Duke's arrival in Sydney there had been much skepticism about his achievements. All doubts had vanished after the Hawaiian's Australian performance. He quoted a Sydney newspaperman's comment: "Kahanamoku has justified all that was said of him. Also, his sportsmanlike actions and good nature have made him very popular here."

The Sydney newspaperman knew that, despite Duke's being ill from the region's frightful heat, he never refused a race. Once the Islander even raced with a badly infected ear—against a doctor's advice.

From Duke's optimistic letters to this family one would never suspect he was enduring any great stress or strain. To his father he wrote: "Here in Allora, all is well with us. Swam here yesterday...in the 440 and won easily...We are heading for Brisbane...We'll swim at Rickhampton, Maryborough, Mount Morgan and then back to Sydney. After Sydney, we'll swim at Melbourne, then in New Zealand. My aloha nui to all at home."

But that was Duke; he would be the last to cry out. In the dressing room before an event his ear was giving him fearful pain. It only got worse during the wait. Still Duke swam.

Duke   *Courtesy of Tommy Holmes*

11

Poetry in Motion

THERE SEEMED NO END TO AUSSIE APPRECIATION. Duke's treatment was so generous that he felt indebted to every spectator. In his tours and exhibitions he reciprocated by always giving his best.

"Never saw such hospitality," Duke remarked to Evans one day. His manager could see the gratitude in Duke's eyes.

"They love you," Evans responded.

There was nothing the Australians asked which Duke would not try. He and George Cunha swam relays against teams of four men, something that had not been done before. It made for grueling races for the Islanders, but Duke felt he owed it to the people. George felt likewise and didn't hesitate to join in this exhausting swimming.

Melbourne was the next leg. There Duke won the 100-yard sprint in the Melbourne Swimming Carnival. He beat George Cunha, who was second, and Harry Hay, who was third. However, in the 100-meter handicap Duke and Hay swam a dead heat. Athletically and socially, Duke was accepted as a quality human being.

After remarkable performances in other cities, particularly Brisbane, Duke hit upon a novel way of doing something special for the folks "Down Under." He saw that they were not using surfboards, not taking advantage of their wonderful big surf. He decided to introduce the sport of Hawaiian kings to Australia.

The first and only surfboard imported to Australia at that time had come to C. D. Patterson from Honolulu in 1912. The contrivance had been tried—obviously without success—and had wound up as an ironing board in the Patterson home.

To Duke this was heresy. He picked out some fine sugar pine from George Hudson and made a demonstration board. He trimmed it to eight feet nine inches in length and made it concave underneath. The finished product weighed eighty pounds. It didn't compare to his own board back home in Waikīkī, but it would serve for exhibition surfing.

Duke selected Freshwater Beach (now Harbor) for his first demonstration. In February 1915 he put on a surfing show that captivated the throngs of Australians who crowded the shore. He soared and glided and drifted and side-slipped. He combined flying and sailing as only experienced surfers can. Duke was poetry in motion, board and surfer a single unit.

His grace and control riding the steep, long swells of Freshwater made the Aussies shout. They had never seen anything like it. Duke's exhibition turned them to making their own boards, introducing a sport that has since become an Australian addiction. But in truth, he gave Australia more than a great introduction to surfing. Duke created an interest in swimming the Aussies had never before known. His new style of swimming intrigued them, and they wanted it for their own. They were infatuated.

When Duke was ready for New Zealand and still more exhibitions, Fred Williams—often called "The father of surf-bathing in Australia"—paid the islander a great compliment. He said, "Duke Kahanamoku has left something, the great worth of which will be demonstrated in swimming seasons to come. The instinctive genius of the young Australian is well known. Already hundreds of him may be seen practicing the 'Kahanamoku Kick,' a method of propulsion different from other methods."

The Aussies hated to see Duke leave, for he had brought much to their land. In all he had won twenty-five of his thirty-three races (some handicap) and had always given people sparkling performances. They were grateful and he was appreciative of the hospitality bestowed. He felt he had evened things up a little.

At the farewell dinner, Duke complimented those who had been cheering him. "I've had a great time down here," he said. "I hate to leave such a wonderful place. I think, if I return to Australia in a year or so, it might be to be beaten."

After Duke took his bow, Fred Williams said, "What a wonderful knack he has of suiting himself to any position. This was especially noticeable at all gatherings and picnics of which he was the central figure." Resounding applause assured the assembly's agreement .

The American trio sailed to New Zealand aboard the *Moerake*. Arriving on February 23rd at Wellington, on the southern end of North Island, they were ready for more exhibitions. The mountains of the land had a majesty when the sun sloped on them. Duke couldn't keep his eyes off their splendor. Here, too, he found a warm, heady hospitality.

However warm the hospitality, they found the waters far chillier than they liked. But swim in them they did. From Wellington the threesome sailed across Cook Strait to South Island and entrained for Christchurch in Canterbury

Provincial District. They were greeted heartily by W.E.D. Bishop, President of the Canterbury Center. The press, dignitaries, and, particularly, the sports fraternity made them welcome.

Again the focus was mostly on Duke. One local paper described the swimmer in part as follows:

> Duke Kahanamoku would pass muster as a Maori [Polynesian aborigine of New Zealand], a rather big handsome Maori, with all the outward and visible qualities of the Native Islander. Only he comes from different latitudes, from a Little White Pearl of the North Pacific, the Islands of Hawaii, which to him is home.

Again hospitality was the order of the day. The swank Surf Club took the three under its care and guidance. They were feted that night at an excellent dinner. The following day they were motored to Rona Bay. After they were taken to Lyall Bay and hosted by High Chief and Mrs. H. Tukino.

They were greeted in true Maori style with, "Haere-mai! Haere-mai!" followed by the nose-pressing ceremony of welcome. An elaborate genuine Maori dinner, with all the trimmings, followed the initial welcome. Duke had the sensation of being royalty himself. This was a far cry from working for a fistful of coins in Honolulu, trying to appear financially self-sufficient.

Canterbury Center officials then escorted the threesome from the Tukino home to the beach at New Brighton. There Duke put on an exhibition in fancy surfboarding that thrilled the onlookers. He found the surf, in addition to being cold, was very fast-breaking. Pointing to his own board, he explained to the New Zealand watermen, "The boards you make will have to be much heavier, wider, and tapered at the ends." He delighted in being able to help the people being so hospitable to him.

They served Duke's group tea at the Surf Club, then took them back to the Tukino home. There Duke received more tribute. Mrs. Tukino addressed the Americans and the others. Chief Tukino entered a Maorian inscription into Duke's personal autograph album. Pictures were taken of Duke holding a baby. Finally, Duke was honored with a *haka* on the lawn and was told they were adopting him.

It was a day of honest fun. Duke had been feted like a Maori prince. As he and his party left there was more nose-pressing, more cries of "Haere-ra!,"—and not a few tears.

The stay at the Tukino's was followed by train south across the Canterbury Plains, parallel with the sea. They rode through Ashburton, Temuka, Timaru, Camaru, and Palmerston to Dunedin. Duke swam an exhibition at Dunedin and got to meet an old Hawaiian friend who had been living there for years. Renewing the friendship, he felt more at home than ever. From Dunedin he and his party went north by train, then took a boat across Cook Strait back to Wellington. From there they made short stops at other towns, finally arriving at Auckland in the middle of March.

George and Duke swam a few exhibitions and races in Auckland. By this time the Maori were calling Duke "The Human Fish." He thanked them by again breaking the world's record for fifty yards. Supplying this kind of showmanship inclined Duke to accept the native hospitality without guilt. This was the way he wanted his life; he felt he was paying his way.

So, without any qualms, he enjoyed taking several days with his group and seeing the beauties of Rotorura. He was able to leisurely appreciate the spa, boiling springs, living waters, and cooling 1000-foot elevation. Unhurried, he mixed with the Maori—went into their homes, became one of them. They performed ceremonial dances and showed him their big war canoes. In detail, and with real interest, he viewed their workmanship in decorative greenstone (nephritte) ornaments; *Tiki* (greenstone ornament in human form) and ceremonial *Toki Pou Tangate* (greenstone adze with carved haft). Duke was moved by the Maori culture and told his hosts he admired them.

The threesome returned once more to Auckland and sailed from there on their homeward journey aboard the *Niagara*.

"We've had a time," mused Duke quietly to Evans. Once more the brooding began, the brooding about the scheme of things back home, and just where Duke could possibly fit in.

Fear of again becoming a nonentity haunted Duke. He shuddered to contemplate again being of no consequence in a practical world. He looked ahead and thought, "How long will I be able to just rest on my swimming laurels?" He was headed home with a record of forty-five wins in sixty events, many of them handicap races. With all his notoriety and publicity, he still had to find the primrose path to financial success. He sensed that if he could not now achieve a decent-paying job at home, he would feel like a walking accident.

"Can't afford to get bitter," he told himself. "Too much of that, and I'll just crumble."

His thoughts turned to a recent dinner introduction. The master of ceremonies had begun: "We have Mister Swim with us tonight. In addition to his swimming talents, he has genius for another great coming sport. Ladies and gentlemen, do you want to know what a big surf is? A big, booming surf is Duke Kahanamoku. It is this gentleman I now introduce!"

In his present dilemma, Duke asked himself, "How can I capitalize on all the tribute and honor they pay me?" How, when, and where could he trade on his many honors to gain financial security—something tangible and bankable? He despaired at the prospect of always being the low man on the financial totem pole.

Duke Kahanamoku at Waikīkī
Tai Sing Loo, Bishop Museum photo

12

The Dilemma Remains

MUSICIANS AND FRIENDS WERE AT THE WHARF TO MARK THE THREESOME'S RETURN TO HAWAI'I. DUKE, GEORGE CUNHA, AND FRANCIS EVANS ARRIVED AT HONOLULU APRIL 4TH, 1915. They were thoroughly satisfied that the journey had been a success. With their wins and new records, and their reception by the Australians and New Zealanders, they knew the time had been well spent.

The *Honolulu Star-Bulletin* announced:

"Above all, this grand expedition, led by the Bronze Duke of Waikīkī, probably was the greatest creator of international goodwill ever sent out of Hawai'i."

Duke had been thinking hard about his personal situation, concentrating on it while aboard ship. Still as he watched the hazy, peaked outline of O'ahu rise from the ocean, he knew that he was as far from a solution as ever.

He was paying the price for being untrained and unschooled. People still paid him tribute—but not cash. Swimming events, exhibitions, and tours continued to be his only defense. As long as he could be top man in aquatics, he could walk like a man. Without the swimming he felt he was nothing; it was the one area where he was master.

It was not easy talking to his father about the dilemma.

"Do the thing that makes you happy," his father said. "It's your life."

"But I can't swim and surf forever," Duke answered quietly.

Kahanamoku senior looked away. "Happiness is when your heart is in the center of everything. So many people stand aside from life and just stare at it."

"I know, Papa," Duke said. "I know. And I want to enter life. Seems to me that life is a working out of what you are, and what you are is how you react."

"Then go your way, son. You're doing the thing you know and do best."

Father and son, they saw things the same way; they were eye to eye on this.

For three months Duke and George Cunha trained at Waikīkī before they left for the national championship meet at the San Franciso World's Fair.

With Harry Chilton as coach of the Hawaiian team, Duke went out and once again broke his own world record for the 100-yard freestyle. He negotiated it in fifty-one and three-fifths seconds. In later years he grinned when describing that particular race.

"I was swimming against Rathael of Chicago," he explained. "We ended in a dead heat, and there was nothing to do but swim the race again. With only a fifteen-minute rest we took our starting positions again. That time I beat the fellow by a whole body length. People were so excited they pushed Coach Chilton into the pool with his clothes on."

By this time Duke was on a touring merry-go-round. His reputation as a champion plus his great personal style kept him in high demand. He had learned to keep a weather eye open for aquatic events wherever they might be.

After numerous contests on the mainland, he returned to Hawai'i to train like a top-flight fighter. Competitive swimming had become a way of life. In 1916, in open water in Honolulu Harbor, on a relay team he turned his fastest time in the 100-yards. He clocked an incredible fifty-one and two-fifths seconds, earning more reviews.

August that year Duke entered a Y.M.C.A. meet in Honolulu. The local paper exclaimed:

DUKE SETS THREE NEW RECORDS AT YMCA PENTATHLON MEET!

Details followed of how he lowered the "All Navy" marks in the 75-yard swim, the 220-yard swim, and the towing race. In the water Duke could do no wrong. There seemed no limit to his record-breaking. He was truly in his element.

Shortly after, in still another meet, the paper headlined:

THREE WORLD'S RECORDS MADE IN YMCA MEET

The subhead offered:

Duke Kahanamoku Makes World's Record Time in 100-Yard Swim for Tank, 53 25.
YMCA Relay Team Breaks World's Records for 400 and 500-Yard Relay—Largest Crowd Ever in Attendance at "Y" Watches Meet—Kelii, Kruger, Lane, Cunha and Duke Star.

The column said in part:

When George Cunha had finished his lap, the spectators and timers were dubious. They feared that the attack on the record had failed. Duke Kahanamoku would have to break a record to make the time better. It did look bad at first, but when Duke began his event with a fast steady stroke and made a perfect turn on the first two laps, the spectators began to wonder if the record would not be smashed after all.

There were a number of pacemakers giving Duke a race, and the world's champion passed them by, his work on the turns being perfect. Swimming critics had predicted that Duke would flash the 100 in 55. He did, and crossed them by swimming the fastest 100 yards ever marked for a tank. He came within 1-5 of a second of the world's record held by himself, which was made in open water.

It finished with:

Duke had to lower the world's record to tie the mark made by the Illinois Athletic Club, and the spectators will not soon forget the fast hundred made by the champion. "Even Duke can't do it," was heard on every side after the timers had checked up at the end of the fourth relay. But once again the champion proved that he could rise to occasions, and there are a heap of swimming devotees who will change their minds regarding any of the visitors taking the honors home with them for the 100-yard swim which will be held on Labor Day.

So Duke rolled along, distinguishing himself chiefly in swimming, but also spending time surfing and in other aquatic sports. A natural athlete, Duke proved superb at a vast number of competitive sports. Water polo, body-surfing and racing outrigger canoes were longtime favorites. It was not long before he added yachting, barge-rowing, and singles and doubles sculling. Duke even started golfing, and here, too, showed great talent.

It is interesting to note that, prior to 1911, when he had his first triumph swimming, Duke had always wanted to be a champion single sculler. He once told Colonel Edwin North McClellan, a close friend, "I did not think much about swimming back in 1908 and 1909, although I knew I was pretty fast. Since I could not afford a scull, I took up rowing with the locals clubs."

In 1916 Duke could enjoy rowing. He rowed for pleasure, he rowed for conditioning, and he rowed for club wins.

The Fourth of July Regatta at Pearl Harbor in 1916 was one to remember. Duke was entered in three events. He was Number Four in the boat *James L. Torbett*, and assisted the Myrtle Club to defeat the strong Healani Club. He was stroke in the boat *Pearl-C* or *Kahululani*, with George Chillingsworth, which won the Pair-Oar Race. Then in a Scull Class-A Race, Duke battled against Bob Fuller of the Healanis, defeating him in a spectacular finish.

But life was not all swimming and surfing. He had other interests, as any normal young man did. Bernyece Smith came into his life at this time. She came into his life as softly and unostentatiously as she went out of it two years later.

Bernyece was employed by the Public Utilities Commission in Honolulu. She rented a bungalow on Beach road (Kālia Road today)—a stone's throw from where the Royal Hawaiian Hotel was built in 1927. The cottage was the home of Duke's cousin, Maria Pi'ikoi, who had lived there for many years. Bernyece shared it with two other girls and a Japanese housekeeper. Under the coconut trees, with the trade winds gently fanning the beach, they made a happy laughing family.

Duke resided not far from here and was "Big Brudder" to all, spending more time in Maria's little house than he did in his own. When the girls needed a picture hung, a nail driven, or anything which in those days took a man's hand, it was always Duke to the rescue.

Duke loaned Bernyece a camera given to him while on his Australian tour. He didn't know how important that camera would become. Bernyece recorded their free and happy life at Waikīkī with the camera. Fondness grew between Duke and Bernyece. She found Duke toiling in bewilderment about what to do with life. Together they found inner voices for one another and spoke a language none around them could hear.

Bernyece Smith wrote in later years: "Duke taught me to surf, and what a thrill it was when I was able to stand with him on his huge board when catching a wave. I swam with him every day and he helped me with my stroke, and on moonlight nights he would take all three of us for a surfboat ride, after which we would have a swim and go back to our house for light refreshments.

"He was a tall, handsome boy. I called him the Bronze Statue—simple and unspoiled in spite of all the fuss made over him. In fact, he was very shy and hated a show. Nearly every ship brought some celebrities whom the Mayor asked him to entertain, as they all wanted to meet the Duke, who by then was world renowned. He would often dash over to my house and say, 'Come with me. I must take so-and-so out in a canoe,' or 'I'm taking so-and-so home. Please come along.'

"I well remember when Edsel Ford and his little bride came on their honeymoon, and I accompanied Duke when he took them to his house. They wanted to see his cabinet of trophies won in swimming contests at the Olympic Games and elsewhere. And afterward his little brothers played 'ukulele, guitar, and sang, while his sister, Bernice, served refreshments.

"His mother was very retiring and spoke no English, so Bernice always acted as hostess. And Duke was so sweet and natural and won the heart of everyone; even his competitors, to whom he was always willing to show his strokes and help. He was considered the fairest and squarest athlete in the swimming world."

Bernyece's letter made it clear that even working for a living and making time for training and occasional swim meets, Duke still managed to find time for this deep friendship. Loving the out-of-doors and its natural beauty, he took Bernyece on trips by foot and horseback through the beautiful tropical trails of O'ahu. He showed her the caves and lacey waterfalls in Mānoa Valley, a delightful place just to get lost. Another favorite spot was the huge Princess Ka'iulani Estate bordering Waikīkī, with its lovely walks and lush vegetation. Flowers there exploded with color, and Duke always enjoyed visiting.

He taught Bernyece customs of the Hawaiians of ancient days. He gave to her one of his most treasured possessions; a crudely made ivory necklace that had been in his family for generations. It was carved from ivory by visiting whalers, who then smoked it with sugar cane to produce an exquisite amber color. The handmade treasure had a gold-colored silk ribbon with a heart-shaped pendant hanging from it. Duke gave it to Bernyece with feelings he couldn't express in words.

His affection for Bernyece only added to Duke's disaffection with being penniless and without means. He realized that matters of the heart would have to be delayed. He had to find a field of endeavor that would someday assure him of financial security. That would take time.

Duke went to Bernyece on the beach one morning, a little unstrung from the grim internal battle he'd been fighting with himself. He pointed skyward at a flock of frigate birds wheeling and turning against the blue. He said haltingly, "I've gotta be as free as those birds up there, for a while, anyhow."

He was not sure he was saying the right thing and she could see the doubt on his face. Obviously, he wanted her, but he also wanted the freedom so important to him.

Bernyece's lovely features melted into a Mona Lisa-like smile, she studied him for a moment, and then walked away. Both knew a door had been closed that would never again open. Duke stood there, blinking into the sun, and wondering.

Bernyece said good-bye late the next afternoon, in front of the Pi'ikoi cottage. Dressed for traveling with her fashionable handbag, she left without telling him why. She didn't tell him that she was leaving the islands. All Duke knew was that she was leaving, and that she was sorry for him, achingly sorry. She seemed sorry, too, for the dreams they had shared. She left just like that. He was numbed. Suddenly the clouds against the evening sky were an ugly gray and the Hawaiian air was dank. In the hollow days that followed Duke buried himself in training. He swam. He rowed.

Regatta Day of September 17th, 1917 was another exciting event. The Myrtle's white and red colors copped seven races, Duke contributing heavily to their wins. The day had started out in red-letter fashion when Mrs. Ritchie Rosa, wife of Myrtle coach, William L. Rosa, christened the new Myrtle senior crew barge.

"I christen thee *Duke Paoa Kahanamoku!*" she cried, as she broke the bottle on the prow of the craft.

Then Duke and the rest of the Myrtle senior crew proceeded to go out and in front of thousands of cheering onlookers, win a sensational victory against the strongest opposition they had ever met. Cheers at the finish were largely for Duke, for it was apparent that he had made the decisive difference. He went on to win the senior scull with another spectacular finish and he seemed almost indestructible. He did, however, take one loss that day; he and his partner, Arthur Waipa Parker, placed second in the Senior Pair-Oar Race.

Some felt it was good for Duke to lose an occasional event; so it wouldn't be a foregone conclusion that he would be victor whenever he entered.

"It puts the race forecasts in doubt," said one sportswriter, "and makes for more public interest."

The scribe was right. Yet Duke secretly knew that unless he continued a winner he'd lose the recognition he had gained. It was his only stature, without it he'd be just another beachboy with nothing but memories and a nickel-and-dime job. This driving desire to stay on top gave him no rest. He could not afford to be less.

Duke didn't have to travel to be lionized; tourists did that right in Waikīkī. He could hardly step on the beach before people would stop him to shake his hand, talk to him, and have their picture taken with him. He never quite understood the interest. He understood the applause when he was winning a race, but seeking him out on the beach and finding him so exciting was mystifying.

Like many beachboys, Duke took great pride in his surfboard and had his name on it. Since other surfers had begun to fashion boards designed like his, the name helped to distinguish his from the others. It was not publicity, it was just identification.

It was not too long before visitors began asking to have their picture taken alongside Duke and his board. He smiled and obliged, though it all seemed silly. The beachboys he'd grown up with ribbed him and he couldn't help being self-conscious. It became a problem just to get his board off the beach and into the surf. Duke could not bring himself to refuse those who demanded his attention.

The situation went from awkward to worse. One afternoon he left his surfboard leaning against the Moana Hotel pier pilings. Returning, he spotted a lady tourist standing prettily against the board while her girl friend snapped the picture. To compound the problem, others were standing along side, obviously waiting their turn. The sight stopped Duke cold. He retreated some distance, wondering when the sightseers would finish. They were casual and unhurried.

The sea beckoned while the tourists posed. Shyness and heat drove Duke back up the beach. Seeing—and reveling in—his predicament one of the beachboys called out, "Auwē, Paoa! Why you not surf, eh? Big waves out dere!"

Duke looked back at the group clustered around his board. He grinned. "To get that board now?" He shook his head, "Waste time!"

"How 'bout usin' mine?" one of the surfers volunteered.

Duke flicked sweat from his forehead and glanced at the cooling sea. "Why not? Thanks!" He walked over, accepted the board, and headed seaward.

Had Duke known that the group around his surfboard included a reporter, he would have been better prepared for the next days' photo of a curvaceous girl beside his board with this caption:

TOURISTS WANT PICTURE WITH DUKE'S SURFBOARD

Below the caption the column related that Hawai'i boasted many publicity stunts to trap tourists' attention, but that the accompanying photo "outstunt[ed]" publicity angles of the past.

The column cited Mark Twain's lyrical writings about the islands. It quoted some kudos Robert Louis Stevenson bestowed on Waikīkī when he lived there. The writer spoke of the constant literature emanating from the Hawaii Promotion Committee (today the Hawaii Visitors Bureau) about Hawai'i's climate, surfing, volcanoes, aloha spirit, etc. Finally he noted the new fad of visitors having their pictures taken alongside Kahanamoku's surfboard.

Here are two paragraphs:

> These photographs will be mailed to friends throughout the Mainland and will be an incentive to attract visitors to the beach at Waikīkī. When asked about the publicity end of it, Albert P. Taylor, secretary of the Hawaii Promotion Committee, said that it was one of the best plans to bring attention to the Islands that could be obtained.
>
> Duke looked at the proposition in a strange way at first, but after scores of tourists had asked his consent he agreed to the plan and any day one may see pretty young ladies gathered around the board, taking photographs of each other. Of late Duke has been doing more swimming than surfboard riding, as his board has been in constant use. It isn't Duke's nature to begrudge the visitors any pleasure that they may have in being snapped in front of the board which is marked "Duke," so it is expected that in the future he will be kept busy with more requests for his board and will continue his training for the world's championship races in September.

Duke studied the article and smiled at his islands' publicity. He understood that his name and reputation were certainly making a sizeable contribution. "Makes me feel like I'm Mister Hawaii or something," he thought.

That evening at home, after his family had read the piece, his father said proudly, "Duke, you're beginning to be real important to your homeland, right?"

"Yeah," broke in David, the next oldest brother, "pretty soon they'll have to address you as 'Your Eminence.'"

Laughter was never scarce in the Kahanamoku family and all chortled good-naturedly.

"Funny thing, though," Duke commented, "when I'm looking for a job employers walk past me as if I'm invisible." He went quiet and his brown eyes seemed to retreat to another place. Finally he turned, and walked slowly, thoughtfully out of the room.

13

War Rears Its Head

DUKE'S FINANCIAL FUTURE REMAINED UNCERTAIN. HIS LACK OF AN ATTAINABLE TANGIBLE GOAL WAS RAPIDLY DESTROYING HIS SENSE OF VALUE. His inner voice told him that earning a real income was critically important to his sense of self-worth. Despite his high honors, Duke existed in a sort of financial limbo. He continued to protect his simon-pure amateur-athletic standing. A paltry salary from Public Works was his mainstay—a chain of sundry jobs to help keep the Kahanamoku family together. Lack of schooling financially handcuffed Duke as he had never anticipated. Seeking a greater income became an emotional rollercoaster.

Even keeping company with a girl offered Duke problems that, at the time, seemed monumental. Duke had been deeply involved with Bernyece, but lost her when she left. The departure of Bernyece left a deep vacuum in his life. He was not one to forget quickly. The only girl Duke became attached to was Marion "Babe" Dowsett, but, at the time, Duke considered her too much younger than himself to warrant anything beyond friendship.

Babe Dowsett, with wide, soft eyes jammed with character was a lovely girl, willowy and full of fun. She was an excellent swimmer and, in fact, a swimming protege of Duke's. Their first bond had been laughter. Duke found that his loneliness went away when Babe was around. Later his fondness grew. When her mother took her to live in California, his pain was deep and lasting. Duke had now been hit twice by lost love.

James "Alika" Dowsett, Babe's father, was big in the cattle business as well as other fields. Duke's financial embarrassment was heightened by striving to socialize with the daughter of a man of Dowsett's business and social standing. But fortune still smiled on Duke. Alika Dowsett, at least, had cherished him as a suitor for his daughter's hand. Duke had the same deep aloha for the gentle man. Their relationship endured Babe's departure.

Duke was working on Dowsett's Big Island cattle ranch in 1917. The land lay on the western slopes of Mauna Loa. Duke was helping with roping and branding—a delightful change from tourist-filled Waikīkī Beach. At the end of a heavy day's range work, Deputy-Sheriff Lazzaro came up the long slope from the Kona Coast. He was grim countenanced, burdened with a message no one enjoys carrying. The officer huddled at the ranch-house door with Dowsett, telling him

Duke Paoa Kahanamoku in front of Outrigger Canoe Club c. 1919.
Bishop Museum

the bad news. The rancher turned slowly and walked to Duke, who had just come up in his sweaty, dust-laden work clothes. A warning flick of panic touched Duke.

"Hate to tell you this, son," Dowsett said in a controlled voice.

Duke braced himself as the rancher gently gripped his bicep. "Let's have it."

Dowsett went on, "Your father passed away."

Duke blinked and swallowed. "Make?" he said, "Dead?" He had to say it in Hawaiian and English to comprehend the full impact. By now he might have been carved from lava.

Dowsett nodded. "We'll get you down to the coast right away. The steamer Kilauea will be clearing for Honolulu in a matter of hours." With the suddenness of a crashing wave, Duke wanted to go home.

The ranch's best riding horse, Barney, was quickly saddled. The big sorrel stallion seemed to sense the urgency. He stomped his unshod hoofs and champed at the bit. Within minutes Duke was riding Kona-bound, his soiled work clothes still clinging to him.

It was a melancholy ride, with heavy banks of fog sliding along the slopes like walls of dirty cotton. But the mount had trod the route enough years to know his way. Duke hewed to Dowsett's suggestion and let Barney have his head. With slack reins the horse moved unerringly through the fog, past brush and pānini cactus. Meanwhile, the saddened rider tried to sort his thoughts. His heart cried for his mother's anguish. Duke realized he had never really felt pain before.

Rider and horse finally reached Ho'okena on the coast road. Duke's shirt was clammy against his shoulders, and it wasn't merely the ride. He was bursting with the pain of his sorrow and needed to talk to someone at home.

Friends met him and offered a Ford truck to take him south to the village of Ho'ōpūloa. He dropped the reins with someone and climbed in the truck. Voices around him were just a jumble. Duke thanked them for their thoughts, his own voice almost inaudible.

He soon had the Ford rattling southward over the dirt road and within the hour he was in Ho'ōpūloa Village. Although a green squall was working its way across the channel, friendly folks rowed him offshore to where the steamer Kilauea lay at anchor awaiting additional passengers and cargo.

In the interim the faithful mount, Barney, had started back for the Dowsett ranch. No one caught him and reined him in; possibly no one tried. In a few hours the horse made his way back to the gate of the Dowsett property. While Duke sailed the choppy channel waters for O'ahu, Babe Dowsett and her father were struck with the depth of Duke's anguish as they watched their riderless horse nosing the gate open.

"It's Barney!" breathed Babe. "And carrying an empty saddle."

"Right," agreed her father, massaging his jaw in his characteristic way. "It's a measure of our boy's grief."

Duke made it home aboard the steamer *Kilauea*. Every mile of the route was gray and barren. The grief-stricken family would naturally now look to him as the head of the house. It was not small comfort for him to think of his financial situation. The outlook was bleak.

He was met at the dock by his sister Bernice, with, surprisingly, Bernyece Smith. She had come back, and Duke could hardly grasp it.

The girls' eyes were tear-stained as they threw their arms around Duke.

"Papa's gone," Bernice cried softly. "But we have you and David and ..." Her words trailed as she buried her face on his chest.

Duke thanked Bernyece Smith for being there to meet him, for staying with his sister and the family, and just for returning. He had a million questions to ask, but now was not the time.

Duke's grief was slightly eased learning that his father had died peacefully and suddenly in his sleep.

Bernyece told him, "Your daddy came back from a swim in the surf and just lay down for a rest. He never suffered."

"That helps," Duke said quietly. "It really helps."

They drove to the Beach Road home from the steamer wharf. A silent, hollow-eyed family met Duke. His father's body had been moved to the funeral parlor, but the man's spirit seemed still to linger in the gift home Duke had provided for his loved ones.

Devoted to his family, Duke took the loss hard. He doubted his ability to ease the pain of others. He turned to Bernyece Smith for help. "Will you stay the night?" he asked.

"You really want me to, Paoa?"

"It will help. We need you, all of us."

Bernyece spent the night saying the things which Duke could not. She helped the entire family through the initial shock, particularly Mama Kahanamoku. Mama, though deeply distraught, finally offered the Hawaiian saying, "Well, at least, we know that Papa has only taken the canoe ahead."

Duke remained close. He didn't leave Mama until the wash of despair had left her face. Meanwhile, as is Hawaiian custom, there was beautiful music, with friends and relatives coming and going with soft footsteps and hushed voices.

After his father's burial, Duke felt the weight of supporting a family left with no insurance benefits, no cash in the bank, no anything. He turned full-time to earning money wherever he could, totally neglecting his training. His dream of again representing America in an Olympiad withered and began to die.

But fate stepped in, for 1918 was war time. Olympic Games were the least of people's thoughts. Manpower was wanted on land and sea, combat zones, behind the guns. Though needed at home, Duke felt duty-bound to join the military. The Red Cross got to him first. It made sense, for Duke could best serve his country using his great swimming talent.

Duke and other top watermen were organized into a unit touring the United Sates and Canada for Red Cross benefits. With Manager Owen Merrick, former sports editor of the *Honolulu Star-Bulletin*, there was Stubby Kruger, Clair Tait, Clarence Lane, and Duke, a money-making quintet generating relief funding.

From June to September they toured the mainland, swimming and diving at Neptune Beach, Monterey, San Francisco, Seattle, Victoria, Winnipeg, Duluth, Milwaukee, Chicago, New York, Boston, Norfolk, and Washington, D. C.. They toured sixteen cities in the United States and Canada, presenting what was probably the world's first aquacade.

Tait was a particularly fine fancy diver and, because he was a Navy man stationed at Pearl Harbor, he wore his uniform; this made him tremendously exciting to the girls. Lane and Kruger, too, had their appeal for distaff spectators but it was Duke who made the girls babble. He had an undefinable inherent romance about him.

The team offered swimming, diving, and lifesaving demonstrations along with some clowning. They were tremendously well received and greatly helped the Red Cross efforts.

One story shows how the group captivated fans. Clair Tait, a Portland boy who formerly held the Pacific Coast diving championship, acted as trainer for the tour. He once reported to the press, "You should have seen us stage an exhibit at Castles by the Sea, the Long Island resort started by Vernon Castle. A big storm was on and the lifeguards kept everybody from going out except we fellows from Honolulu. Duke took a surfboard out to the last line of breakers, half a mile out, and rode all the way in at express-train speed. The waves were the best ever seen. We gave people something new in the line of body surfing when we rode the crest of the waves for 200 and 300 yards. The shore was lined with enthusiastic people and we were nearly mobbed when we started back for the dressing rooms. There were cameras by the hundreds, and Duke was photographed until he was blue in the face."

Another story was printed in an Associated Press item of August 9th, 1918:

KAHANAMOKU SWIMS FIFTY YARDS IN RECORD TIME OF 20 4-5

Most Remarkable of Aquatic Performances Stated in New York Last Night—Lane and J Kruger Finish Second to Duke—Others Come Close.

Duke Kahanamoku's world record time for the fifty, made in a tank is down in the books as 23 2-5 seconds, while his world's record time for open water over this distance is 23 seconds flat.

If the time given for last night's sprint is correct, Duke has clipped two and three-fifth seconds off his world's record in a tank. While this seems almost incredible, still, it will be remembered that the noted Hawaiian swimmer has on more than one occasion astonished and electrified the swimming world with his remarkable performances in the water and ability to shatter existing records in a manner almost unbelievable.

The tour not only helped the Red Cross fund, but was also publicity for Hawai'i. Duke, Polynesian in carriage, manner, appearance, and humor, especially spread the aloha of the islands.

Exciting traveling with expenses paid was fine, but, for Duke, there was still one hitch in it. There would come a time when he would want to pay his own way.

"I want to feel like I'm my own man," he told Merrick.

The sports editor agreed heartily. During all this moving around Duke now kept an eye open for a field, a business, a means of making a living, where he could be self-sufficient.

At the tour's end, the group broke up in Washington D. C., and everyone went their separate ways. Duke went to the recruiting center to volunteer for the Air Corps. The recruiting officer said that if he stuck around, he might be assigned to training school in Texas or California.

He stayed at the Y.M.C.A., waiting. A great influenza epidemic was sweeping the country at the time. The scourge was unchecked and people died by the thousands. Duke was struck, sabotaging his chance for the Air Corps. He lay deathly sick and unknowing on a cot in the Y.M.C.A. Hospitals were overflowing and Duke lay unattended. He lost fifteen pounds as the influenza developed into double pneumonia. It was touch and go whether he lived or died.

During this nightmare, a miracle happened in Prince Kuhio's Washington office. Bernyece Smith was traveling with politicians from Hawai'i hoping to get some legislation for the islands. She was a secretary and, while searching for stationery in a desk drawer, found Duke's camera. Recognition and astonishment fought within her, for she hadn't known Duke was in the city. She reasoned that he had just passed through and accidentally left the camera.

She asked her boss if he knew if Duke was in Washington. When he didn't, she asked if he would check about the Red Cross team. After going back and forth with newspapers, Red Cross, police, and hotels, they found that Duke was at the local "Y." Bernyece lost no time phoning.

Talking to the manager, she identified herself as an old friend from Honolulu. Before she finished, the manager was saying, "Please come. He's very ill and we have no one to take care of him."

Bernyece quickly taxied to the "Y." Disturbed when she got into the taxi, it was nothing to what she felt entering Duke's little room. He lay in a partial coma, a week's growth of blood-matted beard on his face, and no recognition in his eyes. A wooden table held a jar with less than a spoonful of jelly and some broken crackers.

Bernyece paled and turned to the man who had brought her, "Has he been eating?"

"That's all he's had for days, ma'am. He's broke and pure sick."

Bernyece just nodded her head and dropped to her knees. She took Duke's fevered hand in her own. "Dear God," was all she could mutter.

Duke's eyes opened slowly, his head turned, and he studied her from filmy pupils. There was a faint light of recognition in them. Gray fatigue laced his face.

"Hi, Bernyece," he breathed, then swung his head to the wall and sobbed.

"You're going to be all right Duke," she said, blinking her eyes. "I'm here to help you."

There'd be time to talk later, when his strength was back; time enough for a lot of things. Bernyece spoke to him, not expecting or getting any answers. She just wanted to assure him that she was there, to take care of him, nurse him to health, and get him home to Hawai'i's sunny days and warm nights.

Duke turned to say something, but she quickly touched his lips and shushed him. The two had always agreed that the most significant things are not expressed in words, but by the silences, glances, and gestures between words.

Some life flowed into his face, the old vigor seemed to momentarily course in the clasp of his hand.

Bernyece found the house doctor and had a hurried talk. "Kahanamoku doesn't look as though he'll make it," she said.

The medico apologized, looking guilty. "I just can't handle all the cases assigned," he explained.

She ignored the defense, asking what she could do. "Milk," the physician suggested. "Lots of milk, if you can get him to drink it. And maybe a little brandy."

Bernyece hurried to a corner store and brought back three quarts of milk and a half pint of brandy. It proved a major chore for Duke to get anything down. With patience and will, she succeeded. She then turned to cleaning him up as best she could. It soon became obvious that another sickness also possessed Duke, loneliness.

With no hotel rooms available, Bernyece went to the home of a young man whom Duke had mentioned as a friend. The fellow was out of town, but she talked to his mother.

"Could you take Duke in here?" Bernyece asked, trying to keep the pleading out of her voice. "Just until he's well?"

The woman explained she had just nursed her own son through the influenza and that she was currently helping many others flu-stricken and desperately ill in the neighborhood. "I'm afraid I'd neglect him," she said. "I have only two hands—and I'm already committed to others."

Bernyece countered, "If you'd take him in, I'd come daily and tend him. He'd be my responsibility, my patient."

"If you'll cook for him, feed him, give him..."

"Everything!" broke in Bernyece. "Just please let him have the room. I'll pay you in advance."

The lady wouldn't take any payment; Duke's being a friend of her son was enough. The deal was made.

Bernyece went back to the Y.M.C.A. and arranged for an ambulance to move Duke. He was hemorrhaging through the mouth again and his chances looked slim.

Anxious days followed, with Bernyece arriving each morning to care for Duke. She nursed him with dedication. She later admitted that she had never before seen anyone so close to death. She was a metaphysics student and brought her books to read to Duke and help him in his fight. She also brought in a doctor to see him daily. Gradually the hemorrhaging ceased and Duke improved.

Finally Bernyece could question Duke about why he was alone in Washington. He told her his tale. "The tour finished here and all the boys scattered. I wanted to get into the Air Corps. Two days before I took sick, they asked me to get ready to start ground school in California."

Bernyece was deeply sorry for Duke. She knew how badly he wanted to make something of his life and be something other than just a swimmer, surfer, and beachboy. He had often spoken about wanting "to fly like the birds." This time he had missed.

Time in Washington ran out for Bernyece. She had to leave with her boss for Portland. Fearful of leaving Duke alone, she sought his physician's advice. The doctor decided that if someone accompanied Duke, he could travel to Hawai'i.

Despite Duke's condition, Bernyece managed to get him on a train West. She arranged for a porter to leave Duke's berth always down, and she stayed close day and night. She wirelessed an Olympic Team man in San Francisco to meet the ailing athlete and get him aboard a Honolulu-bound ship.

The first leg of the rail journey amounted to a deathwatch for the Florence Nightingale-like Bernyece. At one of Duke's lowest points, he muttered, "I'll never be able to thank you enough." There was no timbre or resonance in his voice—it showed the depth of his sickness.

"You're going to be alright," she countered quietly, stroking his hair.

He forced a grin. "At a time like this, I feel like one of God's culls. Twenty-eight, sick, and still with no ability other than swimming and surfing."

Her cooling palm came to his fevered forehead and rested. "Duke, you've been honored and applauded by more people than most men will meet in a lifetime. You're loved and you should be grateful." With a smile she forgave.

He closed his eyes and nodded that she was right. When she kissed him, her lips revived old memories. Duke tried to control his pain, but felt pierced by stabbing futility.

Over the next few days Duke began to heal. For a change he looked a little less like a doomed man. Sooner than they wished, Bernyece had to part company. They had reached Salt Lake City, where she and her boss had to switch trains for the Northwest. Duke's gut wrenched as Bernyece left his compartment. For the rest of the trip he listened to the echos of his loneliness. Sleep escaped him most of the time; what he caught was confused, restless, and full of fragmentary dreams. The sad, throaty wail of the train whistle laid a heavy hand on him.

Duke c. 1918
Bishop Musuem photo

14

The Comeback Trail

STILL LOOKING LIKE DEATH, DUKE ARRIVED IN SAN FRANCISCO. Almost out of touch with reality, he didn't even realize that Bernyece had paid the train porter well to give her friend special attention. With the help of an Olympic Team man in the Bay City, Duke boarded the steamer *Shinyo Maru* bound for Honolulu. The swimmer was on the mend.

Armistice was declared while the ship was mid-ocean. When the morning bulletin was posted, Duke read it a little ruefully.

"There goes my flying career," he said. Then smiling widely for the first time in a long time, added, "But I'm glad all the killing and dying is over."

The slow-moving vessel inched on to Honolulu. Duke said later, "When I arrived at the dock, I weighed 175 pounds instead of my usual 190 and more. I was a ghost. Friends hardly recognized me. But I was home—and I knew I would get well. I needed the sun. I needed the surf."

Friends and relatives welcomed Duke home with open arms. He was home with those who knew him best, and their heartfelt aloha would be his best medicine.

Returning home, Duke was again forced to face his financial realities. He was still out of sync with a society that honored him but never thought about where he was supposed to find a personal income.

After months of intensive touring followed by the frightful letdown of broken health, Duke rested as long as he dared. Talk was in the air about the proposed Olympic Games for 1920 at Antwerp. Duke was expected to again represent those who had backed him at Stockholm. With his courage and life-long phenomenal good health, he recovered enough to start training. Island weather acted like a healing balm. With the smoke of war hardly dissipated, Duke swam his way into condition. He began to look like his old self.

Lucrative professional offers were again tendered to the Hawaiian champ. He still turned them all down, feeling that he owed everything to his islands. Throughout his life Duke exhibited an amazing loyalty to his islands and his nation, often with great personal sacrifice.

In the early summer of 1919, Outrigger Canoe Club prepared for its annual

Duke aboard Shinyo Maru.   *Bishop Museum*

swimming and sailing regatta off Waikīkī. The newspapers gave it good play, particularly the long-distance swim where Duke would compete. A gruelling mile and a half open-water contest, it ran from Castle's pier to the Outrigger at Waikīkī Beach. Coral beds abounded in the area, presenting huge obstacles.

Interest in this event was always high, for it brought together top long-distance swimmers for a stirring finish. This time it carried additional promise because the "people's choice" would be testing his strength and condition for the upcoming Olympics. Besides, Duke was challenging distance well beyond his ordinary races. Hawai'i marveled at his audacity.

Duke trained hard for this race, and he knew he had regained much of his old strength. But did he have enough to buck the rough water over such a distance against top competition? He waded out with others at the foot of Diamond Head, and knew this test would measure whether or not he'd be ready for Olympic trials. Public interest ran high, and many were skeptical.

At the gun, Duke hit the tide with his usual long, powerful stroke. He knew this water as his birthright, but so did many of his fellow racers, still others had competed in even rougher waters. Fans on shore gave them all a big hand.

Duke paced himself, thinking his way through the route. There were tricky currents and trade winds, plus shallows where the low tide allowed coral to jut to the surface. It would be pointless to hug the shoreline too closely.

Twelve swimmers took the start, all stroking like machines. Duke gradually branched from the field and took a course nearer to the beach. The wisdom of his move became obvious as the wind and current carried him back to the best path, while others who had begun with the direct line were washed seaward and had to fight the current back.

Duke pulled in ahead of the field, finishing in twenty-seven minutes fifty-two seconds. It was a good time considering the water conditions.

Immediately figurative drums began to herald Duke as the natural swimmer to again represent the United States in the coming 1920 Olympics Games at Antwerp. Dad Center, Bill Rawlins, and other supporters of Hawaiian sport started rustling up money to send him to the mainland for trials.

However, with Duke's having taken a different course in the "Castle's pier to Waikīkī" race, a segment of fans chalked up his win to his having outfigured his competitors. They felt that his speed days were behind him, and new blood was needed. In 1919 several people told Duke to retire, for he was twenty-nine—as sprint athletes go, ancient. Duke began to wonder himself.

One in particular did not go along with this. Dad Center still believed in his

Hawaiian friend.

Center had been born at Kīpahulu, Maui, on December 25th, 1887. Like Duke he learned to swim at Waikīkī Beach. He had also been in the 100-yard race at Alakea slip, Honolulu, in 1911 when Duke first shattered a world's record. In 1916 when Outrigger Canoe Club first organized a swim team, Center became the coach. He went on to develop some fine watermen. Duke had stayed with Hui Nalu until 1917, when he became a member of Outrigger, under Center's watchful eye. The older man did not believe Duke was now less the swimmer than he had been before. He encouraged Duke in his training, polished Duke for the meets which would build to the later Olympics.

Duke was beginning to feel something new enter his competitive life. It shocked him, but, reticent man that he was, he said nothing to the press or his friends. The old story of the public wanting a long-time champion beaten now began. This emotion often rears its head when kings long wear their crowns. It stirred a sense of unease in Duke.

This odd phenomena made its first appearance during the Honolulu Victory Swimming Carnival in June, 1919. It showed in the press. Newsmen, intent upon discovering new stars, passed by the comeback-bent Duke Kahanamoku and gave most of their space to new faces. Duke was mostly overlooked. He was considered an old war horse who had had his day. Readying again for battle was thought absurd.

One example of public fickleness showed when fans and scribes went berserk as John Kelii came close to waxing Duke in the 100-yarder. No one knew that a cold had settled in Duke's neck muscles and he had been lucky to finish at all.

Plaudits were posted for John Kelii and the word was that "Kelii will beat Duke in September." Following newspapers stressed that Kelii was the comer and that Duke had no place to go but down.

Asked about it, Duke said, "Face it, sooner or later the rent has to be paid."

Duke had told no one his brother had needed bottles of liniment to loosen Duke's aching back and neck before the race. Swimming that century sprint had been agonizing for Duke, but less so than the lack of public acclaim for the win. Duke made no complaints, offered no alibis for his narrow win.

Later some learned from Duke's brother about his condition at the race. Word passed to the press and one influential sports writer reported: "Duke deserves credit for his heroic conduct in the meet."

The pardon was a little late, the victim had already been hung...

As Duke's conditioning improved, his extra years seemed not to make a difference. Dad Center and other friends believed that the Olympics would again see Duke representing the United States.

Duke continued to impress everyone. He had the same beautiful body, the old verve, and the quiet charm. He still evoked admiration in all who met him. That year, 1919, nationally-known newspaper columnist John D. Barry visited Honolulu. Sitting on Waikīkī, he wrote:

"Presently an athletic-looking young Hawaiian appears among them, of a velvety bronze his big eyes shining, his thick hair combed back from his forehead, his vigorous shoulders tapering down to a slim waist and slim, wiry legs. He is a great figure in these parts, Duke Kahanamoku, generally known as 'the Duke,' democratically free in his manners, exchanging familiar greetings here and there. Suddenly he runs into the water for a few feet, hurls himself forward where it is still apparently shallow, in a dive that keeps his figure close to the surface, shakes his head like a lion tossing his mane, and strikes out with his long, sinewy arm over arm, face pressed into the water, coming up occasionally for a long breath.

"While I am indulging in these reflections a strong breeze has come up. The Duke, standing close to the shore, points to the reefs. Lines of white are appearing there. The surf is beginning to break heavily. The Duke runs up the beach, makes his way under the pavilion, between the canoes and the outriggers lying on the sand, disappears for a few moments, returns with his big surfboard in his hands, throws the board and himself on the surface of the water and proceeds serenely to paddle out with his hands, his long figure lying flat on the board.

"Eight husky young fellows are drawing out one of the outriggers. The effort strains the muscles in their shoulders and arms and legs. When they get the boat into the water they paddle towards those reefs, where the Duke is evidently headed. They are the first to reach the surf. A big wave lifts them into the air and causes them to disappear. Soon they are turned around and going full tilt. A big white wave is holding them up, drawing them down, hurling them to one side, threatening to upset them, righting them again—no, over they go, spilling into the sea, vanishing, black heads coming up, faces laughing.

"The Duke is in the surf, erect on his board, arms extended, tearing along magnificently, like a god!"

The words frame a picture of Duke's life at the beach, training and conditioning. He was at home in the sea and found his passion in the water.

The vision of his enjoyment made others wish to share the delights. Always in demand as a swimming or surfing teacher for visiting celebrities, his reputation was such that people seldom offered him tips for fear of offending him, losing him even the income of a beachboy. Still, Duke was always quick to help anyone with their aquatics, rich or poor.

Asked about his income from the beach, Duke once said, "I'd like a nickel for every hour of free swimming or surfing instruction I've given to people who didn't stick around long enough to say 'thanks.'" Remorseful for having sounded so mercenary, he added, "Really trying to make a living out there could be a grubby existence, at least for me."

15

The Everlasting Challenge

HOME IN WAIKIKI, DUKE STILL FOUND THE SEA HIS SHRINE, SWIMMING AND SURFING AN ENDLESS JOY. He regretted that surfing was not in the Olympics, as he loved it even more than swimming. There was something about surfing that he could never explain. Challenging big seas, you became part of the sea, yet still thought of "beating" it. Sometimes it could be terrifying, sometimes a dream come true.

"On a board," Duke said, "I feel like the boss man, I'm in charge when I make the big wave do what I want it to do."

Riding big waves takes skill, strength, grace, and daring. Pitted against the sea's power, if you did everything right, you conquered all that the sea threw at you. You faced panic at times, but you stayed.

"Sometimes I make a mistake on the board," Duke admitted. "Just a little mistake—and I wipe out. Deep in the soup, I still know I can get my board and do it right. I can be boss."

This everlasting challenge pushed Duke to perfecting his surfing, catching the biggest waves for the longest, wildest rides. When storm seas were rioting and thundering, he paddled out to waves that even other good surfers avoided.

"The sea gives me life," Duke used to say, "With my board I feel like I own the ocean and I am king." He smiled, and it was easy to picture his ali'i ancestors standing there.

He loved the tradition that went with surfing. Ancient Polynesian chiefs, beyond their inheritance of rank, proved their worth through courage and physical strength. To remain in authority, leaders were tireless in schooling themselves in courageous activity.

Surfing big waves was a major sport. Closely affiliated with their religious life, surfing among the ali'i involved sacred ceremonies. When a man of rank selected a special tree for his board, he left an offering of native kumu (goat fish) at the base of the tree. After cutting, it was trimmed to a crude surfboard shape and taken to the halau (canoe house) for finishing. Handwork on the board took weeks before it was ready for careful polishing. A lasting stain made from kukui nut coats was rubbed in, giving the board color and luster.

When finished, the board was dedicated with prayer and ceremony by the kahuna. With this care and ceremony, the board became a part of the man. Hurtling down a wave they were one. Ancient chants (mele) show that surfing has long been part of the very fabric of Hawaiian life.

Duke felt that his natural surfing ability flowed from his Hawaiian heritage. Early Polynesians had sailed thousands of trackless ocean miles in great twin-hulled canoes, navigating by sun, moon, stars, wind, and waves. Those that reached Hawai'i were skilled watermen, past masters at riding the glassy slopes of swells and catching the curl.

In Hawai'i, before Queen Ka'ahumanu ended the kapu (taboo) system, ali'i had beaches where they alone were permitted to surf and swim. Commoners were forbidden, under threat of death, to use these selected areas. Men of royal blood had the opportunity to develop into top surfers. Religious aspects of the sport, along with one's expertness, were a symbol of status.

Commoners surfed wherever there were waves and they were not forbidden. Many became highly skilled. They held meets with sometimes substantial wagering. The missionaries, arriving in 1819, looked upon surfing as a waste of time and the sport was discouraged. Not until the reign of David Kalākaua (1874 to 1891) did surfing again see public support. Kalakaua gave the hula, mele, and other Hawaiian forms of cultural expression back to his people. When Kalākaua died, in 1891, surfing again declined. Not until the turn of the century, when Duke was in his teens, did the sport again come into its own.

Duke became a fixture on his board in the waters off Waikīkī. His long graceful rides delighted visiting tourists. He encouraged both local boys and arriving haole to take up the sport.

When big waves came, the word flew. Good boardsmen left whatever they were doing and plowed through shoal water where the green water was building. Sometimes waves broke like long lines of ridges, stretching across Waikīkī Bay. The excitement caught shore-bound spectators as well as surfers. To this day, with six distinct breaks in Waikīkī, a surfer can often pick the waves he prefers. Canoe surf is directly offshore from the Moana Hotel. There the greatest number of surfers work the rollers. This water got its name because it's where the outrigger canoes shuttle tourist back and forth. It's also often called Bone Yard by those not desiring to chance being caught in tangles of surfers, boards, and swimmers, all adding to a confusion that can easily break bones.

There is Poplar Surf, twice as far out as Canoe Surf and more toward Honolulu. There better surfers get bigger, faster rides.

The third area is Queen's Surf, left of Canoe Surf and a little closer to shore.

Used mostly by younger and less experienced surfers, it's a fast-breaking right hand, fun for its short distance.

The three other major areas are best left for hardcore surfers. Cunha Surf is far Diamond Head (southwest) of Queens' Surf. Public Baths-Elks Club Surf is even farther toward Diamond Head. Finally, Castle Surf is to the left of that. Each represents fast and wild rides for good surfers.

It was at the latter where Duke made a legendary ride, still spoken of with awe. The magnificent mile and three-quarter ride began at the fringe of Steamer Lane. It was a day of big "Bluebirds"—mammoth waves that seldom occur; sometimes unseen for years. They plunge from the outer Diamond Head region across in a solid line to as far northwest as Honolulu Harbor. They're high, steep, and fast, and when they crumble, they're killers. Few chance their fury.

This historic day, Duke caught one, got to his feet, and looked down the glassy slope. Sliding left along the monster face, Duke didn't know he was beginning his most celebrated ride. He knew that this was the tallest, bulkiest, fastest wave he'd ever ridden, and its curl would be tons of sea water that could break or kill you.

The swift, silent water coursed forward as Duke cut and shot into Castle Surf, which built and added to the wave he was on. Spray spumed from the rails of his board. He rode it city-long blocks, the wind sucking at him. Diamond Head rushed in from the right.

Then he was slamming into Elk's Surf, still sliding left, fighting for balance and position. He was not sure he would survive this ever-steepening mountain. A curl broke to his right and almost trapped him. Duke swung further left, backing on the board to avoid pearling (burying the nose of the board in the wave).

Left, left, into the back of Public Bath's Surf. Speed blew his hair back. He wondered when the wave would finally flatten. Angling farther 'Ewa (northwest), hoping to catch Cunha Surf, he felt the board vibrate. To his right was nothing but white water. He slanted some more, working farther left by shifting his weight. Skidding into Cunha, the wave was flattening, but not much. To make Queen's Surf would be monumental; the ride to end all rides!

He grabbed Cunha Surf for all it was worth, gaining more. He might just make it. One off-balance move could spill him into the froth to the right or leave him without enough movement left. He chanced a more head-on direct route, plunging down—and then he was sliding and bouncing into Queen's Surf. He looked shoreward at the people standing there, shading their eyes from the sun, watching him.

Duke made the shallows, lifted his board, and lugged it to the beach. He didn't take any bows. He wanted to sit and think about this ride. He wanted to remember this one for all its glory, a shining memory that he could savor in years to come.

"Great ride!" called someone.

"Must've been a couple miles!" another yelled.

Duke saw faces, their eyes fixed on him. He grinned his thanks. He looked at the far surf and could hardly believe the distance. A little bewildered, he walked away with his board, applause and cheers ringing.

"Aye, brah!" shouted a friend.

"Yeah, champ!" screamed others.

Duke smiled and kept going, arms locked around the great board. He would retain the image of today's fantastic ride, a once in a lifetime experience.

Duke didn't know that soon his stature as a surfer would lead to his teaching royalty surfing. That was as it should be; who but the king of surfers should teach royalty to surf. It would be one more stroke of fate in Duke's life.

16

A Royal Visit

THIS WAS A DAY WHEN THE ELITE CAME TO MEET AND GREET THE ELITE. Duke was half of the act. Duke enjoyed doing things for people, often those whose lives were very distant from his own. On April 13th, 1920, the British warship *Renown* sailed into Waikīkī waters and dropped anchor off the Outrigger Canoe Club. His Royal Majesty Edward Albert, Prince of Wales, was aboard. That noon he landed at Pier Eight, Honolulu Harbor.

A coterie of officers and dignitaries, including Admiral Sir Lionel Halsey, came ashore, with the prince. They were all driven to 'Iolani Palace to pay a formal call on Governor McCarthy. Following that, they proceeded to the Moana Hotel. There the prince said that he wished to meet the heralded Hawaiian swimmer, Duke Paoa Kahanamoku. The former beachboy's fame had certainly spread far in relatively few years.

His Royal Highness told newsmen interviewing him, "I would like to witness Kahanamoku surfing. Is he available?"

When Duke was told, he felt complimented and was glad to comply. Dad Center, captain of the Outrigger Canoe Club, arranged for four canoes to be beached in front of the Moana. Each was manned by two or three members with the remaining seats left vacant for guests. One canoe had movie cameras lashed in the bow, for Fox-Pathe Studios wanted pictures of His Royal Highness enjoying the surf. They had a beautiful day, the sky above was crystal clear with high-piled thunderheads looming beyond the Ko'olau Range.

At the Moana, when the British Consul introduced Duke and the prince, Duke felt right at home. He had already met and liked royalty. Duke saw a discerning, polite young man. After the amenities, the prince said, "I would like the honor of being taught surfing by a world's champion."

Duke saw this was not just idle conversation. "My pleasure, prince," he said. "I haven't had an heir to the throne on my board for quite a spell."

The Prince's party laughed at the unexpected sally—with Edward Albert himself laughing hardest.

With the guests boarded in the beach's shallows, Duke took the steering position at the stern. Forward, he saw Dad Center's best paddlers; all strong and adept. The prince was given the place of honor behind the steering seat.

Paddler's bent to their work and the canoe moved seaward through the breaking surf. Duke smiled at meeting royalty again. Deftly he steered to the best surf. While momentarily flat, he swung the canoe to wait for a choice swell.

The prince spoke with casual, genuine friendliness. He talked about Duke's Stockholm victories and asked about his plans for the Antwerp Olympics. Duke answered and added, "I've been lucky."

His Royal Highness grinned, "That's just your humility, but I admire you for it."

Duke watched the swells with a practiced eye. Several slid underneath before he spotted the one he wanted.

"Dig!" he yelled, and sunk his own blade with a strong thrust.

The outrigger canoe came alive while the prince braced himself. Surging forward, the craft pushed through water under the impetus of flailing paddles. The stern rose above the forward-lifting swell. The steep and shiny slope of water pitched the bow down at an exciting angle and the shoreward rush began. Paddlers shipped their blades at Duke's command. At the stern, with ironlike wrists, Duke wielded his paddle rudder fashion, watching the break of the water and keeping the craft at a breath-taking downward slant.

From behind Duke came shrill whistling noises. The young Hawaiian man knew that the young British man was as excited as anyone. Duke was tempted to enjoy the sight of the prince's excitement, but the speed of the canoe demanded his full attention. Speed increased as the breaker loosed its full power, sending the outrigger to the beach amidst hissing. It was a long, fast, exhilarating ride.

As the pace slackened in the shallows, the prince shouted "Tremendous! Simply stupefying!"

"Glad you liked it," Duke said.

"Shan't we have another go?"

"As much as you like," Duke answered, and brought the outrigger around in a graceful sweep.

Backs and arms bent once more to the blades and the canoe headed seaward. To one side was the camera canoe, with cameramen signalling they wanted more. For the photographers and their own sport, the paddlers headed out for more fast, breath-taking rides while Duke and the prince laughed and talked as though they had grown up together.

Dad Center brought Duke's big surfboard out to the shallows and waited. The royalty-laden canoe made a final ride into the shoal waters. Duke turned to the prince and suggested a tandem ride on his board.

"Is that the way you teach surfing?" the prince asked.

"It helps to get the feel of it." Duke offered his big Hawaiian smile, freighted now with a challenge. His Royal Highness took the bait.

"I'll chance it."

Duke climbed out of the canoe, thanked Dad Center, and waited for the prince. He said, "Dad, I never felt so comfortable with a man. We have a big aloha for each other."

Dad nodded quietly, "Why not? You're both right guys."

There was no hesitation by the prince as he splashed through hip-deep water and climbed onto the heavy board. "What have I got to lose, except my life?" he quipped.

Duke grinned. He showed the prince where to lie, then mounted himself. With deep, strong strokes he paddled seaward. The prince paddled, too, fully a part of the adventure.

"Hang on," Duke said as dying breakers came head-on. "Tandem stuff is just to give you an idea of the balance you'll need."

"Good!" said the prince, ducking through the breaker without trouble. Duke continued. He explained how its better to lock the rails in a firm grip and raise your chest and head high, allowing the oncoming breakers to pass beneath.

"That way," Duke pointed out, "you won't get hit in the face by the board."

The prince agreed and the next comber was negotiated with greater ease.

They shoved through more as they made their way out. Past the swells where it was relatively flat, Duke sat up and straddled the board. With legs and hands he brought the board around to face the shore. Swells first lifted and then slid beneath the board.

"We'll wait for a big one," Duke said.

"The bigger the better," agreed the prince.

"We'll ride to the beach," Duke concluded.

The prince looked shoreward and shook his head. To him it seemed no board, surfer, or even breaker could possibly go that far.

"This one looks good," Duke called. "Remember to hold tight, and just get the feel of things. I'll work the board." Duke moved to kneel, with his passenger still prone. "Forward a little more, please."

Duke dug hard, wrist-deep and pulling. As the silken-green water formed into a sloping hill, Duke dug harder, faster. He set the board at the base of the hill of water. The slope steepened and lifted. Duke thrust faster and brought the board to the proper angle on the glassy surface. The ride developed into a mad, seething journey as the water hissed on both sides.

"We go-o-o-o!" cried the prince in ecstasy. "We go-o-o-o!"

Duke was thrilled that it meant so much to the prince. It was good to know that human beings the world over were alike in enjoying simple things.

Like a big cat, Duke sprang upright on the board. He stood with his left foot ahead of his right and both knees slightly bent, like a boxer's stance. The swell raced forward, propelling board and cargo with incredible speed. Duke shifted from time to time, balancing the board and guiding it along the face of the wave. He saw Diamond Head to his right, and wondered how many thousands of rides he'd had in this surf.

He saw Prince Edward grip hard at the rails and rise to his knees. Duke admired him, yet knew this audacity could send the board out of control.

"Stay put for the first one!" Duke yelled.

The prince resumed his former position as they swept into the shallows. Laughs mingled, and hands clasped over their successful ride. They turned the surfboard for another trip.

"I never want to leave," Prince Edward said wildly.

"Stick around," Duke came back. "Lotsa big surfs—all free."

They went out again, turned, and caught another swell shoreward. This time the prince would not be denied. He rose to kneeling during the first part, then rose again to his feet—and that ended it! With the prince's unsteadiness throwing away all hope of balance, the board went out of control. Bouncing first right, then left, it nosed down and "pearled" to the bottom. Both men splashed into the foam, tossed as though trapped in a washing machine.

When the comber rolled on, Duke and the prince treaded water. Seeing that neither had been struck by the stampeding surfboard, they laughed.

"My fault, I know!" the prince gasped.

"Happens in the best of families," Duke grinned.

They swam to retrieve the board, still bobbing in the surf like fish trying to shake a hook.

First gathering in the lost board, they then obtained an extra—smaller and lighter than Duke's—from Dad Center for some solo riding.

Resting his own board on the sloping sand, Duke stood on it. "Let me explain," he said, "with a dry run."

The prince nodded, obviously an eager learner.

"First," Duke began, "you balance and steer your board lying face down, then advance to the same thing kneeling. When you've picked up sense of balance control, you're ready for the waves"

"Makes sense," the student agreed.

Duke dropped prone on the board, explaining again. "This is the beginning position. At the base of a slope of water, you dig in hard." He swept his arms into imaginary water. "When you've caught the swell and have got the right angle and speed, you grab the rails and get to your feet left forward, right to the rear." In one liquid motion Duke went from prone to one-knee and then upright. He stood again like a fighter, one foot extended, body bent at the waist, and hands at his side for balance.

The prince lay upon the other board, copied Duke, and showed that he at least understood the principle. He was on his feet in the center of the board, awaiting more instruction.

Duke went on, "It's a sliding motion along the face of the wave that you want. It gives a longer, faster ride than just heading straight toward shore. Ride at the end of the curl and slide away from the break." He went through the motions, arms out, simulating a fast, downward ride. "When you're on a swell and it starts to break, you move away from the break and slide just fast enough to avoid the soup." When the prince raised his eyebrows at the word "soup," Duke added, "That's the broken water—the surge and froth where you dumped that first ride."

The prince laughed, for an instant looking seaward. "We got pounded out there, didn't we?"

"Right." Duke went on, "You put your weight far enough back to make the board ride high on the wave. By shuffling your feet you shift your weight to get the speed for sliding across. Try not to run down the wave, it'll lose some of your control, and you'll be unable to pull over in case it breaks across the whole front. If the wave does break over, you want to avoid getting trapped, so step back and put your weight on the side to which you are sliding. That will get you safely out."

"I think I get the idea," Prince Edward said, eager to try his own board.

Duke again went through the routine, watching his royal student. The two headed once more for the ocean, this time with individual boards. Offshore waters had temporarily flattened, letting them paddle leisurely and do more talking.

Prince Edward lay on his stomach paddling. He looked from Duke to Diamond Head. "What a paradise." Waxing confidential, he added, "This is the first time in a long while I've been alone; seldom a moment away from the crowds, official groups, advisors, bodyguards."

"It is good," agreed Duke. He, too, looked at the vast blue water. "Good land; good sea."

They enjoyed the silence, then Duke went on explaining the mechanics of surfing. Prince Edward listened closely. They turned and got into position. They allowed two waves to go past, then Duke pointed.

"We'll take this one."

The prince flattened out on his board, dug hard, and started his first solo ride. Duke also caught the swell. On separate boards they dropped together down the face of the wave. It was a fast drop, but the Prince gamely got to his feet. Duke was up and wanted to applaud his pupil—for the few seconds the latter remained erect. The Prince teetered, flailed wildly, lost his balance, and nose-dived. Man and board came up in the exploding water, tumbling free of each other.

Duke stomped heavily on the tail of his board for a hurried "kick-out." Seeing his guest safely treading water, he paddled for the loose board. With both boards he greeted the Prince: "At least you survived."

"I say," Prince Edward muttered, treading water with one hand on his skull, "that was something of a knock on the head."

"Hurt badly?" Duke asked, pushing the loose board toward the swimmer.

The prince shook his head from side to side. "No, I'll just have a knot to help me to remember my first surfing mistake."

Duke laughed and then explained, "Here's how you went wrong. Picture taking the board onto a steep hill-side. When you let go of it, it starts sliding down, just like a board will slide down a wave's face. Paddling to match the wave's speed and to get the board sliding the face is your job. When you've caught the wave, the sliding starts and all you have to do is control it."

"Sounds simple," broke in the Prince, looking eager to try again.

"The only thing," continued Duke, "the surfboard can slide faster than the wave travels. If you head straight in the nose will pearl right on through the flat water below you and probably hit bottom."

"That could be disastrous to the board, couldn't it?"

"To you, too," Duke grinned. "To avoid pearling you move back on your board and keep its nose up. On faster, steeper waves even this isn't enough. You've also got to turn your board. Paddling hard and catch the wave on an angle instead of straight ahead. Another way to turn is to lean on one edge of your board, making it come around."

"How will I remember all your directions sliding on a wave?" the Prince asked.

"Some people get it instinctively. You could be one of them." Duke smiled.

"A vote of confidence!" laughed His Royal Highness. "Praise from Ceasar is praise indeed. I'm complimented, thank you."

"Don't thank me, Prince. Thank God."

"I shall, I shall!" the royal guest said, climbing onto the board.

"You're still a learner," reminded Duke, "So don't try anything fancy for a while." Like two kids at a picnic, both were enjoying every moment. Duke turned serious again, feeling the responsibility of a good teacher. "It's easier to turn on your knees, so forget standing up for now."

"I'll take it slow and give it my best."

Duke nodded. "If you miss a wave it'll be for one of three reasons; you quit paddling too soon, you were too far back on your board, or it was too flat a wave and you should not have tried it in the first place."

They paddled seaward again. Duke congratulated the Prince on his nerve and knew the fellow could become a good surfer. "Last time you were too far forward," he repeated. "It was a good lesson."

Prince Edward smiled, ready for more instruction, and more practice.

For several hours Duke worked patiently, explaining and demonstrating. By later that afternoon the Prince had become quite adept, falling only occasionally. He had quickly become a devotee and just could not get enough. On the beach again with Duke as the sun was sinking, he was bowlegged with fatigue.

"I've truly had a time," he said, extending his hand in thanks. "I'm grateful for all your help."

"Think nothing of it," grinned Duke. "I'm richer for knowing you."

They parted as the prince rejoined his anxiety-laden cortege descending from the front of the Moana.

The following day, April 14th, 1920, the *Renown* sailed. Prince Edward left a message for the press saying that he departed with great regret, having had so short a stay in "Paradise." Another message was delivered by the British Consul, "His Royal Highness has enjoyed his visit to Honolulu immensely. Especially was he delighted with the surfing. He was frightfully keen about it."

The best evidence of how much the Prince enjoyed Hawai'i surf and Duke's company is that four and a half months later, on August 30th, the *Renown* returned to Honolulu Harbor. His Royal Highness was still infatuated with the local surf and wanted more. The *Advertiser* reported that the reason for the second visit was that the prince wanted more "surfboard riding at Waikīkī."

Again Prince Edward stayed at the Moana, where a ten-room suite was engaged for him and his retinue. Coincidentally with the royal arrival, local newspapers were headlining Duke's world-records at the Olympics in Antwerp. The Prince was not disappointed in his surfing. He again had excellent companionship, this time Duke's brother, David Pi'ikoi Kahanamoku. David was as fine a surfer as Hawai'i could present in the absence of Duke. The Prince stayed three days in Waikīkī, and, except for his formal call on Governor McCarthy, spent the whole time canoeing and surfing.

On September 1, the British warship made her final departure from Honolulu. Through the local press the amiable prince announced: "I have made this second unofficial visit to Honolulu as long as my progress would allow because I knew that Honolulu was a delightful place for my holiday, not only for myself but for all the ship's company of the *Renown*... I'm so sorry that I have to leave... I see, too, that my friend, Duke Kahanamoku and other Hawaiian swimmers have been keeping up the great swimming reputation of Hawai'i for the Olympic Games at Antwerp, and I hope they have more triumphs still to come."

When Duke had later read the item he glowed with pride. To his friends he said, "The prince and I march to the ticking of different clocks, but he loves the sea the way I do and that makes us brothers."

Duke was now three decades old and youth had taken flight. Still he unflaggingly poured energy into conditioning and his swimming. He allowed nothing, absolutely nothing, to curb his enthusiasm. Kidded about his age—now thirty—he grinned, "I don't feel old, not as much a survivor as a guy still on his way."

Edward, the Prince of Wales in an outrigger canoe while staying at the Moana Hotel, 1920. Ray Jerome Baker-Baker-Van Dyke Collections - Bishop Museum.

17

Triumph at Antwerp

DUKE'S REPUTATION CONTINUED TO STRENGTHEN DURING THE PRELIMINARY SWIM EVENTS IN HONOLULU. When Manager George "Dad" Center selected his all-islander team to represent Hawai'i for the Antwerp Games, the 30-year-old Kahanamoku was again on the roster. It was quite a team which Center took to the mainland. Those reaching Antwerp included Duke, Ludy Langer, Harold "Stubby" Kruger, Warren Kealoha, Helen Moses, Pua Kealoha, Norman Ross, and William "Wild Bill" Harris, Jr. All told, the American Olympic Team comprised three hundred athletes. They sailed from New York aboard the steamer Princess Matoika, an Army transport.

Once more Duke found himself racing against top-flight competitors while being watched by royalty. It seemed a miracle that, eight years later, he was again in Europe.

"All these trips are fun," he said to his younger teammates. A bit more grimly, he added, "Maybe I'll be able to make a living later on..."

On August 24th, 1920, before a screaming crowd, Duke battered his own earlier world's record of one minute and four-fifths seconds in the 100-meter freestyle finals. He ripped through the field of swimmers, improving his previous mark by two-fifths of a second. Kealoha was second, and only one-fifth of a second off the pace. Harris was third. The Hawaiian team totally dominated the event.

Duke was also a member of the victorious American relay team. Made up of Kealoha, Harris, Norman Ross, McGillivray of Illinois, and Duke, the team won in ten minutes four and two-fifths seconds, a new Olympic record. Duke, at thirty, had never been stronger. King Albert of Belgium personally presented Duke's medals to him and shook his hand in congratulation.

One thing happened to Duke which he hadn't expected, an activity not listed on the program. This day of his big wins, he wanted a photo of the King in the Royal Box. Photographs from his travels had become one of Duke's passions. He wormed his way through the crowd to get a close shot. He was almost shot himself when police with drawn guns grabbed him. Considering the hundreds of pictures shot of himself, Duke never expected the excited gendarmes.

"J—just a picture!" he stammered.

The King asked about the disturbance below. When his guards told him that the Hawaiian swimmer had tried to take his picture, King Albert ordered Duke brought to the Royal Box.

The officers still had Duke in custody. With new instructions to escort the culprit to the King, they simply strong-armed the athlete forward. Brought face to face with the King, Duke's embarrassment left him tongue-tied. King Albert was quick to understand.

The King smiled. "I regret that you were caught in the coils of my security police. Please accept by apologies."

Duke felt totally silly.

The King continued, "Young man, take as many pictures as you wish."

Duke mumbled, "Thank you, sir," took one hurried picture, and hurriedly left. The Belgians had him mumbling to himself.

When the Olympics ended the Hawaiian team went on to Paris where they scored a clean sweep in all their contests. Duke broke his own record in the 100-meter event, hitting one minute flat. A Paris headline read:

WORLD CHAMPION CLIPS TWO-FIFTHS OF A SECOND FROM HIS OWN TIME. KEALOHA SECOND. FRENCH TITLEHOLDER NO MATCH FOR HAWAIIAN.

After also visiting Brussles and London, the victorious island team returned to the United States. When finally back in Hawai'i, Dad Center and the team had every reason to feel proud. They had competed in twenty-six contests and picked up fifty-nine medals and other ribbons and plaques. They had won at Antwerp, Paris, London, New York, Chicago, Detroit, San Francisco, and other stops.

It was a jubilant team that sailed into Honolulu Harbor. The Honolulu Chamber of Commerce, on behalf of all Hawai'i, honored Dad Center and the athletes with a victory luncheon at the Commercial Club. Chamber President A. Lewis, Jr., pinned a gold medal on each team member. Hawai'i was tops in the swim world.

Again Duke was forced to return to a pedestrian life after having rubbed elbows with royalty and dignitaries throughout Europe. Visitors to Hawai'i looked him up, paid him wonderful compliments, had their pictures taken with him, and got his autograph. Duke still had nothing to secure himself for the years to come. He searched for some way to capitalize on his swimming and surfing fame.

Neither brothers, sisters, nor friends knew of his haggard nights of wakefulness over his dilemma.

Two years dragged by with little progress. The jobs he managed to get were not what he wanted. He was not good with words, and needed something where words weren't important. Finally he found a perfect answer. Silent movies had a small place for him.

Duke signed a five-year contract with a Hollywood studio. It forced him to reside on the mainland, but lead to a series of parts that paid Duke the dividends he could not earn elsewhere. He never became a star, and few will remember his pictures, although he worked with such stars of the day as Wallace Beery, George Bancroft, Anita Stewart, Ronald Colman, Lili Damita, John Wayne, and many others.

He swam all over Southern California, played water polo, and made pictures like *The Wanderer, Lord Jim, Golden Journey, Pony Express, Decatur, No Father to Guide Him, The House Without a Key, Lady of the Hare,* and *The Rescue.* He played Sioux Indian chiefs to Hindu thieves. He later joked, "I've been every kind of a native. But they do make every effort to see I don't get my feet wet; I never play a Hawaiian."

It was paradoxical. A man with stature and dignity of ali'i was invariably cast in the role of an Indian or other native far from his true land. He had hobnobbed with potentates, sovereigns, presidents of foreign countries and the United States, and now made a living portraying indigent tribesmen.

"Funny thing," he used to say, and shake his head and let the rest go unsaid. He was thinking that once they almost offered him the role of a Hawaiian chief.

But though he never became a star, at least Hollywood gave him a living and a lifetime of memories. Duke found that most top-bracket stars of his time had a common touch. If they didn't, he didn't bother with them. In his later years Duke regaled friends with stories of yesteryear's movie greats.

One, involving Wallace Beery and George Bancroft, was set on Director James Cruz's schooner off Catalina Island. After the day's filming, Duke donned his swimming trunks and jumped into the sea to cool off. Enjoying after-work drinks, Beery and Brancroft watched from the boat's deck. Suddenly they saw a long dark object rushing in Duke's wake. It gained upon the swimmer, then submerged ominously within a few feet. Beery and Bancroft shouted "Shark, Duke! Shark!"

Duke was far from the boat and water in his ears cut off all distant sound. The men yelled louder. Voices went ragged when the monster rose to Duke's left and

Duke c. 1920   *Bishop Museum*

Duke Kahanamoku in outrigger. c. 1921

Bishop Museum

Duke with friends (clockwise from back row): Warren Kealoha, Ludy Langer, Duke Kahanamoku, coach Dad Center, Pua Kealoha, Helen Moses Cassidy, and W.W. Harris Jr.

Hawaii State Archives

Outrigger Canoe Club 200 yards men's relay team. Winner of Yale-Hawaii Tank Meet - July 29, 1921 Time 1:39 4/5 sec. Left to right: W.W. Harris Jr., F. Turner, Dad Center, G. Harris and Duke Kahanamoku   *Joseph Brennan photo*
Below: Outrigger Canoe Club with Dad Center standing in front of Duke's surf board.
                                                                        Courtesy of Cedric Felix

Duke with friends.

Courtesy of Cedric Felix

Below: Duke with brothers

Courtesy of Cedric Felix

Duke Kahanamoku at Outrigger Club, c. 1922.
Bishop Museum Photo

began circling.

Frantically the two actors hauled in the dinghy and clambered into it. They leaned into the oars and soon had the tiny craft jumping. Panicked glances over their shoulders showed Duke still swimming, apparently unaware of the dark form fast tightening its circle. Beery and Bancroft caught Duke just as the beast again submerged.

Gasping, the portly Bancroft shouted, "Duke!"

Beery panted, "Quick, climb in!"

The rowers shrieking panic was stark and urgent, doomsday at sea. Duke came to an abrupt halt. He faced the rowboat, "What gives?" he called.

Bancroft screamed, "There's a shark under you!"

Beery pointed to where the dark form had disappeared below the surface.

Duke grinned. "That's a sea lion. Real friendly. Been following me and swimming around." Duke added, "He's absolutely harmless."

Winded from their wild rescue attempt, Beery and Bancroft looked sheepishly at each other. To save face and conceal their embarrassment, Beery said, "C'mon, George, let's get back. We've had our workout."

They rowed limply back to the schooner, claiming a speed record for their emergency sprint. Neither wished to offer details to Cruz, who had come from up below deck with a puzzled look.

"Jim," Beery said, "We just felt like rowing. We've gotta lose weight."

Cruz laughed. "You sure don't look like title-holders to me."

"Well," Bancroft defended, "some people swim, some row." He pointed at the Hawaiian swimming in the distance. "There's one that oughta have his own private pool in hell."

Bancroft said, "Duke'd never find it in the steam."

Later everyone enjoyed a few laughs at the expense of the famous erstwhile lifeguards.

Duke Kahanamoku, 1924 Paris Olympic Postcard   *Courtesy of Cedric Felix*

18

Time Does Not Wait

ONE CAN NOT HOLD BACK THE CLOCK. Duke still worked for perfect fitness. "When I'm working out," he used to say, "I feel I'm slapping time in the face."

Those closest said nothing, but felt he was losing the battle. By 1924, before the Paris Olympics, the world again began to see swimming records fall. New training strategies and new methods had much to do with it. Even in Hawai'i, old records fell by the wayside. There was fear in some circles that Duke had had it. His friends were concerned.

In April of 1924, Honolulu saw Arne Borg of Sweden swim the half-mile in ten minutes forty-three and three-fifths seconds, beating Boy Charlton's record of ten minutes fifty-one and two-fifths seconds with Warren Kealoha forty yards behind him at the finish. They saw the 400-meters go to Borg in four minutes fifty-nine seconds, with Warren Kealoha and Sam Kahanamoku, Duke's brother, twenty-five yards behind. Other records also fell.

Despite his thirty-four years, Duke was still trying to remain in top shape. However, the long stretch of movie-making had been no help. "Maybe I should retire," he confided to friends, "because I've been so lucky in the past—and you can only let the bet ride so often." He knew even he couldn't fight the inexorable tide of time.

With the coaxing of many plus his own native courage, he struck out to qualify once more for the Olympics. Many friends—most, in fact—crossed their fingers.

"I'd give a hunk of my soul," Duke said, "to make the Games once more," as he turned his will to training.

Suddenly the race for places on the American team became even tighter. It was announced that, for lack of funds, the American swimming team would be reduced from thirty-six to twenty-four.

The announcement explained the cut in these words: "This applies to the men's branch. The women's team will number eighteen swimmers. Only the first three men in each final event in the trials will go to Europe, while six others will be drawn from the diving events. It is probable that there will be no American water polo team on the trip to the Olympic Games."

Duke realized that his chances of making the team had been cut by a full third.

1924 Olympic Swim Team   *Courtesy of Cedric Felix*

Below: Duke Kahanamoku with Johnny Weissmuller, 1924 Paris Olympics Postcard
                                                   Courtesy of Cedric Felix

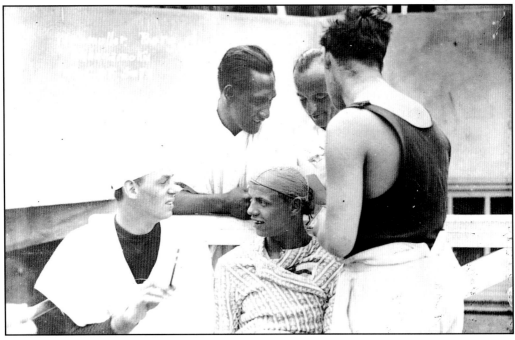

1924 Paris Olympic Village   *Courtesy of Cedric Felix*

U.S. Olympic Swim Team, 1924   *Courtesy of Cedric Felix*

Johnny Weissmuller and Duke Kahanamoku when former took Duke's title away at Paris Olympics.
Joseph Brennan Photo

Real fears of being left began to assail him. To a confidante he said, "If I got left behind I'd feel I was all used up."

He knew he could be a good loser, but that would not save him from feeling destroyed inside. Doggedly he went at his training, hoping he had not too many years on his back. But now he had a premonition that he'd soon lose the world he loved so much.

At the Indianapolis pre-Olympics meet, Johnny Weissmuller broke the world record for the 100-meters in fifty-nine and two-fifths seconds. Hawai'i read that Duke was second, and his brother, Sam, third. The bad news for Duke and his supporters was printed in The *Honolulu Advertiser* of June 6th, 1924:

WEISSMULER NOSES DUKE OUT IN RECORD TOPPING SWIM IN
   THE 100 METER EVENT

Sam Places Third in Event When Illinois Flash Makes Time of 59 2-5;
One Second Lower Than Duke's Antwerp Time

Indianapolis June 5. John Weissmuller of the Illinois Athletic Club today
shattered the world's Olympic swimming record for the 100 meters
freestyle swim, leading a field that included Duke and Sam Kahanamoku
and Jack Robertson. The Illinois star's time was 59 and 2-5 seconds, one
second lower than the time made by Duke Kahanamoku at Antwerp in
1920 when he established the record in 1 minute 2-5 seconds.

In the same event, which was part of the series of final trials for the U. S.
Olympic swimming team, Duke Kahanamoku, swimming for the Los
Angeles Athletic Club, finished second and his brother Sam, who swims
for the Hui Nalu Club of Honolulu, took third place. Jack Robertson of
the Olympic Club of San Francisco was fourth.

This was to be a dress rehearsal for the July Paris Olympics. Young Johnny had the edge in years, training, and know-how. Hawai'i fans resigned themselves to the fact that Duke was a marvel to even be in the Olympic trials for a third time. Twelve years were too many. Duke's friends wanted to close their eyes to what would come.

The Paris Olympics ended Duke's reign as the world sprint-swimming champion. He finished in a French pool. Beaten, he hung at the edge of the pool for a few moments; mute, immobile, void of discernible emotion. Then he made his way to Weissmuller and shook his hand. "Congratulations, champ."

"Thanks," Weissmuller panted. In his characteristic way, he added, "What was the matter, Duke? You lost your way down that lane?"

"No, I managed to find my way." His crown was gone and his world was shattered. Duke groped among the pieces.

Weissmuller tried to repair any hurt he might have caused. "You swam a pretty good race."

Duke forced a smile. "A pretty good race is like a pretty good egg."

With most at home at least partly expecting the news, shock from the Paris report was cushioned. Hawai'i read with sadness the dispatch of July 21, 1924, in both The *Honolulu Advertiser* and *Star-Bulletin*:

> AP Les Tournelles, July 20. America made a clean sweep in the short distance swimming events of the Olympic today. Johnny Weissmuller of the Illinois Athletic Club won the 100-meters freestyle finals in :59 seconds flat, breaking the Olympic record. Duke Kahanamoku of the Los Angeles Athletic Club was second and Sam Kahanamoku, Hawai'i, was third. Arne Borg of Sweden finished fourth in the event and Takaishi of Japan was fifth.

Time had finally run out for Duke. Indianapolis had offered a warning, but Paris made it official. The thing Duke had feared most—being unable to duplicate his feats—had finally come. He was little better equipped to find lucrative employment in Hawai'i than when he had quit school. Professional swimming offers would no longer come in; swimming races and exhibitions were a business for youth.

Duke did the one thing he could do. He went back to the movies. He was modest and practical enough to realize he'd never be a star, but the industry did offer some security and position. He returned to Hollywood, accepting whatever parts were offered.

His memories of being the champion were warm and comfortable. He promised himself to keep it that way. As for the world, well, he was still an almost matchless swimmer and surfer, and no one could meet him without coming away with a great deal of respect.

Film work and surfing took Duke all over Southern California. June 14, 1925, found him on Corona del Mar, a beach some fifty miles south of Los Angeles.

Duke was prepared for some late-afternoon surfing, but not for the surfing he would be compelled to do this day.

He was camped on the beach with friends: the Henry brothers, Bill and Tom; the Vultee brothers, Jerry and Art; Owen Hale; and Henry Chapplett. While the others were unloading the cars some distance from the beach, Duke had lugged his board to the sloping sand to study surf. Resting the big chunk of redwood on the slope, he gazed at the water. There was big surf; bigger than he had seen in some time. Combers were breaking on shore with the sound of a heavy cannon.

The "chuck-chuck" of a fishing boat caught his ear. He could see a charter boat making way parallel to the coast. She was maybe an eighth of a mile offshore, apparently well beyond the breakers. Duke still watched, knowing that swells could, without warning, form farther seaward and endanger the craft.

Suddenly faint evidence of green ridges formed farther out. Duke watched them grow into slopes resembling silken foothills. They rose and mounted, an unseen force hurrying them shoreward. The boat's helmsman must have seen them, too, for the craft came around aslant toward the horizon.

The boat didn't quite quarter the first swell. She teetered, dipped, and settled down the other side. Wallowing in the trough behind the passing swell, she appeared to try to nose into the next. The craft did not handle that one well, either, and shuddered as the wall of water caught her. When she slid down the back, Duke could see only her superstructure. He knew she must be wallowing helplessly and his fear rose at sight of a third wall of water heading in.

Duke could see the boat's foamy wake as the pilot tried to bring the vessel around. The third swell had massive breadth and height, leaning forward in its mad pace. Duke stood transfixed as the great wave curled forward, venting explosive power against the ship's hull.

"Solid water!" murmured Duke, hoping the vessel could take it. "God save them!"

The boat capsized under the crashing water. For an instant the surge hid everything from view, then the craft's bottom rose into the sun.

"She turned turtle!" shouted someone from the rear. "She's done for!"

In one motion Duke had his big board under his arm and was roaring into the surf. Cries for help shrieking from the fishermen bobbing in white water were barely audible.

Those bobbing heads would not long remain above the surface in the churning surge. Duke dug deep and hard, always trying to keep an eye on fully-clothed victims. Swells and breakers often cut his view, and only when the overturned boat and its passengers were lifted skyward could he glimpse them.

He gave all he had, hoping to pick up the victims before their sodden clothing dragged them down. He saw several clinging to the bottom of the capsized craft. Then a sea washed over, and he couldn't be sure if they had survived the cataract. He hit one comber after another, piercing them, pushing on, bucking the next one.

He got into even more explosive breakers; one was like a skyscraper lunging down upon him. He locked arms and legs around the board, heaved hard, and spun upside-down. Protected beneath the board, the breaker rolled over and past him. Duke then spun again, bringing himself and the board right side up.

Through the following comber he found a fisherman rising to the surface, gagging for air and help. Duke swept forward and dragged him onto the board. Two more lost their grip on the slick, overturned vessel, raw fear on their faces. Duke fought over to them, yelled through the pandemonium, "Climb on!"

Pawing clumsily through the foam, they caught the rail and squirmed on. Duke's board could not hold more survivors, so he lay far aft and started paddling. The nearly-drowned men would be no help for the long, backbreaking haul. Another swell lifted men and board high and Duke barked "Hold tight!"

His passengers braced for what would come. Duke drove hard at the water, arms in to the elbows, giving the loaded board a fast thrust. Triple-tandem they shot down the wave beginning to broach and throw one off. Frantically Duke grabbed him, held tightly, and righted the board. Overloaded with half-drowned victims in massive breakers, even Duke couldn't surf without mishap. The board and its awkward cargo swung sidewise to the wave.

"Tight!" cried Duke.

With all four gripping the rails, the board somersaulted, washing and bouncing toward the shallows. Duke's sodden passengers were smashed from the twisting board. Fortunately, by now others from Duke's party had gotten their own boards through the surf. The arriving surfers caught the battered fishermen and took them in tow. Meanwhile Duke turned his board and again started seaward for additional victims.

Once more Duke pushed through the oncoming breakers. He reached the overturned boat and picked up two others vainly struggling to hold on to the craft. He swung around with his new cargo and paddled hard for shore and safety.

Other surfboards were now also propelled seaward to help. The water was full of floundering, panic-ridden fishermen fighting against raging waters that clutched their clothes. Other surfers finally reached the tangle of frantic victims, to grab at waving hands. Some they caught, some they missed—more than one fisherman went under.

Still headed shoreward, Duke planted his board onto the face of a crashing wave, thrusting him and the wreck victims to the shallows. There the board pearled, and all three spewed to where oncoming surfers could grasp and save the fishermen.

Duke scrambled for his now loose board, retrieved it, and once more headed seaward. Cries for help still pierced the racket of smashing combers. Duke passed an incoming board with a surfer and a victim prone, leaned into his own paddling and heard his breath hoarsely. Time was short and his fatigue was already heavy.

He hoped he had the strength to make one more rescue. Feeble calls for help made him dig harder and deeper. He watched one comber on the upturned hull geyser into the air. When the torrent passed, it had wiped off the last of the clinging victims. Duke wondered how many had been trapped below.

Duke re-entered the maelstrom of exploding water. To starboard, the face of a victim rose and started down again. Duke reached and caught a fistful of hair. In one desperate pull he brought the gulping man across the board and held him.

"Good God," babbled the victim, clutching the board's rail and vomiting.

"Hang on!" Duke gasped, his own strength ebbing.

He searched the wild turbulence for other victims. Doubts assailed him. With one man gripping the board, Duke worked through the crazy water to seaward. Two men were hanging onto a hatch cover. They at least had something to cling to. Farther to port, Duke spotted two more dog-paddling weakly, too sodden with heavy clothing to keep their heads above water. Surfing pals Gerard Vultee and Owen Hale were headed toward others inshore, so Duke paddled desperately to reach the exhausted pair.

They were too beaten to even help when he came alongside, so Duke caught the clothing of one. The victim already on his board managed to catch the other.

Again Duke rasped, "Tight, now! Tight! Don't let go!"

Three victims clung like monkeys to the board. Duke paused to suck in air and gasp, "I can get you in." He slid off the stern and rested on his forearms. "Just hang on!"

When he had gotten through, he began kicking. It was awkward, for the board was heavily overloaded. The first man taken aboard managed to sit astride and hang onto the other two while their bodies dangled in the water. All had eyes bespeaking their exhaustion. The cumbersome cargo wobbled precariously. Duke slogged away like a winded horse.

He got into the rolling surf, almost lost his passengers, but pushed through the worst of it. A curling breaker caught the tangled mass in one sweeping rush. It was a jumble of legs and arms that washed onto shore like debris. Part was Duke Kahanamoku, now too exhausted to even grab his board and stop it from surging seaward in the backwash.

Others were there to care for the victims, there to retrieve his board. The beach had rapidly filled with people, for the disaster had been seen by residents all along the shoreline and the alarm spread. Lifeguards were rushing equipment and know-how to the stricken fishermen.

No more rescue work was to be done in those pounding waters. Duke saw there was now ample help on shore. There was nothing he could do that would not be done by police and lifeguards. Soon there would be the questions and the praise, which he wanted no part of.

Wrung slack by exhaustion, he walked southward on the beach, like a man with ironshoes. Later he would come back and rejoin his friends. They would have his board in camp and would be waiting to tell him he was a hero. The thought embarrassed him.

He continued while the sun fought with gray clouds. He passed around the cliffs to where he could not be seen. There he lay on the sand and let his energy slowly return.

It hit Duke that possibly no one had seen him leave. His absence would prompt a search of the very waters he had just worked. The thought of others endangered for his sake chilled him. There was nothing to do but head back for the camp.

Ambulances were on hand as Duke approached. Tom Henry broke from the crowd to meet him, then Jerry and Bill.

Tom spoke first. "Take a bow, Duke. You did a great job."

"Yeah," added Jerry, "you did."

Beyond the surf life guards where diving for the ones they hadn't gotten.

"I did all I could," Duke said. "Then I left." He indicated the beach south.

Bill nodded. "That's all right. We understood."

"You saw me?"

"Right. We knew why. You did more than the rest of us."

"Wish we could have saved more," Duke said. "I feel awful about the ones we couldn't get to."

"You saved eight from grief," broke in Jerry.

Duke's pals had known that he would try to flee from praise.

"What about the reporters?" Duke asked. "Questions from police?"

"Go back down the beach," Tom said. "We'll handle them. Come back when the mob's gone."

Bill added, "You've done enough. Everything's under control."

Duke's three friends turned and went back. Police and newsmen filtered in and out in a subdued hubbub. Duke turned opposite and took a slow thoughtful walk.

He didn't return until the sun was on the horizon. The excitement was off the beach now. Not a fellow in camp said anything about the tragedy. The gasoline cook stove had been set up and there were covered pans on it. A coffee pot rested at its base.

"Hot chow and java if you want it!" Jerry called.

"Thanks," Duke said. He looked to the boat now lying on her side in the shallows. Waves had hammered the hulk shoreward. She was coming apart, timbers splintering, superstructure disintegrating. Men were at the water's edge with heavy equipment to salvage what they could. "Thelma" was painted in black letters on the stern. Breakers chewed at her ribs.

Duke's eyes went to the combers rolling in, the yen to surf today long gone. He walked to the bedrolls. He would sleep, and try to forget the cries of those he had been unable to save.

Making his bed on the sloping beach, Duke tried to sleep, but his mind raced on. His friends talked in low tones, still full of the day's experience. Their words, distinct on the inshore breeze, reached Duke. He learned that five had drowned, twelve were rescued—eight by him.

Sensitive to violence, thin-skinned to tragedy, Duke strove to shut out the words and bring on sleep. Wails of those lost still haunted him, their plaintive eyes still stabbed. At last he fell into mixed-up dreaming that gave him little rest.

As expected, newsmen came that evening and asked for Duke. They were put off by Duke's pals.

"We won't wake him," one of the Vultee boys explained. "He's had a tough day."

"Come around in the morning," Jerry said. "We'll help you get the story then."

But Duke took off early in the morning. He still wanted no interview. There was nothing at the beach for him but June fog and the sad crying of gulls. Taking his board, he drove back to where he was staying, the Les Henry home in Los Angeles.

A newsman was waiting for him there. Trapped, he answered the man's questions as briefly as possible.

In parting, the reporter asked, "Just how did you make all those rescues?"

Duke tried to fight his embarrassment. "I don't know. It was done. That's the main thing."

The reporter made another note, then closed his book with a snap. "Thanks, Duke."

When he left Duke was blinking. Neither had understood the other.

Morning newspapers were full of the Corona del Mar tragedy, loaded with the dramatic rescues of one Duke Kahanamoku, the Hawaiian swimmer from past Olympics. His friends had talked and praised.

The Henrys took turns in reading different columns aloud. Duke felt the embarrassment rising. This was not for Duke. After Duke lived an experience, good or bad, he walked away without looking over his shoulder.

The reading went on. J. A. Porter, Newport Beach Chief-of-Police, was quoted: "Kahanamoku's performance was the most super-human rescue act and the finest display of surfboard riding that has ever been seen in the world."

The reading halted as the Henrys finally looked at Duke. Silence seemed to have burst into the room.

"If anybody wants me, I've just fallen off the world," Duke excused himself politely.

Honolulu papers, too, wrote of the heroic work done by Duke in the tragedy. The *Star-Bulletin* suggested that Hawai'i recognize his valiant deed in a suitable form. It recommended that a medal for valorous action be struck and forwarded to him by the Chief Executive, Governor Farrington.

An editorial of June 30, 1925, took up the cry, saying: "Mr. Robert B. Booth, a lifelong friend of Duke's father, and his uncle Piikoi, both of whom are fine types of Hawaiian mankind, has consented to act as Chairman of a Committee to raise the very modest sum needed for a suitable medal."

Money was raised almost overnight. The gold medal struck by Wall & Dougherty was engraved: "For Heroism" and carried the Hawaiian Coat-of-Arms. Governor Farrington sent the medal to the mainland for presentation to Duke.

The Hawaiian Society of Los Angeles presented the medal to the guest of honor, Duke P. Kahanamoku, on September 4, 1925. To the large and enthusiastic assembly at the Alexander Hotel, President Lorrin Andrews read the Governor's letter. In part: "Your prompt action and disregard for your own safety, a brave and heroic deed, fully upholding the best traditions of Hawaii in the greatest service that one can render his fellow beings... I know that I am expressing the thought of the people of Hawaii when saying that this latest victory of yours in saving human life is greater indeed, than all those you have won in the athletic contests that have made you a world figure."

Following Duke's thanks and bow, Miss Pauline Steele, secretary of the society, placed a bright lei of fresh Hawaiian flowers about his neck. Duke's embarrassment was complete. Being thought of as a hero was something he never quite comprehended.

One thing that amazed him was that not one of those he had rescued had written or phoned any thanks. Nothing came from any of the eight throughout that year. Duke was bewildered at man's ingratitude. He shook his head in puzzlement. "Strange," he said. "Maybe life doesn't mean much to them."

Duke's sense of man's ingratitude was lessened when, on Christmas day of 1925, the Los Angeles Athletic Club presented him a gold watch for his rescues.

Duke's thoughts turned inward. He tried to relate his own life to his picture-making in Hollywood. Filmdom's make believe world was a far cry from reality. Everything was pretend. Where was the picture work taking him? Nowhere, he felt, and sometimes it seemed to smother his mind, dragging down his self-image.

He remembered an elementary teacher quoting Helen Keller: "Life's a daring adventure, or it's nothing." Well, he'd keep an eye open for a field that wasn't loaded with pretense. He wanted something where he could see the end of the tunnel. His chances of real success in the picture world were two—slim and none.

Part-time picture work in Hollywood was a living for Duke, so he remained on the mainland. He had no illusions about becoming a major star, but pay checks were at a premium. The glamour of studio work also helped fill the void left after the loss at Paris in '24. Heralded as a world champion for so long, Duke's current years were anticlimactic.

Between pictures in 1927, Duke accepted an invitation from Hawai'i to participate in the dedication of the World War I Memorial Natatorium, which would open on August 24.

He embarked from the *City of Los Angeles* at Honolulu on August 19th. Brothers, sisters, and friends were ecstatic. Aloha was everywhere. Again and again he was told how much he had done for his homeland.

"No big thing," he insisted modestly. "I had a God-given ability, and I just gave it my life." Still, his brown eyes contained a certain sadness.

Everything seemed to be in the past, yesterday, yesteryear, a lifetime ago. He was an ex-king—with no new kingdom in sight. He kept looking back.

When reporters queried Duke, he gave them echoes of yesteryear—hollow though they may have sounded. Younger, faster swimmers had supplanted him and he acknowledged the march of time, "You know, you just can't stop the clock"

"Duke, where do you go from here?" one *Star-Bulletin* reporter asked.

"I wish I knew," came the laconic reply. Ruefully Duke added, "I've had all this honor, but have wound up with nothing in the pocket. It's late. I've got many medals to rub together, but I'm at the age where it would be nice to rub dollars."

His financial dilemma continued, but it didn't keep him from helping others. He continued appearing "for free" (as he called it) at openings, dedications, and festivities where his presence always added color, excitement, and significance.

Chief among his appearances was the opening dedication of the World War I Memorial pool on August 24th, 1927. The big $250,000 concrete structure had a packed audience that came alive as Duke dove into the 100-meter stretch of water. He showed the rhythmic leg-drive and fluid arm-stroke of his better days. It was only an exhibition swim preceding the competitive events, but the roaring crowd let him know that he was still loved and respected.

As guest of honor, Duke remained to officiate. Attending swimming events was more than just entertainment for him. Encouraging upcoming swimmers was one of his great loves. He witnessed the sensational win of handsome "Buster" Crabbe—half-Hawaiian—in the one-mile swim.

Congratulating Crabbe, Duke said, "You'll be a world champion!" There was joy on the older man's face when he hugged "Buster." He was glad that another fellow-Hawaiian would become a shining light for the islands. Even so, Duke knew that these new swimmers would gradually end public recollection of his wins.

19

A Yesteryear Champion

TIME PASSED AND DUKE FOUND THAT, AS YESTERYEAR'S CHAMPION, HE NOW WORE A DIFFERENT HAT. He would, as always, adjust.

Duke resumed exhibition swimming at aquatic events. He did his share of officiating, watching young swimmers zoom into top spots. He remained in his financial quagmire, engulfed in a financial world alien to him—one in which he felt unable to cope. People began seeing in him the brooding quietness that comes with excessive introspection. Duke was becoming solemn.

Talk began about the 1928 Olympics in Amsterdam. Like an old war horse, Duke wanted to return to battle, despite his being almost two decades past his prime. His sporadic work in Hollywood studios didn't keep him from training daily. He trained in Santa Monica Bay and at the Los Angeles Athletic Club. But fate lowered the boom on his hopes with a severe case of influenza he was slow to shake. Despondent, he sat out the 1928 games.

In 1929 Duke hit an all-time low, disheartened still over his finances. He wrote his brother David: "Lady Luck has gone by and, so long, I've had you, Lady. I've always heard she was fickle, but at least she was something wonderful I experienced—and now I go it alone without her." He felt unwanted by the world.

Finally Hawai'i made an official effort to let Duke know he was always wanted back in the islands. Introduced May 1st, 1929, by Senator Henry K. Aki, the concurrent Senate and House resolution read: "We would welcome Duke Paoa Kahanamoku's return and permanent residence in Hawaii. For, by his honorable conduct and prowess in many lands, this distinguished Son of Hawaii has added much to the honor lei of the fair land that gave him birth."

This show of love triggered Duke's yearning for home. Learning that his mother was not well, he completed his current picture, *The Fire Walker,* and boarded the *City of Honolulu* on December 20th, 1929.

His friend's welcome gave him momentary sense of belonging and success. But he was still without trade or profession to himself. He had given much of his earnings, such as they were, to friends in Hollywood and elsewhere. He felt he had swept his money into a false bottom bag.

Duke shook his head and mused.

Screen star Ronald Colman and Duke on movie location.   *Joseph Brennan Photo*
Below: Duke Kahanamoku and Frank Lacteen as Sioux indians in "The Pony Express" on
location during screen shooting.   *Paramount Pictures*

Duke Kahanamoku as he appeared in the movie "Pony Express", July 1925. Joseph Brennan Photo

Duke Kahanamoku as a Turk.   *Joseph Brennan Photo*

Duke Kahanamoku and Anita Stewart, top screen star of the late 20's and 30's. Shot at Balboa Beach, California on location. *Joseph Brennan Photo*

Duke with brothers Willy and David
Courtesy of Cedric Felix

Duke
Joseph Brennan photo

Duke Kahanamoku in Long Beach, California stunting with a golf stance on his surfboard.
Joseph Brennan Photo

Picture making at MGM Studio in the 20's.   *Joseph Brennan Photo*

Duke on location during his picture making days. Joseph Brennan Photo

Charles Chaplin, Duke Kahanamoku and Paulette Goddard.   *Joseph Brennan Photo*

Opposite page: Duke Kahanamoku and Robert Ripley of "Believe It Or Not" fame at Waikiki Beach, 1925.   *Joseph Brennan Photo*

Duke Kahanamoku with surfboard, Waikīkī.   *Tai Sing Loo, Bishop Museum*

Above: Duke in famous diving stance. *Courtesy of Cedric Felix*

Below: Duke diving into Nuuanu Y.M.C.A. pool c. 1927 *Bishop Museum*

Duke Kahanamoku with brothers: (From left to right) Bill, Sam, Louis, David, Sargent and Duke standing in front of the old Moana Bathhouse, Waikīkī c. 1928.   *Tai Sing Loo, Bishop Museum*

Louis B. Mayer, unidentified MGM star and Duke on MGM lot in 1929.   *Joseph Brennan Photo*

Duke on the beach of Waikīkī.   *Tai Sing Loo, Bishop Museum*

Duke Kahanamoku with Douglas Fairbanks, Richard Arlan and others. January 1931

Bishop Museum

Below: Duke as he appeared in the RKO movie "The Fire Walker", 1929.   *Joseph Brennan Photo*

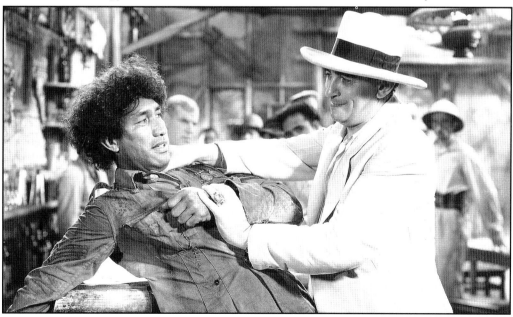

Duke with the long board that he designed, built and owned. This board was a variation of the long board introduced by Tom Blake in 1929. This board was built in 1930 was 10 ft. long, 21-1/2 inches wide, 4 inches thick and weighed about 120 lbs. The board was made of partially hollowed out redwood, which was then decked over.   *Bishop Museum Photo*

Four Kahanamokus: Sargent, David, Duke and Sam, man this Hawaiian outrigger canoe.
Associated Press photo

Five of the Kahanamoku brothers: Bill, David, Duke, Louis, Sargent.   *Courtesy of Cedric Felix*

Duke with surfboard at Waikīkī, April of 1934.   *Bishop Museum*

Duke was still a top athlete in his deep thirties.   *Joseph Brennan photo*

Duke bounding from the surf of Waikīkī Beach in the mid-1930's.   *Joseph Brennan Photo*

Mama Kahanamoku recovered. Duke remained in Honolulu trying to find work. He was offered a position as Superintendent of the Honolulu Hale (City Hall), which he accepted because there was nothing. When he showed up, he found he was "the building custodian," a glorified janitor. Duke was humiliated.

"Serves me right," he said bitterly. "I've just sum myself into a riptide with no return." He was engulfed in despair.

But despair can be a catalyst, provoking a man to search harder. Unpretentious Duke never really believed he was "great." His simple acceptance of both sorrow and joy had provided a life without fear.

When Mayor Wright learned that Duke was unhappy as a building custodian, he stopped him one day in the hall. "Duke," he said, "how come you didn't set your star when you first caught the world's attention?"

The question touched a nerve. "I did, Mayor. I planned to be a champion swimmer—and I made it."

"But a living, a career, a business?"

"I was so young that I wouldn't think about anything I didn't know, and I didn't know anything, so I just didn't think."

The mayor continued, "Why did you drop-out of high school your first year?"

"I lost my way in those school books." Duke struggled not to invent an alibi. He looked away, not wanting to explore the memory. He said, "You're right, mayor. I have only myself to blame. I still want to thank you for your help."

"It was little enough. I'm sorry..."

His Honor walked on, leaving Duke with a broom in his hand and regret in his heart, a dark and lonesome-looking man buried in a rut of his own making.

Duke Kahanamoku with Dr. P. H. Buck at the Bishop Museum.
Bishop Museum

20

An Old Friend

IT WAS A GOLDEN SUNDAY AS DUKE CARRIED HIS BOARD UP WAIKIKI BEACH. The swim-suited blond man approaching ignited memories. "Well, Duke, how are you?" On considered appraisal of Duke's condition, he added, "It's really silly to ask."

Duke grinned, recognizing the husky blond as Charley Paddock, the world record track sprinter from the University of Southern California. "Charley, good to see you!" he said, dropping his board and greeting his old friend from the mainland.

The two shared unforgettable memories. The former "world's fastest humans"—one land, the other water—sat down, cranked up for a sentimental binge. They stretched out on the sand and relived old dreams, checking on old mutual friends. They soon came around to discussing the forthcoming 1932 Los Angeles Olympics.

Paddock exclaimed, "Duke, you look the same as ever, maybe a bit heavier. But you must be pushing forty."

"Forty-one, and feeling great." Duke continued to admire his friend and thought about the track records he had earned. Not long before Paddock had shown his heels to all. "You hold more track sprint records than anyone, don't you?"

"I imagine," Paddock answered, "but there are a lot of new runners coming up."

Seeing Paddock fired Duke with nostalgia. "How old are you, Charley?"

"Thirty-one, but do you know what?"

"What?"

"I'm planning to work into nine and three-fifths second shape."

"Like you say, Charley, there're lots of younger runners, like Eddie Tolan, Frank Wykoff, and George Simpson."

"I know, Percy Williams, too. But I mean it. I plan a crack at next year's Olympiad."

Duke blinked in his characteristic way. Self-conscious, he said, "Funny thing, I've had the same idea." He looked at his muscular legs and flexed his arms. "Of course, there's still Weissmuller and the others to reckon with."

Paddock came alive. "Let's both take a shot," his hand came out to seal the deal.

Duke laughed, but accepted the hand. A sense of rebirth flooded through him. His mind went back to the day he lost his title. "When I lost to Johnny at Paris in 1924, my time was sixty seconds for the 100-meters. Several watches recently caught me in fifty-nine and two-fifths, the fastest time of my life."

"What did Weissmuller do?

"Fifty-nine flat." Duke's hand slid to his thigh as though seeking assurance the old power could still be found. "They've got new training methods and the pools are faster." His voice trailed off. Duke was dreaming, wearing a tight grin, and looking into the porcelain blue sky. For so many years his very soul had been compressed into swimming. He felt it still. "Time's been dragging. I want to get back into the swim. I'll get down to fifty-nine seconds or close, and go to L.A. next year."

"That's the talk!"

Duke got up. "I don't know the future, but I'll tell you what I believe: A man's not old until regrets take the place of dreams."

Paddock, too, got to his feet. "You were the greatest. Maybe you can do it again." He slapped Duke, "I'll bet you're as good today as you were in 1912."

Duke picked up and shouldered his board, his still impressive physique glistening in the sun. He stood, thinking back. "Can't believe it was that long ago."

"It was, Duke. When we met in 1913 you were already champ. Remember how we toured the country with you demonstrating surfing? That's the year I began running—seventeen years ago."

Today's talk had done something for Duke. He knew that if he stopped swimming and surfing the stars would fall. He stood straighter. "It's the old story," he said. "If you quit, you die."

Paddock nodded.

They started across the sand. Athletic gentlemen—younger in heart than body—had much to talk about. Mostly it was about being together at the Los Angeles Olympics.

With all Hawai'i still backing him, Duke planned to condition himself for the 1932 Olympic tryouts. Graying and forty-two, he left on the *Mariposa* for the mainland on June 16th, 1932. He failed to qualify at Cincinnati as a swimmer for

Duke in front of his service station.   *Bishop Museum*

the American team. His valiant effort fell short. He did make the water polo team as a member of the Los Angeles Athletic Club. They lost.

"No alibi," he told reporters. "The legs are gone." He turned away to hide the pain. He had learned that you don't find yourself by going back. Even if you looked until you died there was no going back. He had participated in his fourth Olympiad, covering an incredible twenty-years—that was honor enough. Few athletes had ever competed as long.

He returned to Hawai'i, again casting around for a living. Being a celebrity, friends were loath to offer him minor positions, and Duke had no training for the bigger ones.

Day and night he strove for money to protect himself in later years. He leased a gas station from Union Oil and pumped gas, changed tires, and drained oil. Often he waited on the very people who had earlier cheered him in competitive swims. Tourists snapped pictures of him in his overalls. "Clean my windshield, will you?" one would ask, and snap a photo of Duke in his pedestrian chore.

"Check my tires!" another would say, snapping while he knelt at the tire.

Seldom did people ask permission. Duke felt like an Indian in Arizona, where tourists photographed the natives as though they were exotic animals.

"Maybe now I'm just an exhibit," Duke complained to his brothers. He longed for a way out.

More than two decades after his first records, he still could not accept that, as a competitive athlete, he was finished.

"I guess my star has set," he'd say to friends, hoping they would disagree. But there was no rebuttal. Duke had merely stated the obvious, and everyone, including Duke, knew it.

Some of Duke's friends began insisting that there should be a place of honor and prestige for Duke in the civic structure of Hawai'i. Still self-effacing, Duke couldn't see himself running for public office. It would involve campaigning against others, making promises, and feeling obligated. But his friends continued, and finally Duke was convinced that many people wanted him as Honolulu City and County Sheriff.

In 1934 he ran as a Democrat against the Republican candidate Pat Gleason. He won by about 3000 votes and took office on January 3, 1935. With his father having been in police work for so many years, Duke came to the sheriff's office with a basic knowledge of the work. He benefited from having the respect of the department, so his chores weren't as complex as they might have been.

Taking office, it seemed that Duke finally accepted that his long athletic career was truly over. He realized he could always stay in good shape, but his competitive days were gone.

Duke was re-elected in 1936. Conscientious, he did much to improve jail conditions and management. Living a prosaic life remained difficult for him after so many years of excitement and activity. Losing his mother on June 4, 1936, reinforced his sense of the passing of the years. His mother's devotion loomed large in his life, and her loss was a major event.

In 1937 Duke's admirers conceived of erecting a bronze statue of him on Waikīkī Beach. A twelve-inch model was struck and shown to Duke. He viewed it and said, "I'm still alive, thank you. I don't want a statue of me in public." Pressed further, he added "Maybe when I'm dead, eh?"

This typified Duke. The famous war correspondent and author Ernie Pyle had marveled at his humility. Pyle considered Duke one of his heroes. He wrote: "There is something almost of reverence toward Duke in Hawai'i. His character and his conduct have been so near perfect that he has become almost symbolic of Old Hawai'i...I had luncheon with him at the County Jail...He has never capitalized on his fame."

Serving as sheriff was practically divorced from police work. It put Duke where he could be a goodwill ambassador-at-large. He took pride in that.

Some history is needed here to record the great change that took place in Duke's life while he was sheriff. When Duke made his first great swim at Alakea Slip—the splash heard round the world—a pretty little girl was attending high school in Cincinnati, Ohio. She knew little and cared less about swimming. She had, with her parents, traveled through every state in the Union, Europe, the Hawaiian and South Sea Islands, and Australia before she was seven years old.

This attractive little traveler was Nadine Alexander, daughter of vaudeville actor George B. Alexander. She was a school girl when her hometown paper ran a large photo of Duke and Douglas Fairbanks, Sr., on the beach at Waikīkī. The handsome men caught her fancy and she clipped the photo for her scrapbook. From time to time other pictures and items on the island swimmer were also clipped. Secretly the schoolgirl hoped to someday meet him.

Her real first name was Nadjesda (meaning "Hope" in Russian). Her father, who had an unusually understanding wife, had named the infant for an old flame, Princess Nadjesda of Russia. Curiously, Nadine once came close to becoming a Russian princess herself. During her younger years in Paris she had been engaged

Duke with his board.   *Joseph Brennan photo*

to Prince Youka Troubetskoy, brother of Igor Troubetskoy (once the husband of heiress Barbara Hutton). Later, under the name "Norma Allen," she taught dancing at the Arthur Murray studio in New York City.

Through the years, Nadine had kept her Duke Kahanamoku dream. She decided to revisit Hawai'i, which she had known only as a child.

When she arrived to make Honolulu her home her secret hero was still the Bronze Duke of Waikīkī. To support herself she taught dance at the Boleyn-Anderson Studio in the Royal Hawaiian Hotel. It was not long before she met the man she had idolized so long.

Very soon after they began dating Duke was wholly enchanted. She was fair and beautiful, dancing into his skull at night. She laughed a lot—deep, bubbling laughter. When he looked at her his heart rolled over. By this time Duke's hair was iron gray, but he still had his golden smile and athlete's body.

Each was dedicated to their own field. She was as focussed on her ballet and ball-room dancing as he had been on his swimming and surfing. Both sought rhythm, precision, form, and beauty in their efforts. It was no wonder that acquaintanceship grew first into friendship and later into deep love.

In the years before Nadine's arrival Duke's zest for life had slowed. Duke hadn't thought of marriage since Babe Dowsett had left. Now nothing else mattered. Except that he still didn't have any money. Nor did she. But money would have to wait. Like others who have long been without love, Duke felt he must have this woman or be haunted for the rest of his life.

After a year's courtship—with Duke just days from his fiftieth birthday—he took Nadine as his bride. In the historic church of Moku'aekaua at Kailua, Kona, Hawai'i, they were married on August 2, 1940.

The bride was ribbed about having won the heart of someone so famous. Ever the quick wit, Nadine laughed off the teasing, "They always said Duke was half fish, looks like I caught a big one!"

Duke would light up. He'd say, "A life without love is no life at all," a long speech for him.

Wishing to avoid ostentation they had a simple ceremony. Had the marriage been on O'ahu crowds would have come to witness. On the Big Island only close friends and relatives attended. Among them were Mrs. Duke Cromwell, Sam Kahanamoku, Ralph and Mrs. Fitkin, Arthur J. Stillman, Ernest Richardson, and Lorrin P. Thurston (publisher of The *Honolulu Advertiser*). Senator Francis I'i Brown was best man, Winona Love and Bernice Kahanamoku were attendants of

Duke Kahanamoku and Nadine, the day they were married in Kailua-Kona, Hawaii on August 2nd, 1940 — just a few days before his fiftieth birthday.   *Joseph Brennan Photo*

the bride, and the Reverend Stephen L. Desha officiated.

Duke appreciated the extraordinary girl he had married, but, like others late-married, was still surprised to find he had given up bachelorhood. Any possible regret was quickly banished. The wedding dinner at the home of Arthur J. Stillman served as a prelude to the two-week honeymoon spent at the estate of Senator Brown at Keawaiki on the Kona coast.

Nadine was good for Duke. She gave him the balance he needed and the freedom he could not do without.

If Hawai'i was surprised by Duke Kahanamoku the married man, it was far more so when he suddenly became Republican. Marriage had brought some drastic changes. August 30, four weeks after the marriage, Duke jolted Democratic circles by announcing that he would next seek reelection as a Republican. He asked friends to notify GOP leaders in Honolulu. He had served as a Democrat since 1934.

Upon their return to O'ahu, reporters quizzed the bridal couple. Most queries had to do with Duke's sudden change of parties. A *Star-Bulletin* reporter quoted Nadine saying, "Duke's going over to the Republicans is my fault. I'm strong on the GOP. You can blame me."

Kidded about his late marriage, Duke grinned, "I've still got a lot of good years."

Duke   *Joseph Brennan photo*

21

Pearl Harbor Nightmare

IN HONOLULU AS A MARRIED MAN, LONG-TIME-BACHELOR DUKE TURNED TO MAKING ADJUSTMENTS. He had not had much opportunity before an even greater change occurred. Japanese bombs fell on Pearl Harbor.

Sunday morning December 7, 1941, brought vast changes to every man, woman, and child in America, but especially so on O'ahu. Two Japanese carriers 200 miles north had sent off 360 planes, blasting United States military bases on the island.

Twenty enemy fighters had swooped to within twenty feet of the ground at the Marine Corps Air Station at 'Ewa and machine-gunned forty-nine closely-lined planes burning thirty-three and reducing the balance to unflyable junk. In desperation grounded marines emptied their pistols at the victorious Japanese.

A minute before the 8:00 a.m. hoisting of colors above the ninety-four vessels in Pearl Harbor, dive bombers roared over the Ford Island base in the middle of the harbor and caught the seventy planes sitting there, smashing thirty-three of them.

Seconds later dive bombers and torpedo planes moved against the giant warships in "battleship row," hammering the unalerted ships. An inferno of flame and smoke belched from the ships for a solid 30 minutes. In a half hour of murderously sustained assault all seven of the major ships were hit hard. *California* was down at the stern, *West Virginia* was sinking rapidly, and the *Arizona* was in ruin and on the bottom.

In a second phase after a short lull, the *Tennessee*, *Pennsylvania*, and *Nevada* received additional hits, while *Oklahoma* capsized after taking four torpedoes. Other ships were badly hit and left sinking. Harbor waters were coated with burning oil. Dead, wounded, or trapped in vessels were 2,500 men.

Meanwhile other planes attacked Hickam Field, adjacent to Pearl; Kaneohe Naval Air Station, on the windward side; and Wheeler Field, adjoining Schofield Barracks in central O'ahu. While bombs whistled down and anti-aircraft guns returned fire, rescuers fought through flooded ships to reach the wounded. Sailors blasted off their own ships reported for duty on other vessels. Airmen died trying to get planes off during the strafing. It was a heartbreaking fight for the men who had been caught so unawares.

Honolulu police received their first report at 8:05 a.m. when a man phoned that his kitchen had been hit by a shell. Hundreds of reports quickly followed. With smoke billowing over Pearl Harbor and explosions shattering the morning air, Duke raced to his desk at the Sheriff's Office.

With the office wires jammed with hysterical calls from citizens making ridiculous and impossible demands, Duke wound up working in the morgue. One of his major duties was the Office of Civilian Defense mortuary committee, and he now had plenty to do. There was no thought of rest. The morgue and hospitals were jammed. Throughout the day and night trucks and busses rumbled back and forth with human cargoes both living and dead. Cadavers and bleeding men made up the lot. Women and children were rushed from military posts to points where attacks were not anticipated. It was a feverish time for people who still could not comprehend that their homeland had been attacked.

Governor Poindexter hurriedly broadcast a state of emergency. Before noon the Army ordered commercial stations off the air so their broadcasts could not be used to guide Japanese planes for further attacks. The ensuing silence was even more nerve-racking than earlier frantic announcements. Figures showed the severity of the beating the United States had taken. The disaster took 2,008 Navy, 109 Marine, and 218 Army men. Injured included 710 sailors, 69 Marines, and 364 soldiers. American casualties totaled 3,478, while Japan lost less than 100 men. The Americans lost 188 planes, whereas Japan lost but 29. Such were the bloody results.

Duke assumed many new duties. Nadine also put endless days and nights into the war effort. The two were a team. She was particularly involved in special service work at Fort Ruger, for which she was later awarded the Medal of Merit. The great military effort and arrival of personnel, installations, and equipment forever changed O'ahu. War was close and very personal in Hawai'i; everyone was touched by it.

People gradually adjusted to night time blackouts and sentry's shouts in the darkness. This was not the peaceful, quiet Hawai'i where Duke had grown up. Along with all the others, Duke worked and worried during the war, doing his job as best he could.

Duke Kahanamoku *Joseph Brennan photo*

Duke Kahanamoku with Dorothy Lamour, Juanita Guerrero (far right), Mrs. Alan McGuire (second left) and unidentified other.   *Tai Sing Loo, Bishop Museum*

22

The Year of Coasting

THE YEARS AFTER THE WAR WERE SLOW FOR DUKE, IN KEEPING WITH HIS OWN YEARS. The lethargy prompted him to take a leave of absence in 1948 and go back to Hollywood to make one more picture. Twenty years had passed since he'd been in movies and the industry had changed. Still, he did a good job, working with John Wayne and Gail Russell, in the *Wake of the Red Witch*, where he played a South Sea Island chief.

In Honolulu again as sheriff, Duke once more found himself wondering why, with all of his publicity, he made so little financial progress. Business did not seem to be among his talents.

To finally attain some financial status, he licensed his name to an aloha-shirt manufacturer. It was 1950 and he felt time pressing upon him. The arrangement involved Duke going to New York to launch the nation-wide promotion.

Duke was lionized the "Big Apple." He was delighted to find he was still remembered for his swimming records. Whitney Martin reported from New York on January 19, 1950:

> The first thing you notice about the Duke is his hands... They are tremendous mitts, long and broad and thick, and you have the idea they aided him no little in winning two Olympic titles and breaking every freestyle swimming record from fifty yards to a half mile... It is Duke's first visit to New York since he returned from the 1924 Olympics in Paris, where he finished second to Johnny Weissmuller in the 100-meter freestyle. He won the event in the 1912 and 1920 Games. For the past fifteen years he has been sheriff to the city and county of Honolulu, and so great is his popularity, his election every year is a formality.
>
> Duke is still an imposing figure of a man for all his fifty-nine years. He's six feet and one inch tall and weighs a well-distributed 220, and his dark skin, topped by graying hair, gives him added dignity. And those hands!
>
> For six years after his return from the 1924 Olympics he hung around Los Angeles as a movie actor, playing in numerous colossal epics of the

period.

Tiring of that, he went back to Hawaii where he endeared himself further to his fellow-citizens by his generosity and his role of unofficial host.

All his records have been broken now, he believes, and he has only one answer to the improved marks: "They work harder at it now."

He's watched the current swimming sensation, Furahashi, and as near as he can figure the Japanese ace achieves his spectacular results by speeding up his arm action.

"He digs in with his hands and pulls with his arms like this," Duke explains, demonstrating with those big paddles which pass for hands. "It's like a propeller set to a faster pitch. I was watching him from above, and as far as I could see his kick was the same as we use. He just works harder, that's all."

The famed Hawaiian is not unconscious of the size of his hands. In fact, he consciously developed them to their gargantuan proportions.

"I used to paddle a lot," he says. "The paddles we used had big handles, much larger than ordinary paddles, and I'd grip the wood and flex my fingers and hands to strengthen them."

The swimming world was fascinated by the form used by the competitors from Honshu. Duke was frequently questioned about it.

He was quoted as saying:

"I saw them [the Japanese team] in Honolulu just before they left for the States. I was watching them from a boat. Their style did not seem revolutionary; it is just that they moved their arms faster. They're great swimmers, and the only way swimmers can beat them is by training seriously all year 'round."

Before Duke had been in New York a week, Earl Wilson's column noted:

A big town visitor getting the full treatment these days is that great Islander, Duke Kahanamoku. Duke, here to publicize his colorful sports shirts, has been doing things that even native New Yorkers seldom get around to doing.

Nadine and Duke Kahanamoku   *Courtesy of Tommy Holmes*

"I gave Gypsy Rose Lee a *lei*," Duke said. "I explained to her husband, Julio de Diega, that it is a custom to kiss someone when you give them a lei. He agreed, and I kissed his wife. I also had my picture taken with Eleanor Holm."

Duke hadn't been to New York since 1924 when he was here with the Olympic team. That's when the biggest thing in town was a puny Woolworth building.

When he landed here the other day the acting mayor shook his hand and remarked later: "I shook the Duke's big fin—and I'll probably never get over it."

Everybody entered into the spirit of making Duke feel at home. The management of his hotel pinned a big star on his door, emblematic of his sheriff's star. It made the place look like a theater dressing room. Even Billy Leeds, the tin plate heir, got into the act. He phoned Duke at 4 a.m. and announced he wanted to give a party for him. "I hung up on him," Duke said, and I disconnected the phone."

Meanwhile, he's been getting his picture in every paper and appearing on radio and TV shows.

On Arthur Godfrey's television program he willingly shucked his shoes and did a hula to Arthur's ukulele strumming. Godfrey shook his head and said, "Aren't those Island people wonderful?" The audience agreed with him.

Duke plans another TV appearance Sunday night and will head for home Monday. "I'll probably be back in Honolulu Wednesday," he told me. "When I get to Los Angeles I'll see Bing Crosby and a lot of other friends."

I asked him what else he'd done here. He's been eating oysters. He's been at Lindy's and Toots Shor's and a lot of other places, and it seems he's always ordering Bluepoints, because he can't get them at home.

He's been to see *South Pacific*. I asked Duke if he'd been doing much drinking.

"I never was much of a drinker," he explained. "If I drank, how would I stay in shape like this?"

But there was one thing this great big city couldn't offer the Duke. Back home he swims every day. But he couldn't here—on account of the water shortage.

Duke returned to Hawai'i after great success in the public relations promotion for the aloha shirts with his name on them. Only time would tell if, at least this effort would provide the income Duke so desired.

Duke Kahanamoku surfing on his 60th birthday at Waikīkī.   Joseph Brennan Photo

23

Birthdays Pile Up

RETURNING TO HAWAI'I, DUKE RESUMED HIS DUTIES AS SHERIFF AND RETURNED TO HIS FIRST LOVE—SWIMMING AND SURFING THE WAIKIKI WATERS. Surfing had always helped Duke keep in top shape. Tourists continued to marvel at the silver-haired, coppery man riding the waves. What time he could spare from his duties was spent in the surf.

Duke was entering his sixth decade in 1950. Like most ageing men, he wished to pretend it wasn't really happening. His Outrigger Canoe Club buddies wouldn't allow it, they wanted to party!

On August 24 they threw a birthday party for him larger than anything the club had ever before attempted. Over five hundred people came for the steak fry and entertainment. Duke was presented gifts, publicly lauded, and wound up personally serving everyone a slice of the mammoth birthday cake. Duke was further honored by the city of Honolulu when people set aside a Saturday for "Duke Kahanamoku Day."

He was stopped on the streets, applauded, and draped with lei by people he had never met. He laughed and his eyes were wet as he enjoyed his public acclaim.

Through the first half of the 1950s Duke remained much the same. He joked, "I'm like the man who bought a farm and spent his life watching the goats butt heads."

In midsummer 1955 city fathers arranged for Duke and his cousin Leon K. Sterling, Sr., (City and County Clerk) to take an extensive mainland publicity tour for Hawai'i. Though Duke was basically quiet, he was always worth untold thousands of dollars in advertising for the land of aloha.

In connection with the mainland to Hawai'i Trans-Pacific Yacht Race that year Duke shipped his twenty-foot catamaran Nadu to San Pedro, California, sailing it in the coastal waters as an added attraction. He attended the Shrine Convention in Chicago and made numerous appearances on TV shows, such as Arthur Godfrey's, spreading the fame of Hawai'i and aloha throughout the mainland. Duke was in high gear.

On Duke's return to Honolulu, Red McQueen, sports editor of The *Honolulu*

Advertiser, wrote a birthday column on the man he respected as an athlete and loved as a friend. McQueen always insisted that he considered his long personal friendship with Duke one of the finest parts of his life. Their friendship began when McQueen sold programs at swim meets at old Pier 5-A, where Duke first started smashing records. McQueen honored his old friend with these words:

> Like the long drawn out arguments of the greatest golfer of all time, Jones, Hagen, Hogan or whosis; or the timeworn feud over the greatest fighter, many have tried to compare Duke and Weissmuller. It can't be done. They came in different eras where they surely would have improved with the trend of the time. As for Duke, in his prime, he might surely have set better marks except that he seemed only to swim good enough to win. Certainly they'll never see a more colorful athlete in any form of sport. He exuded color and magnetism.
>
> They used to rise as one when he took his mark; never sat down and tossed their sugar planter's hats, pheasant leis and all, into the harbor as he won, which was always and invariably in record time.
>
> So let's rise and toast this great Hawaiian on his sixty-fifth birthday today and wish him many happy returns of the day.
>
> P.S. And a second toast to his sweet wife, Nadine, who has been a sparkling addition to Duke's life.

As best as anyone knew, Duke was healthy day in and day out. It was a shock when the morning paper of December 3, 1955, headlined that Sheriff Duke Kahanamoku had suffered an apparent heart attack and been rushed to Queen's Hospital. Phone calls swamped the hospital switchboard. Duke's physician, Dr. L. C. Beck, reported in the evening paper that his patient was "Still pretty sick but should be out of the hospital before too long."

Throughout Duke's hospital stay the papers ran daily accounts of his improvement. Not until he improved did the public learn that Duke had been treated for years for heart problems. Angina pectoris had sporadically troubled him after his years of competition. The doctor's statement came as a surprise. It was typical of Duke not to have informed anyone.

Ten days of bed was were all Duke could handle. He was eager to get back to Waikiki Beach where he was sure he could more rapidly recuperate. On his demand, he was discharged and taken home. His doctor gave Duke firm orders to abstain from any athletics.

People received him back as a hero returned from the dead. Even those who had taken him for granted now wanted to do something special for him. In early 1956 talk began again about erecting a statue on Waikīkī Beach. Hawaiians and kama'ina wanted a hall of fame; some wanted it at the capitol, some at 'Iolani Palace, and some preferred City Hall. Others wanted a book be written about Duke while he still could give his own factual account of his life.

One group actually did something tangible. The city needed a name for a new beach at Henry J. Kaiser's Hawaiian Village Hotel, just 'Ewa (west) of Waikīkī Beach proper. It just happened to be adjacent to the old Kahanamoku home, exactly where Duke learned to swim. Kaiser, the industrialist and hotel tycoon, had dredged out the offshore coral in front of the hotel, creating a beautiful artificial lagoon. Tons of white sand were trucked and graceful coconut palms had been planted along the shore. Outrigger canoes rested on the sloping sands.

Many haole protested naming the beach after Duke. They said "Kahanamoku" would be difficult for visitors to pronounce. Research was quickly done, finding that while many mainlanders couldn't pronounce "Hawai'i" correctly, most could spell and pronounce "Kahanamoku."

On May 10, 1956, the City and County of Honolulu Planning Commission wrote Duke Paoa Kahanamoku's name on the sands of time—courtesy of Henry J. Kaiser's sand. Duke was pleased, as usual, beyond words.

Another tribute was paid to Duke in 1956 when, on October 25, he and Walter F. Dillingham were awarded Hawai'i's "Order of the Splintered Paddle" for "distinguished service to mankind." They were the third and fourth to receive this honor. The second had been "Uncle George" Lycurgus, longtime host at the Volcano House. The first was President Eisenhower, honored earlier the same year.

Governor King presented the awards at the Honolulu Chamber of Commerce's quarterly meeting. The governor praised Dillingham as "An industrialist, corporation executive, civic leader, humanitarian and builder of Hawaii." He cited Duke as "A famed Olympic swimming champion, Sheriff of the City and County of Honolulu since 1934, and the City's unofficial ambassador of good will."

For those who did not know, it was explained that the "Order of the Splintered Paddle" derived its name from the events leading to the law of King

Kamehameha I providing that "the old, the helpless and the young may sleep by the roadside and none shall molest them on pain of death."

The award honored those whose daily lives exemplified the spirit of Kahamehama's law. Governor King and the Chamber originated the order in 1955 after both David K. Bray, Sr., and the Reverend Henry Judd had substantiated the splintered paddle legend and endorsed the order as a continuation of Hawaiian tradition.

A third honor came to Duke in that year in the form of an invitation to him and Nadine to attend the Olympic Games at Melbourne as guests of the Australian Olympic Organizing Committee. A warm letter from Sir Frank Beaurepaire, former Lord Mayor of Melbourne, advised that the official visitation would be . forthcoming.

Duke wrote back; "It is a great honor to be invited as official guest of the Olympic Organizing Committee. It is wonderful of them to make it possible for me and Mrs. Kahanamoku to attend the Olympic Games. I am very appreciative. We are greatly honored."

The Kahanamokus made the trip to Australia and attended the games at Melbourne. Treated royally, Duke renewed old friendships with people he had met years back while swimming and introducing surfing. He was astonished at how surfing had taken hold. The sport had become an Australian obsession. They had developed six new types of surfboards which had proven highly successful.

Addressing a large audience, Duke said, "It gives me a lot of satisfaction to know that what I showed you has become a national past time."

He talked on and on about the thrill of surfing and the technique of the sport, setting the crowd afire. He spoke the surfer's language, and people felt close to Duke. He tried to tell them about riding a big wave, but the words were elusive. They'd have to learn from experience, he told them, and somehow they understood, standing and clapping as he left.

After the Games, Duke and Nadine went to Japan for more publicity for Hawai'i before returning home. These activities gave Duke's life that extra dimension that made all the years of effort worthwhile. He was no longer an athlete, but he now felt truly appreciated. *Paradise of the Pacific Magazine* writer Don Mayo picked Duke out for a profile. He wrote:

"Few men in the world achieve greatness—though many strive through a lifetime to do so. Some who do not try become great because of a genius for living; a skill of achievement that comes from the heart. Duke has been 'praised by kings, nor lost the common touch,' awarded a gold medal for heroism in the rescue of eight persons off Newport Beach, California—but never assumed the role of hero.

"He is the intimate friend and associate of many wealthy, influential personages—and he has never been even slightly rich himself, except in friendship—nor has he ever lost his beachboy smile. When the muscles of his sun-browned back and arms ripple as he lifts a huge surfboard and carries it into the sea, even witnesses who do not know him are awestruck by the magnificence of his physique."

All Duke lacked was an income to go along with his prestige and stature.

Duke
Courtesy of Tommy Holmes

24

"This Is Your Life"

A FEW MONTHS LATER DUKE THOUGHT HE WAS ON HIS WAY TO HOLLYWOOD TO BOOST HAWAI'I WITH MORE PUBLICITY. He flew from Honolulu on Saturday, believing that the call was just another of the now-routine request that he help promote tourism. He had been told the trip would involve making an island-travelogue movie. He said good-bye to Nadine and his friends, satisfied he knew what to expect.

En route Duke mused on being constantly on call. On arrival at Los Angeles International Airport, Hawai'i's unofficial ambassador was met and thanked for coming so promptly.

"Anything for Hawai'i," Duke grinned. "Gotta put her on the map."

Duke was whisked to Hollywood in a limousine and put up at the Townhouse near Westlake Park. He was made comfortable with all the service due a visiting VIP. The next day he was picked up and driven out through Cahuenga Pass toward San Fernando Valley. Duke watched Hollywood recede behind him.

"Of course," his host explained, "you realize that picture making, for the most part these days, is done around Burbank."

Duke understood that "Hollywood" was now only a term for the industry, no longer a geographical designation.

The two drove on discussing the migration of the film industry from Hollywood to new locations with cheaper land.

Within minutes the car rolled through studio gates, swung behind a huge sound stage, and stopped. They got out and were met by several men whose names Duke was too rushed to get. A little amazed at the rush, he allowed himself to be stampeded through the back door to the wings of a large sound stage. A few more steps and he was standing in a poorly designed Hawaiian village set. Soundmen, lightmen, and cameramen were busily engaged, the director and assistants checking and double-checking everything.

Duke glanced at the cameras and examined the artificial props. Someone asked in a whisper: "How's this for your native Hawai'i?"

"Huts on stilts?" Duke grimaced, pointing out one glaring error. He walked on observing the set. "Some travelogue," he thought. Everyone appeared too occupied to talk to him. He noticed that strangely, the cameramen were suddenly focussing lenses directly on him.

From the opposite wing stepped a man with a familiar smiling face. His right hand was extended, his left held a leather-bound album. Striding up, he offered a cordial handclasp and said, "Welcome, Duke. This is your life!"

Duke instantly recognized his greeter as Ralph Edwards, mastermind and moderator of the internationally-known "This Is Your Life" television show. Edwards repeated the statement slowly and deliberately in a second effort to get through to a bewildered Duke.

Not until Duke's hand was firmly within the grip of Edwards' was he aware that the curtain had opened and some three hundred packed people were there in the audience. While he was trying to orient himself the applause thundered.

It suddenly penetrated that they were really going to present his life on the well-known, nationally-televised show. Duke struggled to grasp the thought that others had found his life worth all the effort and cost involved in the production. Finally, through the handclapping, whistling, and yelling, he managed, "This is the biggest surprise of my life." Indeed it was a complete and shocking surprise; a tribute to Edwards and his fellow workers. Duke hardly needed an introduction to the eager audience, but Edwards made one anyhow. Still bewildered, Duke smiled and bowed. The stage lights made his shock of white hair look like a miniature explosion.

After getting Duke seated mid-stage, Ralph Edwards broke open the big album with the well-known title: "THIS IS YOUR LIFE!" He gave a succinct resume of why they were featuring Duke plus some laughable anecdotes about the difficulty they'd had in getting Duke on stage without alerting him to the true reason.

Duke's memory went back to the telegram on Friday afternoon asking him to leave Saturday night for Los Angeles. He had to laugh at himself for being so easily duped. He recalled Nadine's anxiety for him to catch the plane. He remembered phoning his sister-in-law, Anna Kahanamoku—wife of Sargent—and telling her he was going to Hollywood for a "travelogue." He wondered; had she known the truth and just played innocent? He wondered about his other relatives and friends to whom he had spoken about the trip; they, too had probably known.

He was still trying to regain his composure when he caught Ralph Edwards in mid sentence: "...and we want to present the life of the great Duke, Hawai'i's

Sheriff and champion Olympic swimmer." Edwards explained that his associates had spoken to Winona Beamer, among others, for her opinion of a show with Duke featured. "She told us that we couldn't have chosen anyone closer to the hearts of the people of Hawai'i. We know she was right."

Edwards continued his thumbnail sketch of Duke's early life, mentioning the overthrow of the monarchy and the creation of the Republic of Hawaii, the annexation of the islands by the United States, and the rapid changes that had taken place.

Duke was astonished by how much information researchers had gathered on the early Kahanamoku family life. Edwards rolled back the mists of time. Pictures which Duke had long forgotten laid a heavy hand upon him. How thorough their research had been! To him it was a complete marvel.

It came out that three solid weeks had been consumed in setting up the show and arranging for people to assist. Secrecy had been the watchword, and everyone had carefully complied.

But Duke had yet only seen the tip of the iceberg. With the unfolding of his life story came surprise appearances of many long-unseen friends. One after another they were brought from backstage and presented to Duke and the audience. Cameras were busily shooting from different angles as the surprises continued.

Nadine came on stage, her eyes a little wet, but her smile very bright. Suddenly they were in each other's arms, Duke mumbling, "How'd you keep the secret?" Then it was his brothers coming on stage—all five—David, Sam, Bill, Sargent, and George. His sisters, Kapiolani and Bernice, entered next in all their Hawaiian beauty and grace. Duke held them close to his heart, and his voice sounded rusty.

Edwards got all of them seated with his fast patter contributing to the fun. He brought on George "Dad" Center, Duke's mentor, and then F. Lang Akana, Duke's Deputy Sheriff. By this time Duke was numb. The show was still far from over. While Duke was shaking hands and hugging, more names, places, dates, and events were being announced. Mr. and Mrs. Leslie Henry, two of Duke's oldest friends, walked on stage and wrapped their arms around him.

Athletes were there, too. Michael McDermott of Chicago, who swam with Duke in the 1912 Olympics, stepped out and paid his respects. Then it was Ludy Langer of Los Angeles, a fellow competitor from the 1920 Olympics. Finally, Johnny Weissmuller, Duke's conqueror in the 1924 Olympics, strode jauntily on stage and Duke gave him his bear-trap of a handshake while the two did a lot of back-slapping. Now it was a party!

Court jester that he'd always been, Weissmuller began ribbing Duke. "Paoa!" he cried. "You're older than an old, old blanket Indian with sore feet!" He gave Duke's thick white hair a fast rub.

Duke retaliated with more horseplay. It was obvious that these two, now way beyond their competitive years, had great mutual respect. Edwards finally broke it up, saying, "There's still more to come." He gently edged Weissmuller to a chair and turned to the audience.

Now Edwards gave a short description of the sensational rescue Duke performed in 1925 at Corona del Mar. Then he brought out three California men who Duke didn't recognize even after they were introduced. Puzzled, Duke stared. There was Fred Hock of Riverside, Edward Sneed of Colton, and Harry Ohlin of Riverside, three of the eight whose lives Duke had saved in the pounding waves off the Southern California coast.

Each shook hands with Duke, who was hard put to find something appropriate to say. "I'm glad we made it," he stammered. Fred Hock hung longest to Duke's hand, saying, "I've waited thirty-two years to thank you." "Don't mention it," Duke said—convulsing the house. He blinked self-consciously as Edwards led the last of the three to chairs. With the house rocking, Edwards started presenting gifts. In rapid order Duke and Nadine were given a luxurious radio phonograph, one thousand dollars worth of records, a speedboat, a movie camera, and a projector. Duke was awarded a gold-plated swimming trophy for the front of his car to replace one that had been stolen some years before. Edwards closed the presentations by giving Nadine a gold charm bracelet.

Laden with gifts, neither Duke nor Nadine had words adequate for their thanks. They offered smiles and handshakes plus a few words that hardly summed up their real gratitude. It was somehow a fitting climax to a life story that had unfolded with ever-mounting drama.

Edward closed the show saying, "We selected you, Duke Kahanamoku, because practically everybody in Hawai'i urged us to. Further, we recognized that your love of people represents the true spirit of your beloved islands."

The audience exploded with applause once more for the humble Hawaiian who had given so much to others. Speechless, Duke wiped his eyes, waved thanks, and turned to the embraces, squeezes, poundings, and words from his many loved ones who had come to be with him.

Duke as grand marshall of (possibly) Aloha Week Parade c. 1960.
Bishop Museum

25

Merit Recognized

By 1958 Duke had become a one-man Hawai'i "Chamber of Commerce" and "Visitors Bureau." He was still sheriff, still Hawai'i's unofficial ambassador-at-large—and still the white-haired gentleman with the incredible body on Waikīkī Beach, always noticed by tourists, malihini, and kama'aina. He was a Hawaiian institution.

Despite all his meetings, greetings, and showing VIPs around, plus the promotional trips away from Hawai'i, Duke never neglected his duties as City and County Sheriff. He and his first deputy, F. Lang Akana, continued to campaign for a new Honolulu jail, the present one at Iwilei being wholly inadequate. Though plans were afoot to abolish his department and transfer the jail to the police department—which Police Chief Dan Liu strongly opposed—Duke still strove to create a work farm for jail inmates.

In the spring of 1960 Duke's next Hawai'i-promoting junket was an eleven-nation tour lasting eighty days. As a member of the "Aloha Ambassadors," dignitaries from Hawai'i, he traveled the Far East distributing CARE packages and strengthening Hawai'i's ties throughout the Pacific basin.

The group—actually six, including wives—left via Pan-American jet. Made up of former State Senator and Mrs. Herbert K. H. Lee and State Senator and Mrs. Kazuhisa Abe, and Sheriff and Mrs. Duke Kahanamoku, it was a good representative delegation from Hawai'i, as Lee was of Chinese descent, Abe Japanese, and Duke Hawaiian.

Traveling at their own expense, they visited Japan, Hong Kong, Thailand, Burma, India, South Viet-Nam, Laos, Singapore, Malaya, Indonesia, and the Philippines. Lee, as frequent spokesman, had said, "It will be our duty to show that America's reality of today was nothing but a dream in the year 1776, just as theirs is today."

Returning to Hawai'i, Lee was unhesitant in claiming, "Our mission was a great success." The "Aloha Ambassadors" had met and spoken with many of the Asian leaders, including Prince Akihito of Japan, the President of South Viet-Nam, the Vice-President of India, Prime Minister of Singapore, and others.

One of the most amusing things that happened to Duke on that tour occurred in

Tokyo when the Crown Prince startled him with: "What type of crawl did you use to win the 100-meter freestyle at the 1912 Stockholm and 1920 Antwerp Olympics?" Duke had never suspected that the prince would be interested in swimming. He soon learned that Akihito was both a good swimmer and followed the sport closely. From there on the two had a great time.

Duke returned to Honolulu to find that he had been named chairman of the Oahu Tuberculosis and Health Association 1960 Christmas Seal campaign. He dove into this duty as he had everything else he had ever done.

Public discussion continued about the planned abolishment of the sheriff's office, and about what could be done for Duke. Hawaii's favorite son was shortly to again be out of a job. Sympathetic people had their suggestions printed on the editorial pages in both newspapers.

The *Star-Bulletin* gave space to City and County of Honolulu Auditor James K. Murakimi, who wrote, "The concern is that we, the people of Hawaii, must do something for Hawaii's native son, Duke Paoa Kahanamoku, whose office as Sheriff will be abolished by the City Charter on January 2nd, 1961. He is the concern of every thoughtful resident of Hawaii.

"The Proposal is to write your Legislator to appoint Duke a roving Aloha Ambassador Extraordinary!

"His name is a symbol of noteworthy athletic achievement, fine sportsmanship, and an inspiration to swimmers over the entire world. He has given his life to Hawaii and has spread goodwill everywhere."

With the mayoralty and other elections coming up, plans for Duke became a political issue. Each candidate wasn't merely trying to curry public favor, they all had suggestions as to what could be done for the soon-to-be ex-sheriff. Duke was promised high level posts, but he knew that much was strictly conversation and political game playing. Candidates Frank F. Fasi (D), Robert G. Dodge (D), and Mayor Neal S. Blaisdell (R) all insisted that they were the originator of the "Kahanamoku for Greeter" idea.

In October 1960 Duke was presented the annual David Malo Award by the West Honolulu Rotary Club for his outstanding public service. The award was one more step toward his being given a dignified and well-paid position with city and county or state government. He was seventy, but still vigorous in his promotion of Hawai'i.

Another award this year gave added emphasis to Duke's importance as a salesman for things Hawaiian. He was in the Kaiser hospital for treatment of ulcers when he learned that he had been elected an honorary member of Pi Sigma Epsilon, the marketing and sales honorary fraternity at the University of Hawaii, "in recognition of Duke Kahanamoku's outstanding work in selling Hawaii and the aloha spirit to the rest of the nation."

To Duke's delight, while still at the hospital he was presented with a gold key and a certificate by the fraternity president. He said he'd overcome any obstacle to get out of the hospital and do more selling.

Advertiser columnist Eddie Sherman, in one of his "Backstage" columns, helped marshal the minds of Hawaiian legislators and contributed to their decision on Duke. He wrote:

AMBASSADOR OF PARADISE

An open letter to the Legislature:

Gentlemen:

If you were asked to name the most popular Hawaiian alive today, I'm sure the name Duke Kahanamoku would come to mind.

If you were asked to name the man who most symbolizes the Hawaiian spirit, your answer would have to be Duke Kahanamoku.

If you were asked to name the man responsible for calling more attention to Hawaii over the years than any other person, that man would have to be the Duke.

Well, gentlemen, this famous son of Hawaii will be out of a job in December. His career as Sheriff of Honolulu will be pau. Next August, Duke will be 70 years old.

Should he be left to retire to his memories?

And what memories!

The Bronze Duke of Waikīkī, Olympic swimming champion in 1912 and 1920 and a top contender in the '24 and '28 Olympic Games. He and he alone put Hawaii on the athletic map and his name became a symbol of Hawaii for all time.

Let's turn back the clock to the mid-20's when Duke was acting in pictures. He was camped at Newport Beach, Calif., with a number of other actors. Going for his morning swim, he noticed a pleasure yacht, the

Thelma, had capsized under the battering of heavy ground swells. Grabbing a surfboard, Duke tore a quarter of a mile out through the treacherous waters. Not once, but three times. That day, 17 lives were lost but 12 were saved. Duke saved eight. His heroic efforts captured the heart of America and Hawaii gave him a gold medal. But he shrugged off the incredible feat.

Just a reminder, gentlemen, that the same heroic heart beats in the same Duke Kahanamoku today.

Duke loves people, and people love him. In December he'll be out of a job. How can he serve the Islands he loves? How about appointing him Hawaii's roving ambassador of goodwill? You, gentlemen, can make this possible. Bestow this title upon him. Let him come and go as he wishes, meet the VIPs who visit Hawaii, and visit VIPs, chamber of commerce groups, and other organizations all over the country.

Personally, I've heard more than one tourist remark after seeing Duke on the beach: "To me, he is Hawaii, and to see him in person makes my trip complete."

Wherever he travels today, he is still the center of attention. When a delegation of businessmen, politicians and newsmen attended the opening of the Sheraton-Dallas Hotel not long ago, most of the thousands of the who's who of Dallas who went to the $100 a plate dinner fussed about Duke as if he was king of Hawaii. Film stars and other notables were almost ignored when he appeared on the scene. This same impact by Duke can be made all over the country, and be a tremendous boon to the tourist industry.

Lawmakers of Hawaii: Duke Kahanamoku has given his life to Hawaii. Now is the time for Hawaii to give a little to the life of Duke Kahanamoku. Aloha

Thanks to the influence of Sherman and others, action was taken. On November 10, 1960 the *Star-Bulletin* reported that Duke would be appointed to a new $12,000 a year job as the Mayor's official representative—a post provided for in the city charter. He would act as official city greeter.

As must be expected, there were those who took exception. Some wrote and phoned the newspapers, City Hall, and the sheriff's office to register their complaints. There was quite an uproar.

Some people insisted that the controversy was simply political. Others called the decision looting of the public purse. Charges were made that Duke was already wealthy and needed no assistance. While this character assassination went on Duke offered no rebuttals, no defense. He was hurt, not angered.

Unfortunately for Duke an item in the *Advertiser* added fuel to the flame on November 11, 1960:

Duke and Arthur Godfrey have gotten together in a fascinating business deal. It'll take advantage of Duke's reputation and Godfrey's loot, and won't interfere with Duke's new job as Honolulu's official greeter. Here are the projects already slated by the two, with Mrs. Kahanamoku, Kimo Wilder McVay and Robert A. Hoffman also involved.

1. An annual Duke Kahanamoku international amateur swim meet to be held during Aloha Week.

2. Founding of a "Duke Kahanamoku Boys Club," to encourage and aid local boys interested in sports, entertainment and business relating to the tourist industry.

3. Establishment of a Waikīkī restaurant and supper club, to be known as Duke Kahanamoku's, featuring Hawaiian royalty decor and Hawaiian entertainment.

4. Manufacture and endorsement of Hawaiian products.

On paper the financial potential appeared astronomical. Certain people decried his going into business while a city position was under consideration. Duke was crushed. Having given his all for Hawai'i he wasn't going to debase himself to prove his worth.

On January 1961 the sheriff's office was abolished and Duke was out of a job. Pride kept him from asking for one from friends.

Paradoxically, in the midst of the attacks, Duke was again being honored. More recognition came when Duke, along with Honolulu industrialist Walter F. Dillingham, was honored at the Oahu Country Club by the Sales Executives of Hawaii.

Named "Hawaii's Outstanding Salesman of the Year for 1960," Duke took pride in knowing that, besides Dillingham and himself, only three others had been so honored (Police Chief Dan Liu, 1957; Governor William F. Quinn, 1958; and Henry J. Kaiser, 1959.)

Duke's citation read in part: The person...has been world famous since his youth... From that first day of international fame many years ago to this day, he has conducted himself in a manner so warm, so honest and so completely Hawaiian that he has won fame for all of us. What could be a more perfect way to sell?"

Further recognition came in April, when the *Star-Bulletin* ran a portion of a letter written by Dr. W. E. Edwards to Senator Oren E. Long:

"Your speech on Kamehameha I was very interesting. You spoke of discharging the debt of the State of Hawaii to the indigenous people of the land." Couldn't the same be accomplished by placing a statue of Duke Kahanamoku in Statuary Hall?

After all, many people consider Kamehameha I was somewhat of a marauder and a tyrant, and to honor him with another statue would be recognition that "might makes right." Duke Kahanamoku has done a tremendous amount of good work for Hawaii and the Hawaiians. His statue would serve just as well, I believe, as "an incentive to visitors to learn something of the man, his people, and his Islands." My second nomination is for a statue of Don Blanding. Next to Duke Kahanamoku, I believe he has done more than anyone else to bring visitors to Hawaii and to put Hawaii on the map. His books and poems are being read all over the world, and they will continue to be read for many years to come.

Duke continued to be harried by lack of funds. Trying to match those he socialized with was no easy task. He was still making an effort to find peace within himself between his ambitions and his limitations—it wasn't easy.

Duke became official greeter for Honolulu on February 1, 1961. Asked to head an eleven-man delegation to Scandinavia in April, he tried to overlook the irony of the recent repeated attacks. The plan was to spread Hawaiian song, dance, and aloha on Pan American World Airway's inaugural flight from New York to Oslo, Norway. In one day, fortified with 10,000 bright travel folders and 1,000 fresh lei, they would fly to Oslo, Norway; Stockholm, Sweden; and Helsinki, Finland before doubling back to Stockholm.

Sargent and Anna Kahanamoku were along, but again it was Duke who proved to be irresistible. Others on the tour were not neglected, but Duke was treated like royalty by the mayors, ambassadors, State Department officials, press, film crews and general public.

In that day, the seven hour and fifteen minute trip from New York to Oslo was considered phenomenal. The arrival was heralded by a mammoth sign: "Pan Am—Welcome to Oslo, the New Gateway to Scandinavia."

A school band, smartly uniformed in maroon played "When the Saints Come Marching In" for their arrival. Duke shivered at sight of the bare legs of the majorettes in unison in the 40-degree temperature. Norwegian military in gray uniforms with red-crowned hats lined the runway as United States Ambassador to Norway Clifton R. Wharton came to meet them. Everyone adjourned to the terminal for smorgasbord, coffee, and speeches from the Mayor of Oslo and Ambassador Wharton.

Stockholm also rolled out the red carpet. Their DC-8 was met by dancing girls in peasant dresses and young men in knee britches jigging and fiddling folk tunes. Stockholm had not forgotten that Duke had won the gold medal in the 1912 Olympics during his last visit, forty-nine years earlier.

Cameramen, reporters, and officials crowded toward Duke. One lanky blond shouldered his way through and clasped Duke's hand,

"Welcome again to our country!"

Duke looked hard to recognize Arne Borg, the Swede he had swum against in 1924. He remembered how Borg had congratulated those ahead of him. Now the two rekindled long-ago memories.

Tulips already bestowed upon him, the Mayor of Stockholm also presented Duke with the key to the city. Then Duke spotted a long banner held by girls in the crowd and it made him feel warm despite the weather, "Aloha to People from Hawaii!"

Flying next to Helsinki, the group received another great reception. The Lord Mayor spoke in both Finnish and English and United States Ambassador Bernard Gufler also welcomed the arrivals. A Finnish police band boosted everyone's pulse with its rousing music.

Spectators were supposed to be there to see the new Pan Am jet, but they seemed to value Duke more than the plane. Duke was surprised they even remembered him.

The evening finished with the tour group putting on a show for the Finnish press and other guests. In addition to Duke, Sargent, and Anna Kahanamoku, there was Stephanie Loo, the Narcissus Queen; Pan American Airway's Miss Ruth Wakai, Ernest W. Albrecht, Clem Kapono, and Harold Kakuole; and Aloha

Airlines' Sam Kanae, Diana Jardine, and Alicia Davis. "Buck" Buchwach of *The Honolulu Advertiser* filled out the Hawai'i contingent.

The Finns loved the hula (Tahitian version) and yelled for more. Polynesian string music and song brought them whispers of warm southern seas. People asked Duke about his islands, about his life, hopes, and dreams.

"How old are you Duke?" one ventured.

"Old?" he smiled. "I've got wrinkles I haven't even used."

The group later returned to both Stockholm and Oslo to entertain and promote the delights and advantages of vacationing in the islands.

In Stockholm the Hawaiians produced an extravaganza at the Swim Club. Top swimmers and divers of Sweden, including record-breaking freestyler Per'Ola Lindberg, came to honor Duke. Members of the 1912 Swedish Olympic team, present when Duke won the Olympic sprints, (including Arne Borg again) also joined the celebrations to salute Duke.

Duke presented Stockholm's borg mastre, the City Council President, a koa-wood platter from Mayor Blaisdell and Governor Quinn. Duke wound up his presentation speech by saying, "Jets such as this Pan Am Scandinavian Clipper will help make the people of Sweden better neighbors."

City Council President Carl Albert Anderson accepted the bowl with enthusiasm saying, "Thank you, Your Royal Highness, Duke Kahanamoku." Duke replied in a low voice, "Thank you, sir, but I'm no royal prince. Kahanamoku is my surname, and Duke is my given name."

This time it was President Anderson who was a little rattled. Plainly a little unclear with his English, he said, "I am sorry you are here for such short time, but that is nothing for me to do about."

While Duke couldn't follow the Swede's conversation, he felt sure that the intent was friendly and let it go at that.

Island Newsman "Buck" Buchwach could hardly wait to get his column off to Honolulu. He had always taken great delight in peoples' misconceptions about Duke's name. This kind of garbled tribute was enjoyed by Buchwach and Duke's other friends. They weren't about to try and distinguish the differences between Polynesian and European royal lineages.

Photographs taken, Anderson offered the Hawaiians pastries, candies, and smokes. Duke's brother, Sargent, was impressed by Anderson's size. As Buchwach reported: "Anderson was of Falstaffian proportions, who looked exactly like a borg mastre should look, with white hair, ruddy complexion and a substantial bay window. Matter of fact, Anderson looked exactly like a haole sumo wrestler wrapped in a worsted suit."

In any event, Sargent finally reached over and lightly jabbed President Anderson's rotund stomach with one finger and said to the startled man, "In Hawai'i we call that your opu." Anderson gulped, fought for a smile, and then said, "Whatever it is called, it is a sign of confidence." Duke and his brother looked at each other in bewilderment; this Swedish dignitary sure talked strange.

Duke with friend Arthur Godfrey.   *Joseph Brennan*

26

The Troubles Come After Scandinavia

DUKE CAME BACK TO HONOLULU—AND TO CONSIDERABLE FUSS ABOUT HIS INCOME. DUKE JUST STOOD BY, WATCHING THE GROWING TEMPEST, TERRIBLY HURT. Now white-haired, patrician, he was less apt than ever to fight back.

Asked about the stories, Duke replied, "I don't think I lean to money...but I'd like just enough."

Gentleman's Quarterly (a fashion magazine for men) had reported that Duke was getting $30,000-$35,000 a year in royalties for lending his name to a line of shirts manufactured on the mainland. While the report was far from true, the *Star-Bulletin* quoted the magazine on October 27, 1960. People were still warring over Duke's being retained by the City. Papers were printing letters from both disgruntled and pleased readers. Things came to a head when Duke's old friend, Arthur Godfrey, visited the islands and came to his defense.

The showman had always admired the islander. "If Duke doesn't love you," he once said, "You've missed a chunk of life." Godfrey was quoted in Duke's defense in the August 6, 1961 *Star-Bulletin* headlined:

DUKE WOEFULLY UNDERPAID: GODFREY.

It went on:

Entertainer Arthur Godfrey is "really burned up" at Hawaii for "the shabby treatment that Duke Kahanamoku is getting."

Godfrey, here to pick out TV film sites, said in an interview: "Hawaii should give Duke $25,000 a year and a car and require him to do nothing but appear at only the proper places." When informed the Duke is on the City-County payroll ($8,256 a year) as the City's official greeter, Godfrey said, "Well, what he's getting is not enough. It's a shame that he has to be the front man for a restaurant just so he can get enough money to eat."

Godfrey was referring to a restaurant which opens next month and will be called Duke Kahanamoku's.

"This is a disgrace," Godfrey said. "For all the dignity and honor that

Duke has brought to Hawaii, giving him $25,000 would be just a gesture.
And that wouldn't be charity, either. Hawaii should think of the payment
as an upkeep for something precious, the same as upkeeping Kapiolani
Park or Waikīkī Beach. You know, what really burns me up is that after he
(Duke) dies, Hawaii will probably go all out in erecting a $100,000
monument. Why not honor a living monument?

"Just think of it, for all the honor that Duke has brought here, he's got
only a trunkful of medals. What good does that do him when he's hungry?
He can sell them, and all that'll bring in will probably be enough to buy a
bottle of beer."

Interviewers finally got a response out of Duke. The *Star-Bulletin* quoted him
in part:

The City official greeter said it is true that "I am barely getting along. I
agree that something should be done, but it is not my part to say anything.
It takes a malihini like Arthur Godfrey to come here, look things over and
speak the truth," he said.

Pulling out a paycheck, he noted, "I'm not getting the salary a lot of
people think I'm getting. They think I'm getting $1,000 a month."

His semimonthly paycheck, he pointed out, gives him $327.50 out of
which he takes home $262.41 after taxes.

He said the $12,000 a year which he thought he'd get as the Mayor's
official representative "didn't come through."

As for reports that he has been receiving $30,000 to $35,000 a year in
royalties for lending his name to a line of aloha shirts manufactured on the
Mainland, he said: "If that were true, I wouldn't be here. I'd be traveling."

He received $1,000 to $1,200 a month when the venture began in 1949,
he said. But one of the two factories producing the shirts had closed.
"Sometimes I don't get anything. Last month I only got $11."

At least his association with a restaurant in the International Market
Place will help, he added. "I'll be able to eat three meals a day," he said.

The former Olympic champ agreed with Godfrey by saying, "I'd rather
have the money now and enjoy life, instead of a monument being erected
when it's too late." He noted that he has given the State millions of dollars
worth of free advertising.

"What have I got to show for it? Nothing. And I'm not going to ask for anything."

Duke was always himself; self-conscious when being interviewed, he made statements only under questioning. He didn't want it to appear that he was whimpering about his deal with the city.

Later that same week the *Advertiser* reported that Godfrey had again stated that Hawai'i shouldn't wait until Duke died to erect a stone monument showing that the state really was aware of Duke's contributions. Godfrey said he felt he'd been "misled some," then ended:

> The TV star said when he came here last week, "I didn't know the Duke was as bad off as he is. He was so depressed I tried to cheer him up, but he was badly hurt.
>
> "He hasn't got much money. It's a shame because you know of his love for Hawaii, it makes you cry. "
>
> As for Duke's beach home in Kahala, it was bought during the depression when prices were low. Thank God he bought it then, because he has nothing."

Duke still had no income from any of the proposed business deals because they were only in the formative stages. As if his public embarrassment was not already enough, the *Star-Bulletin* quoted Mayor Blaisdell as saying, "There is a possibility that Kahanamoku may be involved in a conflict of interest if he becomes associated with a Waikīkī restaurant."

The mayor was only alluding to the legal realities and pointing out a possible pitfall. But it helped fuel those who campaigned against Duke.

Duke read and heard the stories and lived with his anger. He felt so unappreciated by his local public that he said that if he had to make a choice, he would take the restaurant. He explained that he had received as a gift one-third interest in one of the two corporations that bought the restaurant from Don the Beachcomber. He said he had been promised $10,000 a year for the use of his name plus an equitable share in the profits. One of the restaurant partners had said, "Under this arrangement, Duke could conceivably make $20,000 or more a year."

This, together with data on the two corporations, were printed in the August 8 *Star-Bulletin*. Duke never felt more controversial in his life. All he had ever wanted was a decent living.

By this time the newspapers were deluged with letters of complaint. They twisted Duke's words and took them out of context. Offerings from August 16, 1961 included:

SHOCKED BY DUKE

Duke's recent remarks that he is needing three meals a day really shocked me. Imagine, over $600 a month and looking for three meals a day. He has hurt every true Hawaiian and all the newcomers.

I just hope that his remarks don't hit the Mainland. This would prove that we pay for publicity for Hawaii. I do also hope that the poor Duke isn't starving. Just how many mouths is he feeding? I loved that guy for years until he shot off his mouth and now all the boys in our office think he is commercial. I think he should find a job like us if he is in need of three meals a day.

DISILLUSIONED.

ATTENTION, ARTHUR GODFREY

I'm so mad I can't even find pen and ink. All I heard at ladies' luncheon today was Duke. He's so ungrateful.

Wish my husband could lie around on the beach for a year and the City would give him a job at half Duke's salary. And we could go to cocktail parties and get paid for it. My husband's good-looking—and a line-dropper and Hawaiian. Maybe Arthur Godfrey will give him a job.

KAMAAINA.

SAYS DUKE IS UNGRATEFUL

I am most upset over the remarks Duke Kahanamoku made. That man should be made to earn a living. My husband is a laborer and resents his bold remarks. I do, too. How can someone be so ungrateful? We are Hawaiian-born and he has really made us disgusted.

HAWAIIAN-BORN.

SAYS GODFREY DID DUKE NO GOOD

Duke Kahanamoku is one of Hawaii's greats. He has brought much fame to these Islands and, in return, has received considerable acclaim and many benefits. The Duke, it seems to me, is an innocent victim of Arthur Godfrey's attempt to do some good. Unfortunately, Godfrey went about it in a way that rubbed a good many people the wrong way. All the Duke could do was agree with the things Godfrey was saying.

Let's not knock the Duke. To many in the world he symbolizes Hawaii. His wife, too, is a lovely person. Of them it can be said that they spread only goodwill wherever they go. Who could ask more of anyone? How many among us do as well?

FAIR-MINDED

On August 21 another reader took to the editorial page:

NEIGHBORHOOD DISCUSSED DUKE

The $655 a month that Duke Kahanamoku gets and thinks isn't enough should be compared with a veteran in our neighborhood. He gave one arm and one leg for Hawaii and only gets $197 a month.

And do you know he isn't complaining? He is working. I say that if the Duke doesn't like what the State (or City) gives him, let him try working.

As for him spending his life selling Hawaii without pay, we all have. I am glad he will be able to eat three meals a day now that he is associated with a restaurant. But many families with children eat well and live on less. Why can't he? This bold statement he made is the talk of our neighborhood.

INDIGNANT.

The sporadic war ran on with the August 24 *Advertiser* offering a rebuttal from an old Kama'ina:

As to Duke's personal finances, this is his own personal business. However, the Duke is anything but a rich man. Outside of his salary and a retirement pay, he has little or no savings, having spent them unselfishly throughout the years to sell his Hawaii to the outer world...Remember that the typical tourist expects to see some Hawaiians in Hawaii. To most of them, the only Hawaiians they ever heard of outside of King Kamehameha is our Duke. Don't let any of us forget at this point in Duke's long life that he is still working for Hawaii.

Publicity that charged Duke with ingratitude was what most sickened him. He refused to fight back. Asked about his lack of defense, he said: "It's like telling people you're honest." A letter written by one of his oldest friends did more to help than anything else. Alfred A. Apaka, father of the late singer, had a letter published in the August 24 *Advertiser*:

It seems to me that some of the people in our fair State of Hawaii are forgetting just what Duke Kahanamoku stands for in this chaotic world of ours. I think it's very short-sighted of some that seemed to have turned their backs on our Duke, just because he agreed with Arthur Godfrey that he was being underpaid. Having known the Duke for many years, I know without asking him that his remark was nothing more than a humorous one.

I have never known anyone as grateful for what he has than Duke, and it's beyond me how anyone can say the Duke is ungrateful. He has been an inspiration to youngsters all over the world for at least fifty years, and today he stands for the highest ideals of good sportsmanship and good fellowship. I am very proud that we have a man of Duke's caliber representing us in the eyes of the world. As for the Mayor's personal representative, no wiser choice was ever made than this appointment as Hawaii's official greeter. Let us not in any way forget what the Duke has done for us when Hawaii was only a few islands stuck in the middle of the Pacific, young and unknown, and just because of a natural remark in jest.

Alfred A. Apaka.

Duke finally closed his ears to the storm of censure and went on with his life. He helped start the Duke Kahanamoku Foundation, a non-profit organization whose major purpose was to grant career scholarships to deserving youths of

Duke on an outrigger canoe at Waikīkī in 1960.   *Joseph Brennan photo*

Hawai'i. Bishop Trust Company handled the finances and Monsignor Charles A. Kekumano was chairman of the organizing committee.

Duke loved the philanthropic work, particularly with kids. He had always given unstintingly of his time, which made it even harder for him to understand the criticism he'd received. Being hypersensitive and intelligent made things both harder and easier. Harder, because it affected him so deeply, and easier, because he knew himself well and could recognize the injustice of his critics.

Duke's need of an improved income continued even at this late date. Still far from financially secure; he could not shake his fears.

He went with the restaurant venture hoping to supplement his income and help commercialize genuine Polynesian food, atmosphere, and entertainment. The restaurant was expected to also bring top mainland entertainers to please customers wanting something other than an all-Hawaiian show.

Duke's partners were Kimo Wilder McVay; McVay's mother, Mrs. Kinau Wilder; socially prominent kama'aina artist, actress, and hostess Betty Chamberlin; Thomas E. Abrums; James A.H. Wilder; and Robert A. Hoffman.

Duke didn't have to buy in; his investment was his name. Under the care of Kimo McVay, the place opened to a packed house September 1, 1961. In true Hawaiian tradition, the Reverend Abraham Akaka prayed for the success of the venture, asking that it be blessed all its days. Guests watched Duke accept the keys from Don Beach, the owner of the restaurant formerly in the building. Master of ceremonies was Kimo McVay, who read a good luck letter from Governor Quinn.

An impressive entertainment schedule was announced, including: Ed Kenney (Hawai'i's brightest Broadway star), The Surfers (recording, island, and Las Vegas favorites), Rosalie Stephenson ("The Voice and Charm of Old Hawai'i"), Mamo Howell's Complete Polynesian Revue; Chuck Floyd's Orchestra, and the Martin Denney Group would be an extra added attraction.

The supper club filled a need, was well received in the press, and had all the hallmarks of a successful enterprise. Everyone wished Duke and his partners aloha and the best of luck.

Now that Duke was an alleged restaurant tycoon, rumors were that his special job as "Greeter," written into the City's newly-adopted charter, would end when the next administration took office. Close friends were searching for another place for Duke in the city, county, or state structure. Senator Hiram L. Fong noted that Duke would be a natural as a Republican congressional candidate in 1962.

Honored when word reached him, Duke still said "Being a restaurateur and official greeter suit me fine. I advertise Hawai'i in both. I'm not going to run for office." Newsmen pressed for more detail, knowing that most Hawaiians and hords of kama'āina would gladly help him get to Washington.

Duke thanked them for their interest and said, "I'm happy where I am. I think it's better to stay." He simply believed he could do more by remaining at home.

He demonstrated this belief by volunteering as a Christmas Seal ambassador. Flying with the Civil Air Patrol to Kaua'i, Maui, and Hawai'i, they took Christmas trees decorated with greeting cards for children in tuberculosis sanitariums. Duke didn't miss Washington, nor, since he was right there, did the ailing children miss him. He didn't say anything thundering to them, but he smiled and helped brighten many young lives.

A month later Duke was honored at the dedication of the city's new Halawa Valley jail. As former sheriff, he had fought for twenty-six years to obtain a satisfactory place for prisoners. Now it was a thirty-one acre, $1.9 million reality.

Hosting a supper club named after him was a big switch for Duke. At seventy-one he was beginning a new career; most people his age were already retired. More than one friend ribbed him.

"It should be natural," he countered. "All my life I've been going places to meet and greet people. Now, they'll be coming to me."

It worked out just that way. Friends, fans, and autograph seekers came to the restaurant—and Duke loved it. Customers expected to see Duke, so he was there as much as possible. Friends predicted he couldn't keep it up for long. They felt that lending his name to the place should suffice. They hadn't reckoned with Duke's sense of obligation, he would be there if it killed him—and it almost did.

Often staying until 3:00 a.m. closing, Duke became a fixture. He renewed many old friendships and made thousands of new ones. Hawai'i being a crossroads, the restaurant was thriving. It offered the spice which Duke had been missing, and led to many amusing incidents. Local newsmen were constantly there picking up column items.

One in particular came shortly after the opening. It was a crowded, hot night, and Duke wasn't in sight. An old-fashioned fan made of plaited pandanus leaves was doing a fair job of keeping the orchestra and entertainers cool. The Surfers were in the midst of blasting out "The Beer Barrel Polka" when a power failure halted the fan. The Surfers began to melt in the still air.

"C'mon, Duke!" called Al Kalani, the quartet's comic. "Keep pedalling!"

To everybody's amazement, the fan started immediately! The diners laughed and applauded until the building wobbled. Entirely unrehearsed, the minor incident was so funny the Surfers later incorporated it into their show.

Asked about it later, Duke winked and said, "That's why I come every night. I keep that fan working."

27

Brain Surgery!

WITH SEVERAL THINGS GOING, IT NOW BEGAN TO LOOK AS THOUGH DUKE MIGHT FINALLY HAVE FOUND THE FINANCIAL SECURITY FOR WHICH HE'D SEARCHED.

"Things are looking up!" he said, grinning confidently to Nadine. She shared his enthusiasm.

Fate had other plans. Duke suffered an acute attack of stomach ulcers. The seventy-one year old Duke was rushed to the Kaiser Foundation Hospital for nine days intensive treatment. He was released on April 4 with doctor's instructions to go home, rest, and recuperate.

That just wasn't Duke. "Mister Hawaii" was up and around in short order, contrary to all good advice.

Duke immediately returned to sailing, swimming, and all he loved in the water. To him it was therapy. Soon he was racing aboard a catamaran off Waikīkī. Tradewinds were whipping when a fast change of course had the crew ducking as the boom swung wildly. It struck Duke's skull with the sound of a kicked cigar box.

"You hurt, Duke?" came the cry.

Momentarily numbed, Duke gingerly tested his head, then answered, "Nah, just a little slap."

Duke made light of his injury. "Can't hurt an old Hawaiian, you know. Poi makes a man of you."

They kidded a little more. "What was the matter?" one asked. "Couldn't find anywhere low enough?"

Still a bit dizzy, Duke just offered a twisted smile. They all nonchalantly sailed on. The knock on the head was forgotten in the day's events.

Surprisingly dizzy spells continued to bother Duke for the next several days. They worsened to where he finally went to Kaiser Hospital for an examination.

His doctor, long-time personal friend Maurice D. Silver, told Duke, "You've got to slow down, Duke. You're getting to be an old guy."

Duke wrinkled the skin under his brown eyes. "I'm not old, not that old. I refuse."

It had long been their standing joke.

Dr. Silver shook his head at his patient. They began the physical checkup both hoping to find only some minor difficulty at worst. That wasn't the case this time. Duke was told he'd be held for further observation. Duke silently held in his fears.

On May 22, 1962 Hawai'i was startled to read:

"DUKE IS CRITICAL AFTER BRAIN SURGERY!"

Not until then was Duke's May 5 hospital stay for observation of dizzy spells and nausea announced. With three doctors on the case, Duke was given the best treatment Hawai'i could offer. After examination, Chief Neuro surgeon Silver diagnosed Duke as suffering from a subdural hematoma—a blood clot on the brain—the result of a head injury. Surgery was mandatory.

Reporters learned that Duke's heart condition had also been aggravated. Nadine said, "He is resting and conscious but can talk only with effort."

A hospital spokesman reported that Duke had undergone two-and-a-half hours of brain surgery, concluding, "His condition is satisfactory from the point of view of a post-craniotomy, but with his age and other conditions, his general condition is guarded."

Daily reports in both night and morning newspapers, kept the public closely informed on Duke's condition. Next morning, May 23 the *Advertiser* reported Duke still in "critical condition," but that, according to hospital officials, "he has the use of all his senses." Another report used the clinical language, "Kahanamoku's sensorium is clear. There is some weakness in his left side in evidence. His condition is still critical. The clearing of his sensorium means that all his senses are operating and that he is aware of his surroundings."

This reporting went on for days. As late as the 31st of the month, The *Star-Bulletin* reported on May 31:

Duke Kahanamoku is still on Kaiser Hospital's critical list, but seems to have made the turn on the road to recovery, according to a hospital spokesman. He is sitting up every day at intervals and his nutritional state shows improvement. He is not yet out of danger, but for the first time some guarded optimism seems reasonable. Mrs. Kahanamoku said today that her husband had a very bad night last night, but is feeling better today." She added, "Hundreds of get-well cards and radiograms from all over the world were sent to Duke last week."

Ten days later things went the other way. The *Advertiser* headlined:

"DUKE HAS SETBACK!"

The story followed with how a setback had occurred from a recurrence of gastric ulcer symptoms. The public reacted with deep concern. People spoke in low voices about his condition. Those were dark days for Duke.

Then he took a slow turn for the better. He was on the mend. People spoke louder when discussing the Bronze Duke of Waikīkī. Hope rebounded. On June 16, the *Star-Bulletin* ran a headline that thousands had been looking for::

"KAHANAMOKU WILL LEAVE HOSPITAL WITHIN TEN DAYS"

Tom Knaefler reported:

Duke Kahanamoku grinned his familiar wide grin as his doctor pronounced him "ready to go home in a week or ten days."

This announcement was made yesterday at Duke's first bedside press conference held in the Kaiser Foundation Hospital since his life-or-death brain surgery May 21.

The 71-year-old former Olympic swimming champ appeared a bit drawn, but well.

"I feel good," he said. He expressed his thanks to the hospital staff and many, many friends and relatives who saw him through his critical road to recovery.

"It was a long time, I know that," he said as he recalled the ordeal just behind him.

Asked what he missed most while hospitalized, Duke grinned and wiggled his toes—in that order—and said "My bed. This bed is too short. About four or five inches too short. When I lie down, my knee bends. No space for them."

Duke, who stands 6 feet 2 inches, said his bed at home was specially made of koa.

"It's big enough," he said. "Lots of room for me to relax."

Duke wore a blue robe over red bermuda shorts for his press
conference, which was also attended by his wife, Nadine, four brothers
and a sister.

On his feet, he wore white socks, chopped off at the toes.

"The socks keep his feet warm," his wife explained. "But he likes to
wiggle his toes."

In addition to the hospital's medical care, Duke attributes his recovery
to "all that exercise," he got helping to rebuild Tommy Kearns' boat
during the past year.

"That's what gave me the strength—all that exercise," he said.

Dr. Maurice Silver, consultant in neurosurgery at the hospital, said
Duke would be able to resume all previous activity in a little while.

"We'll know more in about a month," he said. "Gradually, he'll be able
to ease into his usual activities, including swimming and sailing."

The doctor said it has not yet been determined what caused the blood
clot in Duke's brain.

He said it likely was brought on by either a blow or fall that occurred
about six weeks before Duke began suffering from dizzy spells and
nausea.

As for the recurrence of gastric ulcer symptoms earlier this week, the
doctor said, "It's still a problem. But he is doing quite well. Duke's diet is
normal, except for some restrictions imposed by his ulcers. The
restrictions include rough or highly seasoned food.

The *Advertiser* reported:

Duke, 71, sat on the lanai of his top floor room, wearing a light blue
robe as he talked softly about his stay in the hospital.

"The whole bunch has been very nice," he said of the hospital staff. "It's
a wonderful hospital." Gesturing toward the yacht harbor spreading out
before his lanai, he added, "You can't get this kind of view any place else.
It's so nice—you wake up in the morning and nobody disturbs you, you
just lie down and take it easy."

But despite the view and the hospital personnel, Duke is tired of being
an invalid. "It was a long time for me to be in bed because I've been so
active," he said. "It's hard to lie still."

Duke has been a model patient, according to his team of doctors, and is now able to sit up two or three hours a day. He spends the time talking with his wife, Nadine, or with his five brothers and two sisters, all of whom have been spending a great deal of time at the hospital.

The doctors say that he will be ready to leave the hospital in a week or 10 days, and then will have to convalesce at home for a month or so.

This has been a bad spring for Duke. He was released from the Hospital April 5 after being treated 10 days for stomach ulcers, and then was readmitted last month for surgery which removed a blood clot on this brain. He was on the critical list for weeks after the surgery, but now appears to be on the road to recovery.

One thing the papers didn't report was the way Duke spoke about his narrow escape. In a halting voice he had told his close family of how he had faced that moment when a man looks into the dark, empty void, and has to fight hard if he wants to go on living.

Nadine didn't have to be told. She had been there, had seen his bone-deep weariness, that flat, vacant look of defeat. He had been like a candle flickering for lack of air.

Between herself, the prayers of the Kahanamoku brothers and sisters, and Dr. Silver, they had kept Duke's heart marching. Morning after morning the Kahanamoku family had waited to hear Dr. Silver's report. Finally he had told them, "The tide has turned. Your brother will be all right."

They all wanted to rush to Duke's room and see him. But he hadn't been quite that well for a while longer.

It had been very close. Troubles had come to Duke that spring, come in giant sizes. However, he had survived.

Duke was released on July 2, 1962. "Complete and uninterrupted rest" was the doctor's order. Duke and Nadine went to Kaua'i, where they stayed with the Milo Marchettis at Po'ipū Beach.

Duke really came back to life on the Garden Isle. His only admission of defeat was saying, "When a man's health goes on the rocks, the rocks are birthdays. Those rocks are here, right here," thumping his massive chest with an equally massive fist.

The ex-restaurateur Milo Marchetti and his wife, close friends, pitched in with Nadine to bring Duke around. Duke's inflamed eyes were still holes against his tight, coppery skin. Even in the soft Hawaiian light he still had a wraith-like look. He had a long road to full recovery.

The first several days found Duke walking with a cane, stooped, and beaten-looking. Marchetti kidded him about the cane. "You walk like a man trying to crank an Essex."

Duke blinked. "I know. But that Essex crack sure dates you, Milo!"

Marchetti agreed, and then said, "Duke, I believe it would take an elephant gun to stop you."

"I don't know, right now I feel older than the stones."

Duke constantly watched the blue water along the Kaua'i shore. He talked of it continually. Skies were clear and blue with only a slight trace of clouds in the west. Duke gestured toward the horizon.

"That's my life. I can't live without the sea, I need it."

"Better wait," warned Marchetti. "There's time enough for that after you get your strength back. Health is your first wealth."

Duke nodded agreement. He'd wait.

Toward the end of his two-week stay in Po'ipū, Duke decided to "hit the tide." Better wear out than rust out was his attitude. "Who knows how many days I've got left?" he smiled. "I say don't count your chickens—eat them!"

Gray-haired Marchetti joined his convalescent guest in Duke's first return to the sea. In swim trunks they walked to the shore. Duke stuck his cane in the sand, and, with Milo gripping his arm to brace him, headed for the ocean. The water was flat with hardly any break.

When Duke's big feet felt the cool of the water he seemed to come alive. This was his cure-all. He shuffled forward in his eagerness to get deeper into the brine. Looking down at his thinned-out legs he almost sobbed.

"Hold it!" warned Milo, struggling with his grip on his friend.

Duke pitched flat on his face into the water, flopping feebly and ineptly. Facing the fact that he couldn't swim almost destroyed him. Marchetti stooped and fought for a new grip on the floundering man who once outswam the world. Heavily-boned and without strength, Duke was no easy lift. But Milo got him to his feet and held him.

"Take it easy," Milo cautioned. "Just walk in the surf at first. Crawl or sit if you have to."

"Old?" Duke thought, "Decrepit?" Half crying, half laughing, he began to accept the truth. He went down to his hands and knees in the shallows, and just crawled around. He took handfuls of the clear, briny water, laved his lips with it, and murmured. "This is what I need. Thanks, Milo," he said. "Thank you so much." In that instant he threw off the memory of the past nightmarish weeks. The man of the sea was back to the sea. He was home.

With more days of this "Mister Hawai'i" slowly started coming back. Duke and Nadine returned home to O'ahu. Duke continued to mend and began to look more like his old self, but it was slow going after major brain surgery.

Duke made no public appearances until he was honored at a testimonial dinner on August 18 at the Waikīkī Yacht Club. Five hundred people attended the gala affair.

The dinner climaxed "Duke's Day" at Waikīkī. Earlier that day Waikīkī had witnessed the first Duke Kahanamoku Invitational Regatta, featuring both competitive-class and sea-going yachts. It was scheduled to be an annual event.

Duke was appointed honorary Official Greeter and Ambassador-at-Large for the State. Governor Quinn personally made the address. He noted that all Duke had ever wanted was to give the world all he had.

Leaning heavily on his cane, Duke mounted the platform and modestly accepted his tribute. In addition to many other gifts, he was presented with lifetime memberships in the Hawaii Yacht Club, the Pacific Yacht Club, the Waikīkī Yacht Club, and the Kaneohe Yacht Club.

Every day Duke became more and more of a symbol for Hawai'i. He had come to accept each of these days as a gift from God. During Aloha Week the planners set up a "day" for him, Sunday, October 21. By November he was well enough to visit the Mainland, spreading more aloha and good will from Hawai'i.

Duke was made an honorary citizen of Greenwich, Connecticut, during a Thanksgiving Day ceremony. Two weeks later he was in New York, spot lighted on the Ed Sullivan Show on a coast-to-coast TV hookup. He was there with Sam Pryor, Executive vice president of Pan American Airways; businessman Elmer Leterman; and entertainer Keola Beamer, then appearing at the Hawaiian Room of the Lexington Hotel.

Duke had seen major troubles, all right—but the "Bronze Duke" had beaten those troubles back one by one.

Duke Kahanamoku in his 73rd year.   *Joseph Brennan*

28

A Time for Levity and Festivity

DUKE GREETED 1963 WITH INCREASING HEALTH AND VIGOR. He was home again after his highly successful trip to the mainland. By February he was attending event after event as master of ceremonies, judge, or simply honored guest. He was in demand everywhere.

The February 4 *Star-Bulletin* column by Charley Young epitomized Duke's comeback:

Duke Kahanamoku has made an amazing recovery from his serious illness. I realized this while standing off the 9th green of the Royal Lahaina Golf Course at Kaanapali last week covering the Sheraton-Maui tournament.

Sam Snead had just sunk a 30-foot downhill putt.

There was Duke carrying a 25-pound motion picture camera shooting pix of Snead's shot.

The husky "name" golf pros were riding their electric golf carts between their shots around the hilly, long 7,300-yard Royal Lahaina course.

But not Duke Kahanamoku, who is at least 25 years older than the oldest of today's oldest golf pros. He walked every step of the way carting that heavy camera, fresh as a daisy, and with that charming smile on his bronzed, leathery face.

But that wasn't all the exercise for Duke for the day. That afternoon he came back to the pro shop with the Reverend Abraham Akaka, pastor of Honolulu's Kawaiahao Church, in tow. Abe, as Mr. Akaka is known to us Mauians who knew him in his younger ministerial days here, was decked out in sport clothes.

Duke told Ned Brigg, assistant pro in the golf shop, he wanted a set of golf clubs and a bag of balls to take Abe out onto the upper nine holes to introduce him to golf and give him his first lesson.

Before going home for the day, I had to go over to the Sheraton-Maui Hotel—and there was the Duke in his famous swim trunks, physically fit, though not quite as erect as he was in 1912 when he brought the United States its first three gold medals in swimming at the Stockholm Olympic Games.

He was getting more exercise swimming in the hotel's pool.

"I can swim in the pool," the Duke remarked, "but the ocean's a little too rugged for me out there these days."

May Hawaii's greatest ambassador of goodwill continue to enjoy good health until he lives to be a hundred.

Duke might be avoiding swimming in the ocean, but his birthdays weren't keeping him off the ocean. He turned ever more to boats, officiating at regattas, running the committee boat, and assisting in every phase of local boating. He even began canoeing again. However, his first try at paddling after he'd regained his health did much to remind him that he still had to take it easy.

Gay Harris' newly remodeled outrigger canoe was to be launched from the Outrigger Canoe Club at Waikīkī. Harris, a former backstroker who had swum in the '24 Paris Olympics, wanted his canoe properly blessed. This was exactly the sort of thing which now made up much of Duke's life. He would be steersman for the launching, with Gay Harris, David Kahanamoku, Charles Amalu, and the Reverend Abraham Akaka aboard, with the last performing the blessing.

Duke secretly arranged with Gay, David, and Charlie, to turn the canoe upside down in the surf after the blessing. The blessing was given while the canoe had negotiated the oncoming swells in good style. Everything pointed to complete seaworthiness of the craft. They even caught several fast rides into shore without mishap. Akaka was deliberately lured into a false sense of security.

"No pilikia!" shouted Duke from the stern. "Everything's okay!"

His crew agreed, for the outrigger rode light and sleek on the water. They paddled seaward once more and made their turn. Steersman Duke glanced over his shoulder, selected a high sloping green hill of water approaching from the stern.

"Paddle!" he yelled.

Everyone dug in with the big flat blades. The canoe lifted with the swell and was soon hurtling shoreward. At Duke's command the paddlers shipped their blades and braced for the ride. In the bow the minister was gripping the gunwales and watching the beach approach at a breath-taking pace. Expertly Duke kept the craft under control for some fifty yards before shouting his signal, "A-l-o-h-a!"

In that instant everyone other than Akaka took hold of the port gunwale and heaved upward. Over went the canoe, dumping the minister into the water. The four conspirators continued to hang onto the gunwales while the canoe was upside down and kept their heads within the hull—all yelling as though they were in trouble.

Frantically Akaka splashed over to the upside-down hull to free the paddlers from their "trapped" condition.

Bobbing up within the hull, he found David, Charlie, and Gay laughing. The minister saw the joke and laughed along with them. He had been well taken in and was the first to admit it. But Duke was now in trouble at the far end of the overturned hull. He had overestimated his strength; too recently out of the hospital, he was struggling under the shell and swallowing salt water.

They instantly turned to getting Duke out from under the hull and setting the outrigger right-side up. Duke clung to the hull as it was righted and then his friends helped him in. With the paddles having floated off, the others gripped the sides and swam the boat to shore.

It was the first time Duke had ever been brought ashore by someone else. Self-conscious, he avoided explaining his predicament. When sometimes obligated to tell the true story, the casualness of his voice never matched the embarrassment in his eyes.

In June Duke felt like a champ again as he arrived at Honolulu International Airport to help welcome President Kennedy. He had brought a tie clasp with the Royal Hawaiian Coat of Arms as a gift for the president.

Duke stood with the official greeters as the president and his retinue, including his ever-present Secret Service guards came down the steps. During the usual introductions and handshaking the moment came for Duke to reach into his pocket and present the president this gift. As he put his hand to his coat Duke was trapped by the steely eyes of the Secret Service escort. He froze, halted midway, as the guards started closing in.

Suddenly the president's hand was extended to Duke. He accepted the handclasp, saying "I'm honored." In his consternation he never heard the president's reply.

The presidential party moved on to more introductions, and more handshaking. Duke later admitted to a friend that "reaching into my pocket was only asking for trouble."

In his own nightclub that evening Duke told the story to some of the presidential party (the president was elsewhere). Duke showed them the packaged gift.

Still shaking his head, he explained "With all those big plainclothesmen glaring at me, I didn't have the nerve to get the gift out."

As the laughs rose one of the president's aides promised to see that Mr. Kennedy received his gift. The aide later brought back a P T-109 tie clasp as a special return gift to Hawai'i's official greeter. Duke was elated.

Duke later had another tricky experience while bearing gifts. One day he learned that Marion "Babe" Dowset, who had meant so much to him years earlier, was gravely ill in The Queens' Medical Center in Honolulu. He lost no time in getting to the florist for a beautiful pikake lei, Babe's favorite.

Duke had forgotten that this was the day his wife, Nadine, served as a volunteer receptionist at the hospital. He had never actually seen her there, so when he walked up to the desk to ask which room Babe was in, he was shocked speechless.

Nadine was almost equally startled. "Whatever brings you here?" she asked.

Like an overgrown boy with a guilty secret he hugged the box a little tighter and stammered, "I came to see someone."

"We have a friend in here?" she asked, adding, as she noticed the box, "Flowers for who, Duke?

He stood silent for a long moment before saying simply, "Marion Dowsett." Through the next long seconds Nadine was mentally scanning names, old and new. Finally, she demanded, "You mean Babe Dowsett? Your old girl friend?" Without even waiting for an answer, she swung to the index file and pulled out the "A to E" list. Scanning the names she reported, "She's in the Kam Wing, Room 22." But there was still a question in her eyes.

Duke saw it. "You'd rather I wouldn't?"

"Of course, I don't mean that, Duke. The woman is sick and an old friend."

Duke nodded and headed for the elevator. His private world was okay, solid under his feet, with everything under control.

Babe Dowsett was propped up by pillows when he arrived. Her pallid cheeks and wasted form struck sorrow into Duke's heart. He opened his box.

Her eyes came alive when she saw him and her breath quickened as she leaned forward for him to hand the four-strand lei around her neck. For long moments the two were speechless. Memories flooded back. Duke had to dry his eyes before he kissed her. They talked and talked. They finally finished, smiling over the distant memories.

Duke left the hospital room with a better understanding than ever before about just how much time had really passed—for him, her, and all their friends.

Duke left the hospital in his new 1963 Lincoln-Continental, a birthday present from Mrs. Kinau Wilder. It had been a timely and welcome gift, as his old car had been giving him nothing but trouble. Thinking about the car, he realized that still another birthday was coming next month—his seventy-third. It scared him a little.

Duke was still slightly depressed as he attended his birthday dinner-testimonial at the Royal Hawaiian Hotel that August 23. The testimonial was part of the public launching of the Duke Kahanamoku Foundation. The foundation's president, Msgr. Charles A. Kekumano, had proudly published a statement of the organization's purpose:

"A beloved son of Hawaii inspired the creation of an institution to help young men and women of this State achieve their desired goals in life. As a full-blooded Hawaiian, Duke Kahanamoku is a heroic figure to all the people of these Islands. As a citizen of the United States, he symbolizes to the nation and much of the outside world as well, the noblest qualities of American manhood. Thus in recognition of these virtues, and in celebration of the 50th anniversary of his first triumph as an Olympic swimming champion in 1912, friends banded to honor Duke Kahanamoku by forming a Foundation in his name, dedicated to Hawaii's youth. It is the hope that, in generations ahead, the Duke Kahanamoku Foundation may help others to bring honor to Hawaii as he has done in his distinguished life."

Duke entered the vast hall packed with patrons with Nadine on his left and his sister Bernice on his right. They stopped all conversation. The people came to their feet and gave Duke a standing ovation. Duke halted in his tracks, his eyes lit up like candles.

He straightened up and made his way alone to the speaker's platform. He took his seat between Governor Burns and Mayor Blaisdell, who shook his hand as though he had just won another Olympic medal.

Speakers, including the Governor and the Mayor, paid Duke glowing tribute. Msgr. Charles A. Kekumano rose and explained the foundation's goals.

Except for David and Kapiolani, the whole Kahanamoku family was there, all so proud of the brother who had brought so much honor to Hawai'i and the Kahanamoku name.

Telegrams were read from President John F. Kennedy, Arthur Godfrey, and other celebrities and dignitaries.

People kept adding to the lei around his neck. Duke received a second standing ovation as he was presented with a priceless traditional yellow-

Duke Kahanamoku and his biographer Joseph Brennan in the office of Duke Kahanamoku Restaurant May, 1963.   *Joseph Brennan photo*
Duke Kahanamoku with President John F. Kennedy at the Arizona War Memorial.
                                                                  Joseph Brennan photo

feathered Hawaiian cloak. It was given by Kinau Wilder, who had been given the heirloom by her late blind, father.

"He used to sit and stroke the cloak with loving hands," she said as she draped it around Duke.

Duke looked his most royal with lei ear high and the shimmering feather robe.

Still a third ovation was given as Duke thanked the audience for this night. Many old-timers who had grown up with Duke thought he was an incurable pidgin speaker, but he could offer pear-shaped tones when he wanted. That night he expressed his gratitude to the honored guests, his wife, his brothers and sisters, and particularly to the doctor who had saved his life the previous year.

Dr. Maurice Silver, the surgeon, was an invited guest. When Duke asked him to stand applause rose as the modest, heavy-set neuro surgeon with the lifesaving hands took his bow.

Duke resumed reminiscing about his many friends and about old Hawai'i. Then his voice went very quiet and the room went silent. His eyes closed as he softly and eloquently prayed that those who had gone on before be blessed and accepted by their Maker. He concluded, "One day I'll be joining them in the vast ocean."

The following day the Kani Ka Pila Golf Club honored Duke with a lūau at its annual Pa' Aina Hoolau Le'a in the Lanikai Community Center. This was Duke's third tribute since his surgery. At Lanikai on windward O'ahu, hundreds paid six dollars each to attend. Top Waikīkī shows donated their entertainment.

The feasting had already begun when Duke arrived. He entered on the arms of Nadine and Mayor Neal Blaisdell. As soon as Duke was spotted, local entertainer "Lucky" Luck led the crowd in singing "Happy Birthday."

Duke was walked to the center table where all could see him. He raised a gaunt hand and waved thanks to his acres of friends, crying openly.

Island music played throughout the day, with various Waikīkī shows each taking a turn: The Hilton Hawaiian Village Tapa Room group, Sterling Mossman's group from the Barefoot Bar, Ed Kenney and the Chick Floyd show from Duke Kahanamoku's Restaurant, Al Kealoha's "Hawaii Calls" Surfriders, and others all contributed their talent. The afternoon brimmed with music, song, and dance.

As Duke left, again with the Mayor and Nadine alongside, the crowd once more roared out its love.

Duke Kahanamoku   *Courtesy of Tommy Holmes*

29

A Kimo McVay Salute

HIS HEALTH STILL ON THE MEND, DUKE WAS INVITED TO CO-HOST ALONG WITH JOHNNY WEISSMULLER THE WEST COAST SURFING CHAMPIONSHIPS IN HUNTINGTON BEACH, CALIFORNIA. Duke and Kimo Wilder McVay flew to the mainland on September 18 to join Weissmuller.

Even McVay, an entertainer in his own right, was astonished by Duke's reception as he stepped onto the beach stage to award the winners. The crowd howled and cheered.

McVay wrote a lengthy letter to Red McQueen of the *Advertiser*:

"I witnessed a sight that I will never forget. I saw 30,000 or more teenagers, before any introduction was made, get off their 'ōkole, stand and cheer wildly when our beloved Duke, a good sixty years older than most of them, stepped on a stage at the water's edge, to be introduced and award trophies to the winners of the West Coast Surfing Championships. As I looked at these young surfers, boys and girls alike, I couldn't help but notice the respect and admiration on their faces as they actually saw for the first time in their lives, the legendary 'Father of Surfing.'

"I was so impressed, and knowing what a good friend you are of Duke's, I am writing you this letter hoping it might enlighten a few others here in Hawaii as to just how valuable Duke is to Hawai'i. When you stop to think that in Duke we have an ambassador who alone dominates the scene wherever he is, drawing the most favorable and attractive publicity to our entire State, it is truly a phenomenon in this day and age. No other State has anyone to rival Duke, for no other State has anyone that is an immediately recognized symbol of its State...

"In Duke, we have the most revered, respected and admired surfer in the world, and Duke has already agreed to help in any way that he can. This is so typical of Duke who never has a selfish thought!

"Just think of it! Here's a pure-blooded Hawaiian (fully recovered from his serious brain operation of last year), who can leave our shores and simply by appearing in person anywhere in the world, bring Hawai'i to their attention and do it with little or no advance publicity.

"Furthermore, perhaps unnoticed by many of us here (because surfing is a taken-for-granted way of life in Hawai'i), Duke is the biggest thing in surfing, the newest and fastest growing sport in the world today. We think of Duke as being known primarily for his Olympic swimming feats, but swimming has a number of 'greats' including such people as Johnny Weissmuller, Buster Crabbe, Ford Kono, Bill Smith, Keo Nakama, etc.

"However, Duke stands alone and way up on top in surfing, the 'Sport of Kings,' unrivaled and unequalled. There isn't a publication about surfing that doesn't mention Duke or his surfing feats on every other page, and in most cases there are complete chapters about him, crediting him with introducing and popularizing surfing to the world. Duke actually is to surfing what Babe Ruth was to baseball!"

The most heart warming sight to Duke was the youngsters' craftsmanship and skill with their boards. He now saw what had developed in the fifty years since he had first shown surfing to the world.

He watched young surfers who had profited from everything the old-timers had shown. The new surfers used lighter boards but rode with the grace of yesteryear's best.

Duke witnessed grace and speed and advanced surfing that held the crowds spellbound. Peering seaward, he could almost see himself out there.

Duke saw young surfers caught up in the thrill of riding the very face of the sea, sharing the sky and the clouds.

It was good to think that he had done his part in helping them to find this magic.

When Duke and Weissmuller awarded the trophies Duke realized that the kids were proud of their victories, but clearly equally proud that the "father of surfing" was the one handing them their reward. Duke had done more than any other to carry surfing and develop it from an isolated Polynesian recreation to a major international sport.

The trip produced more fine publicity for Hawai'i. Many local radio and television shows featured Duke. He appeared on the nationally-televised Steve Allen Show. Everywhere he was greeted as the most admired and respected surfer and swimmer alive. After finishing in Los Angeles, they flew to Lake Tahoe to attend Arthur Godfrey's opening at Harrah's Club. Duke's arrival was a surprise for the entertainer. Godfrey was playing his 'ukulele in the darkened club, the only spotlight on Godfrey himself. As the Hawaiian melody ended Duke called out, "Hey, 'Ula'ula (Red)!"

Godfrey looked out into the audience, squinting into the darkness, not quite able to believe his ears. Again Duke called out, using his own special name for his friend, "Mino'aka (Smily)"

Since no one else ever called him that, Godfrey yelled out, "Duke!"

As the lights went on Duke rose, waving. Godfrey stopped the show and met Duke with an outstretched hand as they embraced and pounded each other's backs.

After Duke and McVay returned to Honolulu, the latter announced, "It would be impossible to put a monetary value on the benefit Hawai'i will receive just from this one short trip, but if the State had had to pay for the publicity, it couldn't possibly be less than $100,000 worth if you only computed the newspapers, radio, local, and network TV coverages that Duke got free for Hawai'i.

"To sum up the entire trip, I thank the Good Lord that He gave us Duke, for in Duke, we truly have a living legend, known and loved throughout the entire world, whose very presence on this earth has benefitted, and continues to benefit in some way, all of the people in Hawai'i. To the world, Duke is Hawai'i!"

Duke said little about his West Coast trip. But he grinned as he added two more beautiful silver plaques to his collection. One read:

THIS PLAQUE IS GRATEFULLY PRESENTED TO DUKE KAHANAMOKU IN RECOGNITION AND APPRECIATION FOR OUTSTANDING LEADERSHIP AND CONTRIBUTION TO THE SPORT OF SURFING
UNITED STATES SURFING ASSOCIATION
SEPTEMBER 1963

And the other:

TO DUKE KAHANAMOKU—HONORARY DIRECTOR
FOR OUTSTANDING CONTRIBUTIION TO THE SPORT
OF SWIMMING AND WATER POLO
INLAND NY PIKE WATER POLO CLUB
LONG BEACH, CALIF - 1963

The plaques and his memories of the California surfers told him that he still had a niche in aquatics' Hall of Fame.

In his, as he called them, "alone moments," he well realized that all his old records had long ago been broken; Weissmuler, Crabbe and Cleveland—and more from across the seas—had all surpassed his times. The new surfers with their new boards were spectacular!

He wondered what was the reality of the "Kahanamoku" image? Had City Hall, the Chamber of Commerce, the Hawaii Visitors Bureau, the newspaper, the airlines, and the hotels only built his image to publicize Hawai'i? Was that all? Did the tourists, as many claimed, really count their vacation complete only if they found him on the beach, shook his hand, or had their picture taken with him? How was he to know what the people of Hawai'i really thought of him?

There was no way for him to know that when a disgruntled tourist asked a parking lot attendant why "that white-haired Hawaiian" didn't pay, as Duke cruised past the waiting motorists, the attendant would shrug, "Eh, bruddah, dass dah only king we got!"

30

A Sentimental Binge

ONCE MORE DUKE'S LIFE RAN FULL THROTTLE. He was asked to be race-committee chairman for the Waikīkī Yacht Club's second annual Duke Kahanamoku Invitational Regatta. The event involved twelve racing classes totalling eighty-five boats, all the best.

On a bright tradewind morning the fleet lay spread like waiting seabirds. Duke's passion lit him up like a lamp. Duke was not content with supervising. He insisted on being aboard Commodore Frank Operman's race committee boat, the *Sashimi*, putting all of his strength into getting the buoy markers into the water and later wrestling them back aboard.

The rugged routine lasted the weekend. Duke gave as always—without sparing. He kept up with the youngest, biggest, and strongest. At the finish, he allowed winning skippers to toss him into the harbor. He even stayed for the award party that night and presented trophies to the victors.

But his fatigue didn't keep Duke from his appointment with the author early next morning. Duke came with a tired smile on his face. Limply, he clomped to the far end of the living room, halted and looked out to sea before sitting down at the table for breakfast. Three times a week for the past six months Duke had come to talk of the past, present or future. Today conversation took a holiday.

After Duke had eaten, he lay down on the pūne (couch). At two-thirty in the afternoon he was still there.

Seriously concerned about Duke's condition, the author studied the tired face.

"Who's your doctor now?" he asked.

"Doctor Lin."

"I'm going to phone his nurse and arrange for him to check you."

Duke just nodded and closed his eyes.

Dr. Lin's nurse said to get Duke to the hospital and he would be examined immediately. Told of the plan, Duke looked away, his eyes sad. He got up shakily, indicating he wanted no help. He walked to the door, shoulders a little stooped, hands dangling at this sides. His legs carried him slowly to the elevator. He would accept no assistance.

"I want to go on my own," said Duke.

Still worried, the author let him drive only on condition that he would go very slowly and carefully.

Duke arrived at the hospital without incident, underwent a quick examination, and was promptly put to bed. Through the room windows tall clouds decorated the western sky, but Duke had no taste for beauty this day. He knew that he faced the possibility of another long hospital stay.

Duke was held for observation and testing. Mostly, Duke caught up on some much-needed rest. Other than hospital staff and Nadine, he saw almost no one. There was no talk of writing, business, or problems, only swimming, sailing and surfing.

After a few days he was allowed out onto the lānai where he could look out on the harbor and bay and watch all the ocean activity. He spent hours at the rail, enjoying the constant trade winds.

Duke watched the busy traffic of canoes, sail- and powerboats through the channel and felt that life was passing him by. He walked around on the hospital lānai in his bathrobe and studied numerous surf breaks visible from his ninth-floor vantage point. He had never expected the vast numbers of surfers he now viewed riding the near-shore waves. Waikīkī couldn't begin to hold them. Surfers were now regularly traveling out to the North Shore.

Duke remembered the years when surfers seldom resorted to the North Shore. Waikīkī had been uncrowded, the shore waters not dotted with boards, boats, outriggers, and swimmers. Back then there had been room enough for a man to feel alone with the sea.

He considered the dozens of different boards the surfers had begun using, and decided that it was all for the best, "Progress." Duke knew the 1963 International Surfing Championships would be held off the Mākaha shore this year, December 21-29, and be televised by a national network for the first time. Duke felt that when it happened he belonged there.

His view shifted and he examined the island's newest surfing spot, between the Hilton Hawaiian Village and the new yacht harbor. Produced by the recent dredging through the reef, the changed currents had created a new surf.

Duke contemplated the changes wrought by man in his islands just during his lifetime. High-rise buildings stabbed the sky in every direction, the long curve of Waikīkī shore now crowded with towering hotels. Only two blocks from his hospital Hilton Hawaiian Dome showroom had taken the land where his home used to be.

"Mama and Papa would never believe it," he thought.

He walked back to his room, hoping to get his hospital release soon. He lay down and started making plans for a goodwill tour of Australia. He and Nadine had been invited to Sydney to officiate at the Australian surfing championships November 22-23. As the man who first introduced the sport to Australia, Duke was recognized there as the father of surfing. The K. G. Murray Publishing Company wanted him there to help publicize their new book, *The Australian Surfrider*.

Rest meant nothing to Duke as long as he could be out promoting surfing, sailing, or swimming. The sound of the surf joined the smell of the spray drifting up to his high window. He saw a "V" of nēnē geese cutting the sky, their quavering calls drifting down. He had places to go, things to do.

Duke Kahanamoku 75 years old.   *Joseph Brennan photo*

31

Back to Loved Ones

DISCHARGED FROM THE HOSPITAL AND TOLD TO TAKE IT EASY, DUKE WAS PROBABLY THE ONLY PERSON IN HAWAI'I WHO WASN'T WORRIED ABOUT HIS HEALTH. Once more he thought of himself as indestructible. He kidded that "The doc gave me a dirty bill of health—but I'll outlive the doc."

Those close to him still fretted about Duke's health, welfare, and what was left of his future. His brothers and sisters and particularly the ever-alert Nadine, at Duke's side now for twenty-three years, were full of concern. Others worried about his rightful place in Hawai'i's history. Some were even concerned with what would become of his many trophies, his medals and his surfboards.

Dr. Edmund F. Madden, a well-known local physician, wrote the Advertiser and asked sports editor Red McQueen to do something about preserving Duke's famous koa board. He reminded McQueen of his column item that Duke was to surfing what Babe Ruth was to baseball. The doctor pointed out, "Duke no longer picks up those first breaks off Diamond Head; nor is he able to use that beautiful board weighing over 200 pounds. That board is still in the Duke's locker at the Outrigger Canoe Club. The Club is soon to move. The board will be lost or discarded because fiber boards have replaced the heavy ones. Red, please, that particular board belongs in the Bishop Museum. Will you please get the ball rolling and put that board in a place of honor such as the Duke is in the hearts of all Hawai'i?"

The sports editor was quick to note in his column that the Duke's board plus his trophies and medals, would be preserved in a place of honor. He wrote: "The movement is already afoot, initiated by Councilman Herman Lemke, to establish a Duke's Trophy Room in the foyer of the City Hall."

McQueen then posed the question of Duke's association with the upcoming New York World's Fair and its Hawai'i display. The sports editor wanted Duke to make at least intermittent appearances. He finished, "We can only hope that Hawai'i isn't too late in really realizing what Duke P. Kahanamoku means to the Islands. We've already missed the boat more than somewhat."

When these plans were brought to Duke, who seldom read anything about himself, he said, "What difference? There are new and better surfers and swimmers since my time."

Gay Harris, long-time Outrigger Canoe Club member, also felt the trophy room idea had merit. Cornering his old friend, he said, "Think of it, Duke. Here we are in Hawai'i with all this water, a natural gymnasium, and yet we didn't land a single berth on the U.S. swim team at the 1960 Olympic Games." Harris went on. "Since the 1912 Games, the 1960 Olympiad was only the second time that our islands had no representation."

Duke nodded. "That's right. The other shutout was in the '36 Games at Berlin."

Harris said, "You know we dominated the swimming contests at Stockholm, Paris, Los Angeles, Helsinki and Melbourne. Where are our national caliber swimmers today?"

"We've got top teachers," Duke broke in. "There's Sakamoto..."

"I know!" interrupted Harris. "But the kids have to have something else to fire them up; something else to push them to be champs. Duke, all the kids look up to you. You're the one who can inspire them in water sports."

Duke thought about it. He knew Gay was right. He wished he had the health to actually help train kids. "I'll do all I can," he said, "that's a promise." Duke thought more of what he owed to Hawai'i. All the Kahanamokus had been gifted with strength and character. His brothers typified the still present greatness of ancient times; the finest of a dwindling race of full-blooded Polynesians. Hawai'i could no longer claim more than 9,000 who, like the Kahanamokus, were of pure Hawaiian blood. Duke mentally inventoried his brothers. Sam had been one of the world's top sprint swimmers during the golden twenties. Louie, football star at Kamehameha School, had later become outstanding in surfboard paddling and canoe-racing. David had starred on the 1924 Olympic swimming team and won many more swim trophies over the years. Bill, too, was excellent in the water, far above average. Big Sargent had been another of Hawai'i's extraordinary swimmers and was currently one of her noteworthy golfers.

The Kahanamokus were symbols of a great era in Hawai'i. Duke also recognized other fine families that had contributed to Hawai'i's athletic history: Blaisdell, Wong, Smith, Minn, Lai, Kono, Kim, Kaulukukui, Wise, Kalili, Pung, Kneubuhl, Crabbe, Cleveland.

Duke reflected how Clarence "Buster" Crabbe was named the "Greatest all-around swimmer in the world" for winning three U.S. AAU senior championships and creating new world records for the one-mile, the half-mile, and the 300-meter medley.

Duke remembered the Kalili brothers, Maiola and Manuella; Warren Kealoha; Bill Smith; Dick Cleveland; Keo Nakama; and so many others. Where was the current crop of potential Olympic swimmers? Maybe the sight of his many medals, cups, and plaques—possibly a couple of surfboards—would encourage today's youngsters to real determination in water sports. Maybe a trophy room would help.

Duke left for city hall within the hour. His desk wasn't far from Mayor Neal Blaisdell's office, so he stopped there first.

"Mayor," he began, "they're talking about a trophy room to be set up.."

"I know," the Mayor broke in, smiling. "Councilman Herman Lemke, Red McQueen, Dr. Madden, and others, including myself, are back of it."

"I'm complimented," Duke said. "I've been thinking about it. If it'll help the kids, I'll round up all my stuff."

"It should help the kids," Blaisdell confirmed.

That was enough. He went to his own desk to see what work they might have for him; who to meet today.

This was the kind of thinking that was Duke's greatest therapy. Still weakened and underweight, Duke flew with Nadine to Sydney on November 20 for the Australian Surfing championships. He left with the doctor's proviso-laden approval, but Duke wasn't letting anything interfere with his watching those "down under" surfers. This sport his forefathers had handed down to him—and he was going to see it perpetuated.

Duke appeared at the contests and presented the awards. Then, although reluctant to leave the great generosity of the Australians, they jetted back to O'ahu in time to award prizes at the International Surfing Championships at Mākaha.

At seventy-three Duke Kahanamoku was still building for tomorrow with no thought of his own health. Despite his heavy white mane and lost weight, Duke mostly still fit the picture an Olympic observer had long ago described: "Six feet two...with the rich features of a high Polynesian type. All in all, a handsome specimen of Hawaiian manhood—easy, nonchalant, modest, inspiring friendship."

Unless Duke was away again on another tour, or greeting important visitors at the airport or the docks, he spent most of his time at the Waikīkī Yacht Club. He didn't sit in the lounge, pin-neat and posing as front man for Hawai'i. More likely he'd be stripped to the waist, straddling an empty keg, paintbrush in hand, helping a friend repaint his boat. Duke loved boats the way he loved the surf, and he'd turn to like a deckhand whether it was sailing or repairing.

He was Hawai'i's beloved number-one citizen, a man who had been praised by kings and enjoyed the adulation of admiring throngs but never lost the common touch.

A local paper wrote: "For years the Duke has been a one-man tourist bureau and chamber of commerce."

Duke was news just because he was Duke. When people saw him or read about him, they thought of Hawai'i. He was always ready for a mission to promote surfing, swimming, sailing, or goodwill for Hawai'i. That was his joy.

Duke showing Lowell Thomas how to eat poi at his Sunday Luau, 1963.   *Joseph Brennan photo*

Seated from left to right: Duke, Nadine and Red McQueen. Standing: William Coffman and Joseph Brennan. Taken at Banyan Court, Moana Hotel, August 15, 1964. Duke was selected Sportsman of the Year that evening.   *Joseph Brennan photo*

Chinn Ho, Fred Van Dyke and Duke, 1966.   *Joseph Brennan photo*

32

A Touch of Trouble

NINETEEN SIXTY-FOUR WAS A FINE YEAR FOR DUKE. It began when he won the Red McQueen Sportsman of the Year Award for 1963. Sportsmen Hawaii, an organization of local sports enthusiasts, saluted him at a testimonial dinner in the Banyan Court of the Moana Hotel. Both Governor Burns and Mayor Blaisdell were on hand. Duke took his bow and accepted the award to standing ovation.

Duke and Nadine went as invited guests to the Tokyo Olympic Games in October. When they returned, Duke told the local press, "You just don't know what it means to be remembered."

His health continued to mend. Once more he presented trophies at the annual International Surfing Championships at Mākaha in December.

In September '65 Duke revisited the United States Surfing Championships in Huntington Beach, California, as awards presenter. The same year he was selected as a charter member of the new Swimming Hall of Fame at Fort Lauderdale, Florida. The award included an invitation to appear at the opening on December 27. With national and international TV coverage, Duke's recognition was complete. Other tributes and recognitions might come, but Duke had given up trying to anticipate them.

Duke's fame was such the January 3, 1966 Honolulu morning paper featured this:

STATUE OF DUKE RIPPED FROM CAR

A small, gold-plated statue of Duke Kahanamoku in action on a surfboard was ripped from the hood of the Duke's car in Waikīkī New Year's Eve. The car had been lent to George Patton of Los Angeles, vice president of the Duke Kahanamoku Corp., for the evening by Kimo McVay, corporation president.

The statue was stolen when Patton stopped briefly outside the Edgewater Hotel to pick up a guest. Duke is in New York for an appearance on the Ed Sullivan Show.

"The statue has great sentimental value," said McVay. "I will personally underwrite a $100 reward with no questions asked for its return."

How many people in the world get newspaper coverage for the theft of a hood ornament? Duke was constantly being photographed with royalty, commercial tycoons, sports celebrities, and assorted dignitaries. Queen Mother Elizabeth of Britain danced the hula with him during her May 1966 visit to Honolulu. The picture was cabled around the world. The photo of their laughter was yet another testimonial for Hawai'i.

When it seemed as if there were no honors left to be bestowed upon Duke, he was made a "Charter Member Number One" of the Surfing Hall of Fame. He was flown to Los Angeles for ceremonies at Santa Monica by International Surfing Magazine. Hal Wood, sports editor of The *Honolulu Advertiser*, was with him and, on June 22, 1966 wrote:

> "We walked down the aisle with Duke and his manager, Kimo McVay. As the spotlight was turned on the Duke, the crowd rose to give him a standing ovation... Surfers, young and old, men, women and children, came up to shake his hand, touch his jacket or just stare at the great man in admiration."

Duke continued in his role as city greeter and presided at important surfing and swimming events. In September 1966 he again went to Huntington Beach, California, where he was the guest of honor for the fourth consecutive year at the United States Surfing Championships. The following week Duke was in San Diego where he was honorary chairman of the World Surfing Championships.

While on the mainland, he sandwiched in appearances on radio, television and at clubs. He continuously answered the many calls upon his time

Nineteen sixty-seven began with great promise. Duke's health seemed optimum, and he had a comfortable income. He was like a fine old stallion out enjoying the pasture.

Feature articles on Duke appeared in two major national magazines, Life and Sports Illustrated. He was still good copy.

Duke was sailing happily along until February 16. The *Honolulu Advertiser* headlined:

DUKE UNDER SURGERY FOR ULCERS

Below it:

"Duke Kahanamoku was operated on for bleeding ulcers yesterday at

Kaiser Hospital.

About 40 percent of his stomach was removed and he underwent five blood transfusions. The hospital said the 76-year-old former Olympic swimming champion was in satisfactory condition last night. He is in the hospital's intensive care unit and is not permitted telephone calls or visitors. The surgery was performed at 4 p.m. yesterday. Kahanamoku entered the hospital Sunday. His wife, Nadine, said last night doctors told her recovery is expected, but she added, 'A few prayers wouldn't hurt.'"

Duke was hospitalized for several weeks. Newspapers supplied a daily account of his condition. It was touch-and-go the first few days and nights. Only Duke's great heart kept him living and breathing, but he fooled those friends who were afraid that his years had finally caught up with him.

After some home convalescence Duke was up and around again. His golden smile was more welcome than ever around town, at the yacht harbors, and on the beaches.

He got so well he accepted an invitation to the World Sports Banquet in the Beverly Hilton Hotel, Beverly Hills, California on June 24. The $100-a-plate dinner was sponsored by the City of Hope Sportsmen's Club and billed as the "Academy Award of Sports." Greats from every major sport were invited. Many, like Duke, were ex-Olympic heroes. Fancy large trophies were presented. Besides Duke, others honored included: Paavo Nurmi, Rafer Johnson, Bob Mathias, Casey Stengel, Willie Mays, Sandy Koufax, Joe Louis, Max Schmeling, George Carpentier, Lou Meyer, Red Kelly, and many more internationally acclaimed athletes.

Duke returned with his weighty trophy and said, "It was a beautiful affair, and a thrilling event. I met so many old friends and world champions." He was happy they remembered him and that he had been counted among them. But as the *Advertiser's* Hal Wood reported, "With his bronzed skin and his beautiful shock of white hair, the Duke was an imposing figure in any crowd—and that would include one of sports celebrities of the calibre of Dempsey, Schmeling and Nurmi."

In 1967 one more party was thrown, this outdazzling all the previous ones. For Duke's seventy-seventh birthday party (August 24) 10,000 people were invited. Engraved invitations went out from Mrs. Kinau Wilder, Mr. and Mrs. Kimo Wilder McVay, and Mr. and Mrs. Don Ho.

Richard Boone and Duke at Duke's 77th birthday party.   Photo by Bob Johnson, Joseph Brennan photo

Duke at his 77th birthday party where over 6,000 people attended the event, August 24, 1967.
Joseph Brennan photo

Duke's 77th birthday party (August 24, 1967) at Waikīkī. Left to right is Don Ho, Duke, Nadine, Kimo Wilder McVay, Kinau Wilder and Betsy McVay.   Joseph Brennan photo

To try to cope with parking for the anticipated throng, the entire Waikīkī Terminal Building was reserved. Additionally, air-conditioned buses were hired to shuttle guests from secondary parking near the Waikīkī Shell a half mile away.

In spite of the parking problem, the turnout was phenomenal. The thousands who came were soon, cocktails and pūpū appetizers in hand, having the time of their lives.

On Duke's arrival he was presented with a brand-new Silver Cloud Rolls-Royce, courtesy of "Kimo, Kinau, and Don." Transportation for a king!

For hours Duke's friends ate, and listened to the music of Don Ho; and heard speeches from the governor, mayor, and other dignitaries. Duke and Nadine sat high on the stage in king and queen thrones. Guests were the elite of Hawai'i and visiting mainland VIPs. They thronged about Duke, wishing him well on his seventy-seventh milestone birthday.

Bandmaster and crooner Don Ho, in his white velour shirt and tight jeans, announced, "I've been to a lot parties, but this is the biggest!" Everyone roared, and Ho led the band into "Happy Birthday." Duke stood and saluted the assembly.

Later in the party, an almost-life-sized portrait of a youthful Duke surfing was unveiled. Silence fell as the cover dropped from the framed portrait. Artist Margaret Keane (of "big-eyed children" fame) had worked long in executing a wonderful likeness of the old champ. He was balanced on his board, hands wide, with every silken muscle of torso, arm, and leg shining out in bold relief—a tower of strength.

Duke at Waikīkī Yatch Club, January 9, 1968. Picture was taken by L.A Draper of Chicago. Note: Duke suffered his fatal heart attack on January 22, 1968.   *Joseph Brennan Photo*

A Man Apart Takes His Leave

THERE IS NO DENYING DUKE IN THE AUTUMN OF HIS YEARS. He spent much of his time at the Waikīkī Yacht Harbor aboard his new powerboat, the NADU K II. The beautiful twenty-eight foot twin-engine sportfisher gave thrust to his life the way his body had given thrust to his swimming. He was still gracious and unassuming. Although he hadn't competed for more than thirty years, his fame was undimmed. His friendliness and aloha spirit were legendary. In many ways to many people he was Hawai'i.

In the afternoon of January 22, 1968 radio and TV broke the news: "DUKE KAHANAMOKU IS DEAD!"

It was traumatic for those who knew him well. It shook even those who merely knew of his exploits and character. It was the end of an era.

Through newspapers and over the air, the detailed facts were made known. After seventy-seven eventful years the great champion's heart had stopped. Duke had suffered a heart attack in the parking lot of the Waikīkī Yacht Club. He had struck his head first on the toneau of his car and then on the pavement. At the end he had been hard by the sea he had so loved. Flags throughout the state were lowered to half-staff and tributes were offered by civic leaders. Governor John A. Burns said:

"All Hawaii today grieves the passing of Duke Paoa Kahanamoku; his loss leaves a void in our community and in our culture that cannot be filled. More than any other person in our modern Island history, Duke embodied all the fine and ennobling in the Hawaiian culture.

"He reflected great credit and honor on our Polynesian people. His athletic accomplishments set standards of the highest order; he gave unselfishly of himself for many years as a public servant; his career was rich in a wide variety of experiences. Duke was the friend of royalty and countless numbers of other people from all walks of life.

"He was recognized throughout the world as the symbol of Hawaii and of the aloha spirit that is the hallmark of our society. His humility and the dignity which characterized his life shall remain an inspiration for all our citizens. We shall miss Duke as we miss few others whose friendship we were privileged to enjoy. His passing is a great personal loss to me. To Nadine and Duke's family I extend heartfelt condolences and sympathy."

Mayor Neal S. Blaisdell said: "A great patriarch of the Hawaiian people, an honored public figure and a beloved personal friend of all the thousands of people, great and small, who knew him, died today."

"Duke Kahanamoku was an indomitable man. The courage through which his athletic prowess carried him to international fame was second only to the quiet fortitude with which he boar the recurring illnesses of later life."x

"And through all of his life, his simple dignity, his gentle strength, his kindly good will to man made him a living symbol of all that we admire in the Hawaiian spirit. He was a true Hawaiian warrior. He was a man for all time, and all Hawaii mourns."

Funeral services were held at St. Andrew's Episcopal Cathedral. A thousand people jammed the church. Over one hundred honorary pallbearers attended. The Very Reverend John J. Morrett, dean of St. Andrew's, recited a passage from St. John as the procession moved up the aisle from the rear. The Right Reverend Harry S. Kennedy, bishop of the Episcopal Diocese of Honolulu, gave the first part of the services. A schoolboy sounded a single tone on a nose flute. The sixty-five-voice Kamehameha Boys Concert Glee Club sang the Hawaiian hymn "Hawaii Aloha;" starting as a dirge, it grew into an anthem of happiness with only a suggestion of sorrow—just what Duke would have wanted.

Arthur Godfrey gave the eulogy, telling of his own and the world's love for Duke. He outlined the Duke's Olympic successes of the early 1900's and called Duke "the soul of dignity—ali'i o ali'i, a son of natural-born kings." He spoke feelingly, saying, "Duke gave these islands a new dimension. He gave Hawai'i her very first measure of international stature. He was a godlike creature in a way and yet a mischievous boy at heart. As big and strong as he was, he was as gentle as a baby."

After the services a mammoth motorcade with a thirty-man police escort moved across town to Waikīkī Beach in front of the Royal Hawaiian Hotel. While thousands watched, beachboy services were led by the Reverend Abraham K. Akaka, pastor of Kawaiahao Church. The solemnity was lightened only by remembering that just having known Duke was a joy in itself.

Rolling black clouds sagged down from the Hawaiian heavens and a light sprinkle of rain fell. "This was a man," Mr. Akaka reiterated. While the beach stood silent, an ache in every heart, Mr. Akaka strewed white sand over the urn

Duke Paoa Kahanamoku just before his death.   *Hawaii Visitors Bureau*

holding Duke's ashes. It was the signal for the beachboys to begin singing the Hawaiian song of farewell, "Alohe Oe." There wasn't a dry eye along the shore.

The urn was taken to a waiting outrigger canoe and, accompanied by an armada of other canoes and small craft and surfers on boards, paddled out to sea. Mr. Akaka, Nadine Kahanamoku, and Dean Morrett were in the urn-carrying canoe with Sargent Kahanamoku as steers man. The paddlers were Duke's brothers and close friends. Additional canoes carried more relatives and loved ones. Talk was hushed and low.

Only the dip and splash of paddles accompanied the flotilla. The lead canoe halted and Duke's ashes were reverently put over the side. Many strew bright lei upon the water. Soon the sea was an undulating carpet of plumerias, carnations, orchids and pīkake. The eerie quiet was suddenly broken when the Coast Guard cutter's horn wailed solemnly and Polynesian mourners began droning a soft chant. The Reverend Abraham Akaka's voice lifted: "Paoa was a man of aloha. God gave him to us as a gift from the sea, and now we give him back from whence he came." As though in blessing, a rainbow brightened the shoreward sky as paddlers swept the canoes to the beach.

Duke was now where he always longed to be. The sea had been his passion and his shrine. Singing began to lift up from canoes. Happiness and thanks crowded away the sorrow. It was good to have known Duke Paoa Kahanamoku. He will always be the legendary Duke of Hawai'i—a man apart.

EPILOGUE

MONTHS BEFORE THE LATE DUKE'S POSTHUMOUS 100TH BIRTHDAY ON AUGUST 24TH, 1990, PLANS HAD BEEN AFOOT TO CELEBRATE HIS MEMORY IN A VERY TANGIBLE, LASTING WAY. A statue had already been erected in his honor in Australia and in California, so the absence of such a tribute on Waikīkī's shoreline was noteworthy as an abject and sorry oversight. Particularly had the newspapers been beating the drums for a bigger-than-lifesized bronze statue to be erected in his honor at Kuhio Beach.

Anticipating that the cost would develop into a princely sum, contributions had been sought to cover it. A figure of between $120,000 and $200,000 was reasoned to be the amount needed for creating and maintaining the proposed statuary. The Waikīkī Improvement Association committee commissioned the work, with David Carey, the Outrigger Hotels president heading the fundraising effort. A Kahanamoku centennial committee even laid plans for a slate of water sports events throughout August to mark the anniversary.

Sculptor Jan Fisher, a fine artist, was selected to create the statue. He had been chosen from a field of 21 local artists. He fashioned a stunning likeness of the great Olympiad champion, and it was constructed of material that would withstand the beach's natural weather elements of sand, salt spray, wind, rain and sun. The site picked out for its mounting was on the shore between the big well-known Kuhio Beach banyan tree and the police substation.

Meanwhile, the news columns, TV and radio reports continued recounting Duke's swimming victories at the Stockholm and Antwerp Olympics, his shocking and sensational loss at Paris, his saving of eight men whose fishing boat capsized in a raging California surf, his having been a master surfer, canoe paddler extraordinaire, movie star, internationally-known sheriff and official greeter for all of Hawai'i. Nor did the news media neglect to stress and emphasize how all who knew Duke had learned to love him.

Cindy Luis of the *Star-Bulletin* reported: "John Dominis Holt perhaps best described Kahanamoku's mana, his aura and spirit: 'He had a natural grace and he offered his wisdom freely but in a few words. He will stand the test of time as the epitome of the Hawaiian that I feel badly doesn't exist anymore. He had the simple humbleness that ali'i (royalty) possessed, an intuitive intelligence, a lokomaika'i (a kind, gentle disposition).' "

Duke's character was revealed as good-natured, charming and naturally graceful, quietly wise and dignified, effortlessly the center of attention, yet humble in his way. In truth, most every facet of Duke's exciting life was touched upon: particularly was wordage spent on his first breaking the world's swimming record at Honolulu Harbor, and how he swept the swimming events at the 1912 Stockholm Olympiad—the first of his four Olympic competitions over 20 years. Too, the public was reminded that, as a young man, he became a master surfer on a 16-foot koa wood board weighing an incredible 114 pounds—10 times the weight of today's fiberglass boards.

Fred Hemmings, candidate for state governor, former champion surfer and co-chairman with John Dominis Holt of the Duke Kahanamoku Centennial Committee, explained that, for years, he had dreamed of a statue honoring Duke on Waikīkī Beach. Everyone seemed to be toiling like a serf to pay tribute to Duke on his centennial birthday.

The bronze heroic-sized statue was finally sculpted to perfection. It was trucked to Kuhio Beach and placed on the shore just ewa (northwest) of the juncture of Kapahulu and Kalakaua Avenues. It stood there draped in a brown shroud and boxed in plywood to await the unveiling on Duke's century mark. Meanwhile the City Council had passed resolutions to change the name of Kuhio Beach to Duke Kahanamoku Beach. It was resolved to name the nearby Police Building officially as the Duke Kahanamoku Building.

The morning of the dedication, a small fleet of canoes landed at Kuhio Beach to bring a bevy of hula dancers, along with the chanter and a group of beachboys. They formed a wall with a half circle of 14 surfboards as a backdrop for the occasion.

At the unveiling, the crowd of eager faces demonstrated how enthralled everyone was with the bronze memorial. Voices broke into oh's and ah's as the sheen of sunlight bathed the tall figure. Duke's arms were outstretched in welcome, his Polynesian face lighted with friendliness. The muscles of his torso, legs and arms bulged with the strength and energy that once rode there. The whipcord stomach glinted in the morning light. It was easy to understand how the great pantherlike body carried Duke to so many sensational aquatic victories throughout the world. Murmurs and shouts of delight welled up from the people at the sight of the image's true facial and physical likeness to the Golden Man whom they had lost.

The *Honolulu Advertiser's* columnists, Bob Krauss, reported:

"Rep. Fred Hemmings, sparkplug for the drive gave the most eloquent
talk of the day. 'This is a dream come true for all of us.' Hemmings said.
'With 1,000 years of Hawaiian culture behind him, Duke marched into the
20th century. He made his own legend. We have come here to realize the
true greatness in the greatness of the spirit.' "

Gov. John Waihee also addressed the crowd. He said in part, "I remember as a
boy coming from Hawai'i to walk in Waikīkī to look for famous people. One of
them was Duke. He was a role model for young people to look up to."

Among others who addressed the crowd was Duke's widow, Nadine, who
expressed her thanks for the dedication, plus her love of the statue. "I think it's
gorgeous," she told the assembly. "I hope you will all come to this beach and visit
Duke because he doesn't want to be lonely."

Krauss pointed out that Duke's being lonely on this day was a veritable
impossibility—what with this abundance of leis, assorted flowers and soil from
his Kalia home covering his feet. Offerings of ti leaves, ginger, carnation leis and
maile were heaped on the boulder at the base of the statue. The leis draped on his
outstretched arms looked almost too heavy to hold.

That magnificent memorial will remain there on the beach that Duke loved all
his life; a glowing, mute testimony to all that he stood for and believed in. There
it will shine, day and night—an everlasting reminder of Duke's 78 golden years...

Australia's salute to Duke

Statue to stand near Sydney

By Bob Krauss
Advertiser Columnist

Duke Kahanamoku, Hawaii's swimming and surfing legend, now stands in bronze overlooking Freshwater Beach near Sydney, Australia, as he overlooks Waikiki.

The new statue, which rises to a height of 20 feet on a 12-foot high boulder, will be unveiled Sunday.

"I'm thrilled," said Nadine Kahanamoku, 89, widow of the Duke, who will fly to Sydney to be on hand for the ceremony.

"I really think Duke is better known in Australia than he is in Hawaii."

Sandy Hall, a Honolulu resident who grew up at Freshwater Beach, will travel with Mrs. Kahanamoku.

At age 22, Duke, named after the Duke of Edinburgh, won

Duke Kahanamoku

his first Olympic gold medal in freestyle swimming at Stockholm, Sweden. Two years later he toured Australia and gave swimming exhibitions to packed crowds.

But it was his introduction of surfboard riding to Australia that electrified beachgoers.

While staying at Freshwater Beach during Christmas, he fashioned a 65-pound long board of sugar pine and rode the waves for the first time in Australia on Dec. 23, 1914.

Hall said his board is now the prized possession, insured for $1 million, of the Freshwater Surf Life Saving Club and a shrine for Australian surfers.

She said the statue is east of the club buildings. A walkway from the club to the statue is inset with mosaic tiled art celebrating the highlights of Duke's hfe, and honors 25 Australian world champion surfers, most of whom came from neighboring beaches.

The statue commemorating Kahanamoku's place in Australian swimming and surfing history is the result of three years of effort by Paul McKay and the late Malcolm Campbell, Hall said.

And so the memory of Duke Paoa Kahanamoku's fame, stature and excitement continues to be burnished with time.

Honolulu Advertiser, January 19, 1994

CHRONOLOGICAL INDEX